═ THE ═
CALLING

≡ THE ≡
CALLING

The Year in the Life of an Order of Nuns

Catherine Whitney

Crown Publishers, Inc.
NEW YORK

The publisher acknowledges permission to reprint extracts from the following sources:
The Hound of Heaven and Other Poems, copyright © 1955 by Francis Thompson.
Excerpt printed by permission of Fleming H. Revell Company,
Westwood, New Jersey. All rights reserved.
"Morning Has Broken," copyright © 1931 by Eleanor Farjeon. Excerpt printed by
permission of David Higham Associates, London. All rights reserved.
The Saviors of God, "Spiritual Exercises," copyright © 1960 by Nikos Kazantzakis. Excerpt
printed by permission of Simon & Schuster, New York. All rights reserved.
The Roman Missal, the English translation of, copyright © 1973. Excerpt printed by
permission of the International Committee on English in the Liturgy, Inc., London.

Copyright © 1999 by Catherine Whitney

Published by Crown Publishers, Inc., 201 East 50th Street, New York, New York 10022.
Member of the Crown Publishing Group.

Random House, Inc. New York, Toronto, London, Sydney, Auckland
www.randomhouse.com

CROWN and colophon are trademarks of Crown Publishers, Inc.

Printed in the United States of America

Design by LYNNE AMFT

Library of Congress Cataloging-in-Publication Data

Whitney, Catherine.
    The calling : a year in the life of an order of nuns / Catherine
Whitney.—1st ed.
    1. Sisters of Saint Dominic of the Holy Cross (Edmonds, Wash.)
2. Dominican sisters—Washington (State)—Edmonds. I. Title.
BX4337.5.E35W48   1999
255'.972—dc21   98-28759
                                                                   CIP

ISBN 0-517-70854-X

10 9 8 7 6 5 4 3 2 1

First Edition

AUTHOR'S NOTE

This is a work of nonfiction. The events are based on my own recollections, as well as on those of many other people. But there's a caveat. Even a work of nonfiction involves a form of storytelling—especially when it is in the style of a memoir or is attempting to capture the intangibles of beliefs and rituals. My version of events may feel quite different to others. We are all informed by personal points of view. However, I have shared the manuscript with the key participants and have documented the essence of events that I did not actually witness.

In many cases, I've chosen to mask the true names and other identifying features out of respect for people's privacy. Some sisters and former sisters shy away from having their true names in print, although they're happy to have their words and experiences recorded here. Others have died or are long gone; I felt it unfair to make them the beneficiaries of my childhood recollections.

Finally, strictly speaking, *nun* is a term reserved for religious women in cloistered communities. Women in apostolic communities are *sisters*. However, in the past half century, the words have been used interchangeably in colloquial speech. That's the way they are used here.

For my father,

RICHARD H. SCHULER
1923 – 1996

A man of faith and a great supporter
of the nuns. I am sure he is making
them laugh in heaven.

ACKNOWLEDGMENTS

A NUMBER OF YEARS AGO, I WROTE A BOOK ABOUT ABORTION, titled *Whose Life?*, which was published by William Morrow. I loved writing that book. It allowed me to take sharp journalistic aim at a vital women's issue. Although I tried to maintain an unbiased distance from my subject, I know my personal attitudes leaked out of the corners of my prose. I was most affected by the discovery that virtually every major leader of the anti-abortion movement was male—and nowhere was that more plain than in the Catholic Church. The male hierarchy of the church was like a stone wall, carved from centuries of certitude, especially in matters pertaining to women. Those brave women, including members of religious orders, who challenged Vatican decree on abortion and birth control, felt the full weight of that stone wall pressing down on their backs.

I began to view the Catholic Church as an institution ruled by men—sworn celibates who were removed both physically and ideologically from the people they served. I wondered, Where were the women? My own upbringing in the Catholic Church had been dominated by women. Wonderful, mysterious, committed, strong women who filled the convents and nurtured our minds and souls. *Whose Life?* was a wake-up call for me—a reintroduction to the church I had long ago abandoned. However, deciding it was too grim to face, I hit my snooze alarm and was happily writing about other matters when I was called back.

The Calling represents a departure in my writing, as well as in my life. I have been forced to lay down my journalist's pen and take a different road, one that required the words to spring from my heart as well as my head.

This special journey would not have been possible without my agent, Jane Dystel, and her associate, Miriam Goderich, who inspired me to start off, not knowing what I would find. When Jane first called me to discuss the project, she urged me to use my inner eye rather than my journalist's eye. It was a daunting prospect, but I had plenty of support.

Betty Prashker, my editor at Crown Publishers, was determined to do this book. Not only is Betty sharply in tune with the times and a wonderfully skilled editor, I soon realized that I had found in her a kindred spirit. Her passion about the subject and her unwavering commitment to *The Calling* have been an inspiration to me.

My partner, Paul Krafin, has been far more than a rock of moral support—although he is surely that. His creative contribution to the work has been substantial, thanks to his deep spiritual reservoir and his critical acumen. Paul has never met a sentence that he couldn't improve, or an image he couldn't strengthen. Without his generous collaboration, I might have foundered on the rocks of my own emotional involvement in this story.

The Sisters of Saint Dominic of the Holy Cross, in Edmonds, Washington, generously opened their home and hearts to me. It was these sisters, from the order that taught me as a child, that I learned the wonderful secret of the special calling that allows women to live in a state of anticipation, commitment, and growth, even as their number shrink. In particular, I am grateful to Sisters Maureen Rose, Judy Byron, Kathleen Logan, Dorothy Berg, Adella Diederich, Mary White, Margaret Murphy, Honora Nolty, Angelica Weckert, Mary Rosaire Bagley, Fidelis Halpin, Francine Barber, Jean Marie Lehtinen, Anna Kosenski, Barbara Bieker, Joanne McCauley, Perpetua Haughian, Katherine Diederich, Patrice Eilers, Lorene Hecht, Ann Patrick Deegan, and Cecilia Horan.

A special mention for three Edmonds Dominicans who were great influences in my young life but who died before I began to write this book: Sisters Edwina Sweeney, Ingrid (Lawrence) Doyle, and Celestine Haughian.

I am also grateful to the Sisters of Saint Thomas Aquinas, in

Tacoma, Washington, who agreed to share their optimistic perspective on the future of their community. In particular, I appreciate the warmth and frankness of Sister Joyce Roach and Sister Carol Staudacher.

Many others shared their insights and stories. I am thankful, in particular, to Sister Kathleen of the Cross, Sister Susan Kent of the Holy Names Sisters, Bernadette Hillson, Lynn Wilson, Lynn Lauber, Patricia Lowe, Earl and Eleanor LaBerge, Michaela Gill, Celine Nichols, Lillian Friedman, Margaret Lichter, Jon and Annetta Ezelle, Mark and Sarah Phillips, Robert and Teresa Lingafelter, Steve Brazen, and Catherine Welch.

My wonderful parents, Richard and Janet Schuler, instilled in me a lasting sense of social responsibility, intellectual pursuits, and loving kindness, which resonates to this day. They raised all nine of their children—Greg, Jim, myself, Paul, Tom, Mary, John, Margaret, and Joanne to be creative, smart, unpretentious, and optimistic.

I want to particularly address this book to my son, Paul Richard Whitney. He has been the greatest influence on my life for the past twenty-four years. He possesses a curiosity and open mind that is not afraid to allow new ideas and feelings in. He embraces life, with all its peaks and valleys, and finds God's presence in the world every day. He is my constant inspiration.

CONTENTS

THE
CALLING

1

In the Shadow of the Tabernacle

Rosary Heights
Edmonds, Washington

— J A N U A R Y   1 9 9 7

THE PACIFIC NORTHWEST WAS HARDLY A STRANGER TO RAIN, but it was usually more friend than foe. Rain fell often on Seattle, as if from a great lawn sprinkler, emitting a steady, benevolent drizzle. It nourished the crisp evergreen vistas and swept the urban smog from the skies above. The natives had grown accustomed to the damp air, but the recently arrived Californians, lured to the chilly Northwest by Bill Gates's Microsoft and the bottomless riches of technology, despised the weather. They found the rain and unrelenting wind whipping off Puget Sound more agonizing than bracing. Old-timers scoffed at their delicacy and chuckled gleefully when they encountered Californians heading back down to the more temperate south.

But the storms that brewed along the coast this winter were different, ominous. A cosmic shift in weather patterns had battered the Northwest with severe storms since Christmas. First came the snow, piling to over two feet before the warming air from Puget Sound turned it to rain. High winds sent gale after gale of showers pounding down on the city, felling trees, flooding streets and houses, and collapsing power lines. Interstate 5, the main highway connecting the western coast of the United States with Canada, had been barricaded at major points from Vancouver to Oregon because of rock and mud slides. Snoqualmie Pass, the mountainous egress east, was too dangerous to cross. Schools were closed due to rain, which was an unprecedented event for the children of Seattle.

Day after tumultuous day, the swollen waters of Puget Sound crashed against the docks and wood pilings, reducing them to timber and sending hundreds of suddenly homeless seagulls cawing and shrieking across the leaden sky. Weather reports predicted more of the same.

As the sky darkened on yet another storm-tossed night, Sister Helen watched from a large bay window in the meeting room of Rosary Heights, the motherhouse of the Sisters of Saint Dominic of the Holy Cross. The spacious gathering place had been the chapel in more populous times, but it was now kept empty, reserved for lay retreats and community meetings. Wide French doors with spotless glass panes normally provided an expansive sight of the property, but this evening the view was murky and threatening.

Normally, Sister Helen would be serving dinner at a homeless shelter for women in downtown Seattle. But the lone road servicing Rosary Heights was flooded and blocked with a web of fallen branches. There was nothing to be done but to wait out the storm. Helen frowned with concern as she watched the trees on the property sway and dip toward the ground. Every so often, the sharp crack of a breaking tree branch, or the sudden spatter of sharp pebbles and uprooted brush against the glass, sent her heart racing furiously.

Rosary Heights stood on one of the most beautiful pieces of land in the Pacific Northwest. High on a bluff north of Seattle, overlooking Puget Sound, the main building was an imposing red-brick English Tudor-style house. Its twenty rooms featured lovely groupings of bay windows, and an interior of sumptuously polished hand-carved oak paneling. A smaller cottage, separated from the main house by a cobblestone pathway, had once been a four-car garage and carriage house. The sisters had long since converted the upstairs of the carriage house to bedrooms and guest rooms. The downstairs was dedicated to archives containing the entire history of the order.

The fifteen-acre estate had been purchased by the Dominican Sisters in 1956 from the widow of the president of Boeing. Later, eight acres adjoining the original property were added to house the large novitiate, expanding the grounds to twenty-three acres. Some of the land had been sold off since, but the initial acreage remained, keeping the estate secluded and invisible to passersby. A quarter-mile-long tree-shaded road led from the entry gate to a circular front driveway paved with cobblestones. Fragrant gardens and delicate statuary provided small meditation areas along the front of the main building. A winding dirt path behind the carriage house led to a wooded trail, where blue jays, sparrows, robins, and hummingbirds kept up a continual chorus of song, even during the winter months. Around the back, through a trellised archway, was a large yard and more gardens, leading to the commanding bluff and a magnificent stand of stately evergreens partially obscuring the incredible view. The centerpiece of the yard was a tall, slender black cross that rose from a cluster of carefully tended greenery and was starkly silhouetted against the sky.

Directly below the top of the bluff was a tennis court, built by the original owners, and a swimming pool. The swimming pool had been built in the early seventies for a television version of the movie *Diabolique,* retitled *Reflections of Murder.* It starred Joan

Hackett and Sam Waterston. The exterior of Rosary Heights had been rented so it could represent a boys' school where a murder had occurred. A crucial scene involved a swimming pool, so the producers had one installed. After the filming, they donated it to the Dominican Sisters. In the following decades, both the pool and the tennis court fell into disrepair. The sisters couldn't afford the upkeep on either, and many of them were embarrassed by the opulent lifestyle these luxurious accessories represented. The dry pool, paint peeling and fading, was now littered with cast-off tennis balls and dried leaves; there was no longer a net or lines on the tennis court. Neither was even visible from the motherhouse, unless one walked to the edge of the bluff and looked over.

In itself, property meant little to the sisters. Their vow of poverty precluded attachments to land or possessions. But it was impossible to remain detached from the natural beauty surrounding them; an emotional connection to Rosary Heights was nearly irresistible. There was only one way to describe it: *God* was in this land. Although Rosary Heights had once been the estate of a rich man, any scent of wealth had been scrubbed from the floors and walls by hundreds of postulants and novices over the years. They had swept and polished in silence, their humble work a form of meditation. Many a sister had sat praying fervently on one of the benches placed near the edge of the bluff, inspired by the faraway peaks of the majestic Olympic Mountains, or walked along the shaded paths, where one could almost feel a divine presence rustling through the swaying trees. For most young postulants, Rosary Heights represented their first experience of the contemplative life—the state of *being*. No words to lead them, no actions to define their purpose. Just stillness and silence: simple, open living in the presence of the Almighty.

But Rosary Heights was just a piece of land, a space. Spiritual transcendence required more than a space. True inspiration, real devotion to the sacred vows of poverty, chastity, and obedience, had to come from within. Only the heart was capable of remaining steady in its faith and devotion to God. The land was temporal. Still, the existence of an established motherhouse was comforting to those who remembered the itinerancy of the order's beginnings in the Pacific Northwest. In those early years, the sisters had been housed in rickety buildings atop odorous, flooding tidal flats in Aberdeen, Washington. They had been forced to build makeshift novitiate dormitories in empty schoolrooms. Later, they had crammed into tight quarters in Seattle and Everett. At last, with the purchase of Rosary Heights, there was a real motherhouse—a place where one could go to begin a spiritual search, or to follow a call. Even the women who had left the order over the years returned to Rosary Heights on occasion. They were drawn by the powerful pull of the sacred, nostalgia for their younger years, and something else; they were always welcomed by their *sisters*. It would perpetually remain their home, a place where they belonged.

Sister Helen was the de facto Mother Prioress of the order, although in these modern times, she was called the president. She served as the head of the Leadership Team. Along with three other sisters, Sister Helen was responsible for the order's ministry, its common life, and the treasury. Helen was mindful of her place in the shifting continuum of religious history, but she had few of the guideposts of the order's former prioresses—"*real* prioresses," she sometimes called them—whose decisions were supported by the rigid edicts of a centuries-old rule and the iron mantle of their authority. That had all given way to the modern religious order—not just for these Dominican Sisters but also for most of the Catholic religious orders in the United States. Portraits of the prioresses, stern, wise, strong women who had devoted their lives to establishing the order on the West Coast, kept a framed vigil on the walls of the motherhouse. There was Mother Guilelma, the beloved first prioress of the Congregation of the Holy Cross; Mother Angela, who had served two terms and had been responsible for the community's formal acceptance by the Vatican; Mother Austin, who had ushered in a period of phenomenal growth during the post–World War II decades; Mother Frances, whose term had been marked by financial strains but who had succeeded in giving the order its first true motherhouse in Rosary Heights; and Mother Dominick, who had allowed the fresh winds of modern thought to sweep over the dusty traditions of the past. Mother Dominick's final task had been to make her role and her title obsolete. She was the first to return to her birth name when that option became available, and she asked to be called Sister Hilary, even while still the prioress. Sister Edwina, once the formidable principal at Holy Angels Academy, was chosen as the first president of the order under its new leadership structure. Sister Edwina was a brilliant woman, knowledgeable about culture and the arts. Her love of Renaissance poetry, customs, art, and architecture was legendary, but Sister Edwina could also display a caustic wit that was decidedly modern. She had no patience with false piety. Once she was said to have created a near scandal among certain traditional nuns. A group of sisters were gathered in the recreation room, and one of them was railing against a recently published book entitled *Lesbian Nuns.* "It's disgusting," she said. "There are no lesbians in the convents." Sister Edwina responded tartly, "Oh, Sister. What do you think community life is? Don't you think that when women choose to live together for sixty years it implies that they prefer women to men—that they're more comfortable being in a society of women? I'm not speaking of sex, but of preference." The silence in the room was palpable.

Sister Edwina's death from cancer in 1996 was a bleak occasion for hundreds of sisters and former students who had been touched by her rare spirit. Sister Hilary was still alive, and a vital part of the order. She remained at Rosary Heights after she had stepped down as Mother Superior. Although now quite elderly and hard of hearing, her very presence could fill a room with calm and faith. Her eyes were clear and shining, full of love, and set deeply in the creases of her wizened face. She had a wisdom and selfless attitude that assured her spiritual leadership, and Sister Helen turned to her often for guidance and inspiration. A woman of substantial leadership qualities and intellectual gifts herself, Helen nevertheless often felt humbled before the uncertain crossroads that lay before the order.

Sister Helen presided over an order that was undergoing a metamorphosis—although harsher critics described it as a slow death. It required a powerful act of faith to believe the order would ever be resurrected, especially as the slow fading away of the cherished community of the past continued. Sister Helen possessed that faith, although it didn't ease the careworn lines etched prematurely into her forehead. The changes of recent decades had been so radical that they had shaken the very foundations of all religious orders. Their own Dominican order, designated by Saint Dominic himself as the Order of Preachers, was less visible than ever in the teaching and preaching arenas. Their new mission encompassed the world. Few of the remaining sisters taught in schools or nursed the sick in hospitals, which had been the dual missions of the order since its inception. The Dominican Sisters of the Holy Cross could now be found in the homeless shelters, the prisons, the community development projects of urban ghettos; in the isolated outposts of a Mexican trailer park to the south, and a Native American reservation to the north. They were involved in the creative arts, the law, and in counseling, teaching, and studying at the universities. They were engaged in the loving care of the elderly sisters who lived out their final years at Assumption Convent, the order's retirement center; in distant foreign missions; in parish leadership positions and the training of a burgeoning community of lay associates. The disparate paths of the Dominican Sisters were bound only by the ephemeral philosophy of their founder, Saint Dominic—and by their enduring faith.

Sister Helen turned away from the window. The course of the storm was in God's hands. She stopped for a moment to say a prayer in the small chapel off the great room, easing herself onto the padded kneeler and feeling, as always, the transcendent peace— that moment of quiet—that came from being in the sanctuary. The chapel was dark now, except for the flicker of deep ruby and blue lights glowing from the votive candles near the tabernacle. In the daytime, the chapel was bathed in brightness and cheer, even on overcast days. Multiple windows on three sides of the room looked out on well-tended gardens to the north and east, and the massive bluff to the west. When the house was privately owned, it had been the nursery, and it was easy to imagine the delighted babble of children at play in the warm, sunny room. Now it was designed for prayer, with two rows of lecterns, kneelers, and chairs facing each other, and an altar at the end facing east. Sister Helen watched the light flicker and an old saying popped into her head: *The Dominican Sisters always live in the shadow of the tabernacle.* As long as God was in his tabernacle, they were safe. She blessed herself and glanced at her watch. It was 7:30 P.M.

In the recreation room on the second floor of Rosary Heights, a television droned on with endless weather reports that explained nothing. Sister Amanda looked up from her five-thousand-piece puzzle in annoyance. "They've been saying the same thing for two hours. There's a storm. We *know* that. Maybe we should try the radio."

From her rocker, where she sat swaddled in a robe and afghan, Sister Hilary smiled at Sister Amanda. During her term as prioress, one of the most hotly contested debates had erupted over the introduction of television. Many of the older sisters were scandalized when several convents received permission to buy TVs in the early 1960s. But Mother Dominick had been very firm on the matter. She had bought the first television for the order. The world was changing, and they had to keep up with current events. Now, it seemed, television was often irrelevant. It didn't seemed to focus on anything of real importance to people; it had become background noise as reality continued around it.

Across the room, Sister Martha, a frail older woman with almost translucent skin, sat in her nightgown and pale blue bathrobe, sipping tea and talking to Sister Joanne. Martha was suffering from non-Hodgkin's lymphoma, but her weakness had not affected her sweet disposition, or dimmed her spirit. Determined to remain at Rosary Heights, rather than be cast off to a secular hospice or even to Assumption Convent, she continued her duties as supervisor of the kitchen.

Sister Joanne, in a fuchsia sweatsuit, chatted cheerfully, with an animated youthfulness that belied her sixty years. Sister Joanne's face shone like a beacon, filled with the light of her own optimism and spirit. Naturally given to laughter and cheer, this stalwart Canadian refused to let things get her down.

She loved Sister Martha deeply. The two women had formed a bond many years ago when Joanne was a postulant and Martha was postulant mistress. Joanne had never forgotten the day she was assigned to the laundry, where she was washing Sister Martha's habit. No one had told her that the heavy white serge robes were to be washed in cold water, and Joanne had set the machine's temperature on hot. When the robe had emerged, shrunk to half its original size, she nearly had a heart attack. It had been a serious error. Each nun possessed only two habits, and she had just destroyed one of the postulant mistress's. She felt that she might as well pack her bags right then and there. When Sister Martha was told of the disaster, she never displayed a hint of anger. She merely reproached Joanne by saying, "You must remember to wash the serge in cold water, my dear. Else we'll soon be left with nothing to wear!"

Joanne had marveled that Sister Martha had not shown even the briefest fit of temper. "*Anyone* would have yelled and been upset. I know *I* would have." The postulant mistress's gentle spirit made a deep impression on Joanne. She was, indeed, a role model for the young nun, and later became her friend.

As the evening progressed, the recreation room grew chilly. The air seemed to settle. There was a sense of expectation, of impending crisis—the way everything becomes eerily still in the moments before some horrible disaster. And at 10:30 it came—a deep rumbling vibration, followed by a great heaving sensation. The ground beneath the motherhouse lifted briefly, then shuddered. The windows trembled, and streams of cold air poured in through the sills and baseboards. From all parts of the house, sisters hurried to the main floor. Sisters Adella, Amanda, and Magdalene, whose rooms were in the carriage house off the main building, raced across the courtyard, becoming instantly drenched as they stumbled over fallen tree branches, loose rocks, and uprooted shrubbery. The small group of sisters huddled together at the window of the great room and watched in terrified awe as the edge of the bluff broke away, snapping the massive evergreens and tossing them into the angry waters below as if they were matchsticks. For a breathless moment, it seemed as if the monstrous storm would swallow the entire hillside, taking them with it. But the violent destruction stopped just short of the shrine of the black cross.

Peering helplessly from the window into the dark, the sisters were unable to see the true extent of the damage. Only later would they learn that the entire midsection of the two-hundred-foot-high bluff, weakened by the relentless pounding of the water, had spewed out tons of mud, earth, and boulders with the force of an explosion, collapsing and crashing onto a passing Burlington Northern freight train on the tracks below. Five freight cars had been swept into Puget Sound, leaving the rest of the train and its tracks buried under tons of debris. None of this was visible from the motherhouse.

The sisters debated their best course of action. Would the house hold? If they did decide to leave, could they make it safely to the road? If they were able to make it to the road, would there be a way out? Finally, a compromise was reached. Calculating the distance between the black cross and the house, Sister Helen said, "If the cross goes, we'll leave. For now, we'll stay together in the motherhouse."

In the early-morning hours, a second avalanche jolted the

grounds. The sisters sprang into action. There were no longer any questions. They must leave. Sister Joanne ran to telephone 911 and Dominican House, the convent at Saint Matthew's, where they would seek shelter. As the wailing of sirens sounded in the distance, Sister Helen scurried along the hallways, tapping on doors. "We'll meet at the front. Ten minutes. Hurry. We need to leave."

Ten minutes! Not even time to say good-bye. As the sisters drove away from their beloved motherhouse, each one of them privately wondered if they would ever return—or what they might find if they did. Sister Joanne thought longingly of the order's archives—the written records and valuable artifacts of the Dominican Sisters' history in the Northwest. Sister Andrea pondered the fate of her vegetable garden, which she had so lovingly tended over many years. Sister Magdalene fretted over the computers and business files in the office upstairs. Sister Hilary reflected on the shrine of the black cross—the symbol of their fledgling order—which had been erected after their formal recognition by the Vatican. And Sister Amanda worried for the property itself—the order's financial safety net, the one thing of value they had to use for barter in troubled times.

The storm began to ebb the following afternoon, and throughout the Seattle area, the citizenry emerged to measure its losses. The sisters, safe at Saint Matthew's, were shocked to learn that across Puget Sound, on Bainbridge Island, a bluff not unlike their own had collapsed, bringing down a large house and killing a young family. Other homes had been severely damaged, and at least two people had been killed by falling trees. Hundreds of live wires had been downed, making the roads treacherous. It was almost two days before conditions were safe enough for the sisters to return to the motherhouse. As they came down the long drive that led to their home, they were relieved to see that the house was still standing. But no one knew for how long. The emergency workers, who had set up bright orange barriers along the bluff, warned that the rest of the bluff could go at any time. Surveyors and engineers couldn't properly inspect the property and assess the damage until the soil had dried—which could be months away. And there was bound to be more foul weather. For now, the motherhouse stood on an uncertain foundation and a prayer.

Word of the calamitous mud slide spread—widely publicized in the local newspapers, and carried by phone, fax, and E-mail to the outposts, apartments, and modest houses filled with sisters in Chehalis, La Conner, and Everett; the distant missions in Mexico and Alaska; and to the homes of former sisters, now gone from the order to raise families or pursue independent lives. It did not escape notice by some of them that the landslide might symbolize the final collapse of a spiritual foundation that had long ago been irretrievably weakened.

Three days after the storm, on a cold and sunny morning, a small blue Honda Civic came up the circular path and pulled into a space in front of the carriage house. A tall, slender woman unfolded herself from the tiny car and emerged. Barbara had just turned sixty, but she was still beautiful, her face nearly unlined. When she had been a member of the order, teaching in the local parochial schools, the children always called her "the pretty sister." Barbara was simply incapable of looking plain, even when she wore the bulky serge robes and the awkward square headdress that was the order's habit before the change. She possessed a ruler-straight posture that heavy clothing failed to bow. Her long, slim fingers could make a piece of chalk seem like a magic wand as it flowed out perfect script across the blackboard.

Bundled against the icy air and the whistle of chill wind blow-ing up from the Sound, she hurried through the arborway and picked her way along the sodden, muddy lawn. She moved straight against the wind, toward the garish orange barriers standing as warning sentinels across the wounded bluff.

No longer partially hidden by the tall evergreens, the view

across the Sound to the mountains beyond was breathtaking. Barbara got as close to the edge as she dared and looked down over the precipice. The swimming pool and tennis court had caved in, and it seemed that the entire bluff was suspended in the air, as if held by an invisible thread.

Barbara remembered that when she was a novice, she and the other girls used to pin up their long robes, tie back their veils, and sneak out on summer days to climb down the steep traverse—although now she could see it had been a dangerous excursion. Once at the bottom, the young girls would strip to their bathing suits and dive into the Sound for a swim—laughing at the startled looks from conductors as the freight trains sped by.

Her novitiate class had been the first at Rosary Heights, and when the sisters moved to the estate, they tried to maintain a quiet presence. The small sign at the front gate was barely visible from the road. For a long time, many of the locals didn't even realize there was a religious order here. Barbara remembered once standing by the gate in the late twilight of a summer evening, clothed from head to toe in her white novice habit. A car sped by, quickly followed by the sound of brakes screeching. She moved deeper into the shadows; perhaps the car's occupants thought they'd seen a ghost. In time, the neighbors got used to the nuns next door and left them alone. Occasionally, high school pranksters would steal the sign that read ROSARY HEIGHTS—SISTERS OF SAINT DOMINIC and affix it to the gate of the Jewish cemetery down the road, thinking it a hilarious joke.

Barbara also remembered standing on this lawn the first time she ever wore the pure white robe and veil of a novice, feeling the glow of a new maturity and purpose. She was twenty years old, and confident that her life was set on the right course. At that moment, she believed that she possessed everything she would ever need—and perhaps she had. Try as she might, she had never quite managed to recapture that extraordinary feeling of certitude and spiritual calm.

The life of a religious community had suited Barbara, who tended to be shy, soft-spoken, and naturally drawn toward quiet surroundings. Rosary Heights had been a haven; people didn't stare at her there. They didn't comment on the way she looked, or try to coax a smile or conversation from her. They just let her be. At last she was accepted, for no other reason than that she had felt compelled to answer God's call. When she was assigned to teach at Holy Angels Academy, the girls' high school the order had run since 1907, the very idea had set her delicate stomach in turmoil. Three hundred girls, bursting with energy, hormones, and adolescent savvy—it was an intimidating prospect. But she had been given no choice, so she took on her assignment with grit and determination. To her great surprise, the girls seemed to like her— perhaps because she was young and incapable of the stern manner that radiated from old Sister Albertina, or the intimidating aura of Sister Edwina. Eventually, Barbara relaxed into her role and enjoyed her duties.

During what Barbara thought of as the Great Exodus of the 1970s, she had remained steadfast. Her love of the contemplative side of religious life provided her for a time with a learned stillness. She didn't relish the rebellious atmosphere of that period, as some of the others did. She loved the religious life. But as the leave-takings mounted, she began to experience them as a depletion of her own life force—as if members of her family were being taken from her one by one. When Mother Dominick initially advised the remaining sisters not to have any contact with those who had left the order, Barbara had suffered terribly. She felt such sadness and loneliness that she could hardly bear it. She at first tried to offer it up as a penance, but her very soul seemed to be fighting for air. She felt suffocated by Mother's rule. Her first act of rebellion was to take the car on a pretense and pay a visit to a former sister at her little apartment in the University District. In the end, Barbara battled mightily with her dark night of the soul, and she lost. She became the last of her era to leave the order. But she still loved the life; she had never quite been able to stay away.

"It's only land."

Barbara jumped at the sound of the voice. She turned to see Sister Andrea wading across the sodden lawn, dragging a large garbage bag behind her. She was dressed in a baggy sweatsuit and heavy rubber boots. Her hands were encased in oversized gardening gloves crusted with mud. The sight of her made Barbara smile. Andrea was most comfortable in the loose and grubby clothes of a gardener. She had been the first one—way back in the late fifties—to don a pair of sneakers beneath her robe, creating a near scandal around the motherhouse. When she knelt before the severe and disapproving Mother Frances at Chapter of Faults and confessed her transgression—"I accuse myself of wearing inappropriate clothing"—several of the sisters had to stifle their giggles when they saw the bottom of her black lace-up shoes caked with mud and leaves.

Now Barbara greeted her with a warm hug. "I had to come when I heard."

Sister Andrea nodded. "It gave us quite a scare." She pointed down the cliff. "That's where my vegetable garden ended up." Barbara spotted the nozzle of a garden hose and a mottled pile of root vegetables halfway down the slope. "I'll have to find a new place for it."

"Do you think it will cave in? Will the hillside hold?" Barbara looked doubtfully at the streams of water still trickling down through the fragile soil.

Sister Andrea shrugged. "The earth will do what it will do."

Barbara found it hard to meet those steady eyes, and she turned back toward the bluff. Sister Andrea meant it. Imagine such faith, such lack of fear. Perhaps, Barbara thought, suddenly embarrassed, she had no right to cry over lost land. It was she, after all, who had forsaken the motherhouse. But she couldn't help feeling a bond with this place. If Rosary Heights disappeared down the side of the bluff and was consumed in the waters of Puget Sound, she feared that her last link with the sisterhood would disappear with it.

As the sky darkened on another winter night, the Sisters of Saint Dominic of the Holy Cross gathered in their small chapel for evening prayers. It was Sister Joanne's turn as leader. "I have chosen an opening hymn that was originally sung at the morning office," she said. "I felt it had the spirit of hope we needed, with darkness all around us. Page two twenty-seven."

In soft unison, the chorus of voices, trained over time to sing in harmony, began.

> *Morning has broken*
> *Like the first morning,*
> *Blackbird has spoken*
> *Like the first bird.*
> *Praise for the singing!*
> *Praise for the morning!*
> *Praise for them, springing*
> *Fresh from the Word!*

On the second verse, tears sprang to some eyes. Sister Andrea's voice rose above the rest.

> *Sweet the rain's new fall*
> *Sunlit from heaven,*
> *Like the first dewfall*
> *On the first grass.*
> *Praise for the sweetness*
> *Of the wet garden,*
> *Sprung in completeness*
> *Where His feet pass.*

"Let us pray," Sister Joanne intoned, bowing her head. "Lord, who gives us the nourishing gifts of sunlight and rain, we thank you for your many blessings. We ask our father, Dominic, to intercede for us and guide us in fulfilling the mendicant charism of our order, to make the road our home and the suffering of mankind our first thought every day. For this we pray, in Jesus' name. Amen."

As she lifted her head, Joanne caught sight of the giant cross outside the window; it was swaying back and forth in the wind. She closed her eyes again and prayed for solid ground.

2

Faith of My Father

Edmonds, Washington

— AUGUST 1996

MY FATHER'S GRAVE IS ALMOST A STONE'S THROW FROM ROS-
ary Heights, on a grassy hillside in Holyrood Catholic Cemetery.
A seagull's cry coming from the bluff might echo there. The spot,
which he and my mother chose when they decided to buy a
burial site years ago, has as its neighbors an eclectic population
of Asians, Italians, and nuns, and it overlooks a busy thorough-
fare—all highly appropriate for a man who never cared much for
solitude.

The marble grave marker is the design of the moment at
Holyrood, with the beads of a rosary cut into the background. It's
a very tasteful headstone, although my father never liked saying the
rosary. Liturgical repetition annoyed him; it made him restless.

Before the service, the funeral director, wreaking of piety and cologne, approached me and whispered in my ear that he had taken the liberty of placing a rosary in my father's hands just before he closed the coffin. I solemnly thanked him and inwardly grimaced. Sorry, Dad. If only I had known. At least we succeeded in convincing the organist not to play "Amazing Grace." She seemed stunned and insulted by the request. "Amazing Grace" is a mainstay at funeral Masses. Who wouldn't want such an uplifting hymn played? My father, that's who. He hated "Amazing Grace." He thought it was too Protestant. My mother insisted on that one point: "I will *not* have 'Amazing Grace' played at your father's funeral." I was grateful that the organist respected our wishes. My brother Tom, fresh from the wilds of Alaska, threatened to "take the organist down" in midnote if she began to play it.

I started to write this book several months before my father's death, and he was delighted with the idea. Dad's love for the sisters was uncomplicated. They could do no wrong in his eyes. As far as he was concerned, nuns were one of the best things about Catholicism. Although he had initially been wary when they changed to secular clothing, it actually served to bring him closer to the sisters he met at church and through his work. It relaxed the relationship. His best pal in later years was the elderly Sister Pat, who lived alone in an apartment in Edmonds and did good works for Saint Mark's Parish, in spite of being well into her eighties.

My father wasn't raised a Catholic. Richard Schuler was a World War II convert. While serving in the navy in the icy nether regions of the Aleutian Islands off of Alaska, he met a Catholic priest named Edgar Gallant. Father Gallant was larger than life—literally. When he occasionally visited our home in later years, we children were most impressed by his legs. They were so long that he could wrap them around each other like a rope. With that trick alone, he had our rapt attention. For my father, a lonely young man in an isolated corner of a long war, an only child whose father had died young, Father Gallant was a charismatic presence. My father had never had the opportunity to meet a priest before, and Father

Gallant had the qualities of zeal, humility, and good humor that appealed to him. Had Edgar Gallant been at all remote or pious, the connection would never have been made. Above all, my father cherished a down-to-earth quality and good humor in people— the ability to reach out and relate to someone else in a warm and genuine way.

Father Gallant also sparked a dormant intellectual curiosity in my young father. He began reading about the church, and he was most affected by *The Seven Storey Mountain,* Thomas Merton's moving account of his conversion to faith and, finally, monasticism. Although my father wasn't one to talk openly about the experience that precipitated his own conversion, I imagine he felt it as something like a calling—not to a life of religious vocation, but to a religion itself.

He returned from the war a newly minted member of the Roman Catholic church, and almost immediately met my mother. Janet McArtor was the second daughter of a Scottish Protestant family with a traditional dislike of Catholics. There was still a tremendous reservoir of distrust toward Catholics in the Pacific Northwest, dating back to the late 1800s, when the working-class Irish and Italian immigrants first settled there. Catholics were viewed as low-class and vulgar. For one thing, they bred like rabbits. While most modern women were trying to control the size of their families, Catholic women were encouraged to have as many children as they could—to fill the ranks of soldiers in the army of Christ. There was a time when the Archdiocese of Seattle announced that if a family had twelve children, the twelfth would be baptized by the bishop—and many good Catholic couples actually tried to increase their efforts in an attempt to reach this mark. Roman Catholics also celebrated their Mass in an indecipherable babble of Latin, which sounded threateningly occult to outsiders. This strange foreign liturgy heightened suspicions that Catholics were not "true" Americans, because their first allegiance was to the Pope. When John F. Kennedy ran for president in 1960, his greatest barrier to election was his Catholicism. He addressed the matter head-on. Kennedy made it clear that if he was elected, the United States government would *not* be run from the Vatican in Rome.

My mother's family found it hard to resist Dad. He was tall and ruggedly handsome, with wavy blond hair, had a thousand-watt smile, and radiated a charm and decency that was seductive and comforting all at once. Even so, they didn't like the fact that he was Catholic. When my mother converted, too, they made their dismay clear. But my mother let them know that she and my father had fallen in love not only with each other but with a shared faith.

My parents believed they had a calling to raise a big family of good Catholic children. For that, they sacrificed any personal dreams they might have had. In particular, my father had to set aside his art. He was a gifted artist, capable of painting almost anything—from delicate watercolor ocean scenes to corny cartoons to wonderfully realistic portraits. Each of his children received drawing lessons from him. Every Christmas throughout our childhoods, he painted a sweeping nativity scene on the large horizontal mirror in our living room. To this day, whenever I'm home and look at that mirror, I can still see Dad's nativity mural. But the instability of an artistic career didn't really suit his ultimate calling. Once my dad and mom chose their path as Catholic parents, Dad realized he couldn't support a large family, or afford to send his children to Catholic schools, on an artist's salary. So he became a workingman. He never complained about it, or behaved as if he'd been deprived by having to give up something he loved. He possessed, as did my mother, a pure sense of vocation. For many years, he drove one of those familiar milk trucks from the fifties for Foremost Dairy, the kind packed with big blocks of melting ice and with metal racks filled with cold glass bottles—pints of cream and quarts, half gallons, and gallons of fresh milk. Dad delivered cases of them, along with cottage cheese, sour cream, buttermilk, eggs, and ice cream to the stores and schools around Seattle. It was during that time that he started becoming friendly with the nuns. He'd chat and joke with them when he made his school deliveries, and take them "surplus" blocks of cheese and gallons of ice cream for the convents. Of course, the nuns loved him. Later, Dad was promoted to a salesman for the company, and he created a network of goodwill. To him, selling meant service. Each of his clients—be it the smallest mom-and-pop grocery or the largest supermarket—received his full attention. There was never a Christmas morning when Dad didn't receive a call from some store or another that had run out of eggnog, or Foremost's special brand of peppermint ice cream. My father would drive to the dairy, load up his car, and then go to the market and restock the empty shelves. My mother always frowned and said, "Can you imagine? Who would call a man away from his family on Christmas morning to deliver five quarts of eggnog?" Dad would just smile, give her a quick kiss, and head out into the cold—often with a couple of kids in tow. Some of my favorite childhood memories are of those times when I was allowed to accompany my father on his Christmas-morning drives to the dairy.

I was born in 1950, the first daughter, and the third of nine children, five boys and four girls. My parents named me after Saint Catherine of Siena—or so they said, although I always suspected that they just loved the name Catherine, and that I was actually named after Katharine Hepburn. Whatever the source, Catherine was a very serious name for the small curly-headed imp that I was. It was a religious name. In those days, priests would only baptize a child who had been given a saint's name, or the derivative of one. Names such as Ashley, Tara, Fawn, or Cody would never have made the cut. My parents encouraged me to read about my patron saint in the large gold-leafed *Lives of the Saints* that sat on a shelf in our living room, next to the Holy Bible. One quote about Saint Catherine stayed in my mind: "She walked among us like a smile."

We were the prototypical Catholic family of the fifties and sixties. We could fill an entire row at Sunday Mass. My brothers and sisters and I all wore the itchy brown uniforms of Assumption grade school, and my brothers were altar boys. For a time, I had the honored assignment of laying out the priest's vestments for Mass, until Father Felix caught me sampling the Communion wine and banned me from the sacristy.

Our family life revolved around the church, and of course my parents held the hope that they would be giving at least two of their children to God—one to the priesthood and one to the convent. My eldest brother, Greg, was the natural choice for the priesthood. He was an excellent student, respectful, well behaved, and ardent about his faith. Greg was also blessed with a clear, strong baritone, and he loved to raise his voice in song. So, at the age of fourteen, he left home to pursue his religious training at Mount Angel, a Benedictine seminary in Oregon. Greg finished his high school education at Mount Angel, and there he stayed until his freshman year in college. Then, on a summer vacation at home, he accidentally discovered girls. All bets were off after that epiphany.

It seemed that I was the daughter anointed to be the nun. Although I had a clearly rebellious streak and wasn't entirely the "type" most sought after, I was the eldest daughter of a large Catholic family, and I did love the nuns as a child. I was naturally drawn to them out of a pure and unabashed curiosity. I was endlessly fascinated by what I imagined as the mystery of their lives. What did they do when they weren't teaching us at school? They prayed, they ate, they worked, and they slept. What else went on behind those convent walls?

We were taught by Dominicans—the order to which Catherine of Siena was vowed in the fourteenth century. Inspired by the nuns, I formed a romantic attachment to my patron. She was so bold and daring, so holy and humble—mystic, servant of the poor, and political activist all rolled into one. Also, she was radiantly beautiful, at least according to the holy card I carried in my missal. I especially loved the story of Catherine's calling, which she was said to have received at the age of six.

Catherine and her brother Stephen were returning from doing an errand for their mother. They were passing near the Church of the Preaching Friars in the Valle Piatta when Catherine saw the sky open. Revealed before her was a sumptuous chamber spun of gold and jewels, lush with beautifully colored fabrics. Catherine saw Jesus Christ seated on a glowing throne, dressed in garments fit for a king. On his head sat the bejeweled miter of the Pope. Standing by his side were the apostles Peter, Paul, and John. Catherine, staring deeply into the eyes of Jesus, was transfixed. Then Jesus raised his right hand and blessed her. Only when her alarmed brother Stephen tugged at her sleeve and brought her back from her reverie did the vision fade.

And that was Catherine's calling—at the tender age of six. She told no one of her vision or of her avowed dedication to Christ. When she was twelve—and of marriageable age—her brothers found a suitable bachelor for her to marry, but she refused. It was then that Catherine stated for the first time that she was already betrothed—to Christ. Determined that she make herself unattractive, she cut off her beautiful long dark hair, and so was spurned by her potential suitor. (It is said that other committed mystics of that period—especially those cursed with youth, beauty, or a dowry—went so far as to slice off their lips and noses to avoid marriage.) When she was eighteen, Catherine received the habit of the lay order of Dominicans. She did not join a community, but instead made a cloister of her small room in her parents' house, where she daily spoke with her Divine Lover. One holy card in my possession showed Catherine walking hand in hand with Jesus on the garden roof of her home, as if he had been invited as a lunch guest.

In time, Catherine would leave her self-imposed cloister and take on a healing mission. This young woman with no formal education would ultimately be responsible for shaking a corrupt papacy to its roots, and she would become the most famous Christian activist of her time. Catherine and Saint Teresa of Avila were the only female saints ever to receive the further distinction of being elevated to Doctor of the Church. In 1997, Teresa of Lisieux joined their elite circle.

I was pleased that my patron saint was such an independent, passionate, and powerful woman. As I read *The Lives of the Saints,* I found many of the female saints too passive and saccharine for my taste. I was especially unmoved by the virgin martyrs, whose only claim to sanctity was that they allowed themselves to be stoned to death, burned in boiling oil, pierced with a hundred arrows, chopped into pieces, or beheaded, rather than suffer the loss of their virginity. Since none of us knew at that time what virginity was, and since the nuns made no attempt to explain the details, the virgin martyrs' insistence on preserving it created quite a wellspring of confusion. Whatever virginity was, it was obviously worth dying a horrible death to keep. But it seemed to me that if they'd been clever and resourceful like my patron saint, Catherine, they might have found a way to spare themselves such a pointless fate.

Catherine was also a great feminist—although that term hadn't as yet appeared. She lived and died on her own terms; she fought against the tide of convention and outwitted the most powerful magistrates and princes of the church. It was this same spirit of feminist independence that attracted me to the Dominican Sisters who taught in my school. It may seem odd to call them independent; they were, after all, bound by the strict rule of canon law, and their vow of obedience would seem to mitigate against any show of independence. But the nuns were the strongest women I knew. Their power was supreme. When we were schoolchildren, they ruled us as surely as a general ruled his troops. It was useless to even try complaining to our parents about a problem at school. No matter what, Sister was always right.

In spite of their common dress, each of the nuns wielded her power in a unique way. To this day, my brother Greg pales at the mention of Sister Austin, the school principal, who believed godliness had to be whipped into children. She carried her metal ruler like a sword. At the slightest infraction, she would march down the classroom aisle, drag the miserable culprit from his seat to the front of the class, and slam the ruler down so hard on his naked palms that the crack reverberated through the hallways. When I think back on it now, it was the boys who were usually singled out for physical punishment—not just beatings but also more creative torments, which we could only imagine as having been taught in the convent. The Special Punishments for Sinful Parochial School Students course must have been packed. I particularly remember a perpetually stern old nun named Sister Martina, whom we nicknamed "Sister Martini," for no particular reason other than silliness. If a boy was talking in class, she would call him to the front of the room, draw a circle on the floor with chalk, and order him to stand in the middle of it, bent over and clasping his ankles, for a full hour. In today's world, this would be called child abuse. But at that time, it was an acceptable practice.

If they received an excess of punishment, the boys were also the objects of an excess of fawning. The nuns just loved boys. It was perfectly clear. The eighth-grade teacher, Sister Manette, so adored my brother Greg that she tormented every Schuler sibling who followed behind him. When I struggled with geometry, she simply shook her head in disbelief. She couldn't imagine that the sainted Greg's sister could be so imperfect, so unlike her brilliant brother. I can still feel the sting of her red marker pen cracking against the top of my head whenever I gave the wrong answer to a math problem. "*Greg* was so good at math," she wailed, perplexed by my inabilities. I never resented my brother for Sister Manette's behavior. It wasn't *his* fault that she loved boys.

A friend who attended Catholic school in Lima, Ohio, recalled that her fifth-grade teacher, Sister Benedict, had an unusual custom that she called "boy of the day." This was during the late fifties, when *Queen for a Day* was on television, and she would use the same tune as they did on the show. Each afternoon, toward the end of the class period, she would sing a little ditty: "Boy of the day, who will it be . . . ?" Then she would name the boy who had pleased her the most that day. The chosen boy would have to get up, go to the front of the classroom, and kiss Sister Benedict on her cheek. Apparently, there was an unfortunate episode when the boy of the day refused to cooperate and tried to jump out a window rather than press his lips to Sister's hairy cheek. She dragged him back from the window's edge by his hair, took him to the front of the room, and beat him soundly.

Girls were often spared the worst of the physical tortures, but we weren't excluded by any means. We still carried the burden of our sin. My first-grade teacher, a young woman with the oddly glamorous name of Sister Loretta, strongly impressed upon us that earthly life was nothing more than a ladder to heaven, which we were called on to climb. Our entire lives were to be spent trying to get to heaven. Each sin we committed—lying, stealing, cheating, being disobedient, giggling in church, talking back—caused us to slide backward down the rungs of the ladder. The more we sinned, the deeper we would fall, until finally the weight of our sins would send us plummeting into the fiery flames of hell. This had a powerful effect on a six-year-old! For a long time, I was sure that I was doomed. After I stole a candy bar from the local market, I was mortified. I cried myself to sleep that night with the knowledge that I might die in this state of sin and be sent to hell. The worst part of it was that I couldn't undo my sin. I had already eaten the candy bar.

The nuns believed that the best way to set young children on a godly course was literally to scare the hell out of them. The major event of first grade was the preparation for our First Holy Communion. It was exciting. We got to wear frilly white dresses and veils that made us look like tiny brides. But it was scary, too. Sister Loretta loved to tell horror stories about children who broke the rules surrounding Communion. The main rule was that we were not to bite the Host. We were to hold it on our tongues until it melted of its own accord. She soberly told us of the young boy who bit into the Host. Blood spurted from his mouth in rivers— he was eating Christ's crucified body, after all—and he choked on the blood and died. There was also the little girl who decided she could keep Jesus, so she took the Host out of her mouth and wrapped it in a handkerchief. On the way home from Mass, she was struck by a bolt of lightning. Fortunately, the priest saw her fall and managed to rescue the Body of Christ, which he returned to the tabernacle.

My second-grade teacher, Sister Camilla, introduced us to the best protection from our own evil instincts—our guardian angels. Today, guardian angels are ubiquitous in our culture. They are pictured as gentle, benevolent spirits that hover about trying to keep us from harm's way. But the guardian angels of my childhood were more ominous and demanding beings. Their role was not so much to surround us with light as it was to knock us over the head if we started to sin. According to Sister Camilla, our guardian angels were perched on our right shoulders. She forced us to sit on the far left edge of our seats so that our heavenly protectors would have room for their substantial wingspans. This seating arrangement made it difficult to sit, much less to write. Our desks were the old-fashioned one-piece style, with the curved armrest on the right. You'd slide into the narrow chair from the left. I, unfortunately, was left-handed, so the armrest was of no use to me. It simply provided my guardian angel with additional room to lounge. Since I was squeezed over to the left side of the chair, my writing arm hanging out into thin air, I was forced to perform a near-acrobatic act to get my hand over to the page. Sister Camilla was constantly cracking me on the head with a ruler because my lettering was so erratic. It never occurred to me to blame my guardian angel for hogging the seat. It never occurred to Sister Camilla to move my guardian angel to my other shoulder so I could get closer to the desk. As I'd been reminded many times before, the left was *sinistre,* sinister, bad. I was lucky they let me use my left hand to write.

The nuns didn't seem to make any effort to protect our young psyches from the hard truths. Sister Camilla also informed us that we shouldn't bother making friends with Protestant children. After all, they wouldn't be going to heaven, so we might as well nip any relationships in the bud. Only Catholics went to heaven. She never warned us away from Jews, but maybe it was because there were so very few of them in Seattle that the chances of befriending one weren't that great. Because of Sister Camilla's warnings, I felt compelled to break the terrible news to my next-door neighbor Randy Minkler that I couldn't marry him after all. I was devastated when he shrugged indifferently and informed me that he had a new girlfriend at *public* school. It was my first experience with the quixotic demands of the heart and the vicissitudes of love.

My parents, in part because they were converts, were by-the-book Catholics who shared this stern attitude toward Protestantism. When I was eight and reading every book I could get my hands on, I once checked out the biography of Martin Luther at the library. I didn't know he was a heretic. My parents soon set me straight. They wouldn't have that book in their house. I had to take it directly back to the library—which I did, crying with shame that I could have made such a terrible error.

The nuns never let us forget that we were soldiers in Christ's army. We had an obligation to reject the evils of atheism and fight the nonbelievers. In the third grade, we marched around the circumference of our classroom, singing the battle song of the Catholic youth crusade:

> *An army of youth,*
> *Flying banners of truth,*
> *We are fighting for Christ the Lord!*
> *Heads lifted high,*
> *Catholic action our cry,*
> *And the Cross our only sword!*

From our earliest years, we were subjected to intense recruitment drives to the religious life—especially during March, which was designated Vocation Month. Each day, we would say the Prayer for Vocations, and at the final line—"Grant to our youth true generosity in following thy call"—Sister would try to make eye contact with a deserving young girl. My friend Mary Anne Dwyer always got many meaningful looks during Vocation Month. She was sweet-tempered, a very good student, and the niece of a nun.

I got my fair share as well, although the looks were far more ambivalent in my case, since I was something of a troublemaker. When we were in the fifth grade, Mary Anne and I, along with several others, were chosen to be in an archdiocesan vocation pageant, where boys and girls were dressed in the authentic habits of the various orders of priests and nuns. I was dressed as a Sister of the Sacred Heart, and I still remember the suffocating headdress. It fit so tightly that my naturally round cheeks bulged to bursting. The heavily starched edges cut into the sides of my face, and the crisp wimple squeezed my forehead into a perpetual frown. The guimpe was fitted around my neck with the force of a chokehold. In the photograph, which was published in the *Catholic Northwest Progress,* my eyes are looking into the camera lens reproachfully, my mouth is set in a tight line, and my face is very still. Perhaps I was afraid that if I moved too suddenly, the guimpe would crush my throat.

Needless to say, my father was thrilled with this front-page display of religious fervor, and he went around calling me "Sister Catherine" for a while. At the pageant, the bishop made it known that God had a plan for us and that the Lord was revealing part of that plan today. Those of us who had been chosen to wear the sacred habits should consider seriously whether it was a sign that God was calling us. We'd been chosen by well-meaning nuns and priests for this honor. Maybe they could plant the seed of inspiration, stir the latent desires of a couple of likely aspirants. A vocation to religious life was supposed to be that way; mystery and surprise were its romance.

God pursued his chosen ones like an obsessed lover. To paraphrase baseball legend Satchel Paige, a great favorite of the nuns: You could run, but you couldn't hide. This theme was oft repeated by Sister Martina. She made all of her students memorize "The Hound of Heaven," a poem by Francis Thompson, which I can still recite by heart:

> *I fled Him, down the nights and down the days:*
> *I fled Him, down the arches of the years;*

I fled Him, down the labyrinthine ways
Of my own mind; and in the midst of tears
I hid from Him, and under running laughter.
Up vistaed hopes I sped;
And shot precipitated,
Adown Titanic glooms of chasmed fears,
From those strong Feet that followed, followed after.

The poem goes on at great length to detail the futile efforts of this poor soul to escape God's clutches; how his life was ruined at every turn, his world collapsing around him, until finally he had nothing, at which point the running "Feet" catch up with him and God says:

"Ah, fondest, blindest, weakest,
I am He Whom thou seekest!"

Sister Martina regarded her sixth graders through narrowed eyes when she read the poem, as if accusing us in advance of trying to run from God. She made being called seem like a curse. If you were chosen, that was that. Your life was no longer your own. And if you refused the call, God was going to wreck your life. Of course, we were all scared to death that we might be called. There was really no way of knowing in advance whose name might appear on his list. It was as if God ran a giant draft lottery, arbitrarily spinning the wheel of fortune, watching the numbered balls pop up.

The happiest day of Sister Martina's life—short of the election of an Irish Catholic boy to the White House—came with the news that Dolores Hart was joining a cloistered order of nuns. This, to her, was proof positive of God's powerful domination. He was using a young film star as one more example of his influence. Dolores Hart was the prototype of early 1960s beauty—shiny blond hair pulled back, her trademark bouncing ponytail—a cross between Grace Kelly and Debbie Reynolds. She had long, dark, curling eyelashes that framed dazzling azure blue eyes, with a pert nose, lush lips, and flawless teeth. She also had a perfect figure, both demure and seductive at the same time. She was best known for the movies she starred in with Elvis Presley, who was treated as though he were some sort of a god himself. Their chemistry in the movies appeared to be so real that rumors spread about a love affair. Then, at twenty-four, Dolores Hart abandoned the movies and the glamorous life of a star. She even left Elvis behind. She disappeared into a Benedictine monastery and resides there to this day, now a still-radiant woman in her sixties.

Sister Martina showed us a picture of Dolores Hart, supposedly taken just before she departed for her life in the convent. The photograph was dramatically lit, as if a heavenly beacon were shining directly down on her. She was in a prayerful pose—her clear eyes lifted upward, her perfect mouth parted slightly, her exquisite face seeming to glow like polished ivory from within. Apparently, Elvis had been no match for the Lord Jesus Christ.

I remember staring at that picture endlessly, trying to read something in her face that would give me a clue. I wanted Dolores Hart's mysterious calling explained. How did she know she'd been called? The way I saw it, the problem with believing you had a religious calling was that there really wasn't any way of knowing. What if it was just what *you* wanted? What if God didn't want *you*? It used to be, in the good old days of mystical visions, that Jesus himself, or his mother, Mary, would appear before you and call out. "You. Yes. You." It was clear as a bell. But things had changed dramatically. The present-day calling, the nuns explained, could be hard to recognize; it could be a little tricky. Maybe it was a thought that wouldn't leave your head—God's name playing over and over like a broken record. Maybe it was as simple as sitting in an almost-empty church faintly resinous with the odor of incense, staring at the flickering votive candles, and being drawn into a state of dreamlike meditation. Maybe it was a deep craving of some kind, or a burning curiosity you just couldn't satisfy. Whatever the calling was—and it was apparently inexplicable—if you were called, you'd know. For a long time, I did my best not to let God enter my thoughts, for fear he would hear me thinking about him and call me.

A couple of years ago, I asked my brother Greg how he experienced the calling. Did he remember what it was that led him into a seminary at the tender age of fourteen? He wasn't really sure what had happened. It had become an inevitability, a presumption that had gained surety over the course of the years. I had always assumed that Greg's desire for a priestly vocation had been a false alarm, since he decided to leave the seminary when he was nineteen, and later married and had children. But he told me that he never really stopped wanting to be a priest. He would gladly be a priest today if the church would allow priests to be married. It was a revelation to me. After all this time, it turned out that Greg still had a true calling.

Fearful as I may have been about the idea of being called, there was also a sense of intrigue. Like most young girls, I was impressionable, innocently romantic, and unintentionally melodramatic. And I actually believed in a personal Jesus—that was a crucial factor. One cannot underestimate the irresistible lure of a mortal yet transcendent God. And I wasn't alone in my love for Jesus. My classmates seemed to feel the same way. We were able to give Jesus all of the qualities of our most romantic dreams. He was strong yet sensitive, demanding yet compassionate—and, most important of all, he listened to everything we had to say and read our every thought. The idea that such an incredible being might single one of us out for special attention was enough to make us weak in the knees.

Such mystical fantasies also served to add excitement to an otherwise mundane life. My parents had created a stable, secure home for us, but it was a busy one, with constant chores. There was almost never a time when there wasn't at least one infant or toddler in the household, which meant my mother spent hours in the steamy basement, wrestling heavy wads of freshly bleached diapers through the ringer of her manual washing machine with a large stick. These diapers, by the hundreds, it seemed, would emerge in clean piles for me to fold. As the eldest daughter, I was the utility caretaker, adept at all aspects of child care, including bottle-feeding, burping, and changing diapers. I loved the babies, and I didn't object to the work, but I also knew from a young age that I would never willingly choose my mother's life—saddled with a demanding brood, all personal wants and needs sublimated. In that respect, the nuns also offered a valid alternative to the life of wife and mother. They were well educated, respected, fearless, and dignified—fantastic role models for a young girl. For a long time, I believed that the only way to escape my mother's fate was to become holy enough to warrant a higher calling. There was only one major stumbling block in the carefully laid out path of my plans.

I wasn't very good at it. I had too much of my father in me to maintain a pious pose for long. Being holy seemed to require a level of submission I wasn't genetically capable of sustaining. I just couldn't stomach being submissive, no matter how hard I tried. Besides, I couldn't keep silent long enough to master the contemplative spirit. The Schuler household was a boisterous place, where everyone vociferously talked, argued, and laughed at a decibel level that could offend more delicate eardrums. Like everyone else in my family, I had not only learned how to hold my own; I loved to talk. A nun who taught me when I was fourteen recognized me instantly thirty-two years later: "Oh, Catherine. Yes, I remember you. You were *always* talking."

Holy Angels Academy, a high school for girls run by the Sisters of Saint Dominic of the Holy Cross, was not my first choice. It was located all the way across town in Ballard, a run-down blue-collar neighborhood of single-story houses and crumbling docks. It was a highly unusual eyesore in the beautiful city of Seattle. I would have preferred to attend Holy Names Academy, where my friend Mary Anne Dwyer was headed. An elite girls' school perched high on Capitol Hill, it was run by the Holy Names Sisters, considered to be the cream of the crop among the many orders of nuns.

But Holy Names was expensive. Holy Angels was cheap—only three hundred dollars a year—so that's where I went. I never was able to get very far away from the Dominican Sisters.

Holy Angels was a modest plant, to say the least. The entire school was squeezed onto the top floor of a three-story brick building that primarily housed Saint Alphonsus elementary school. The aging structure always seemed to be in danger of collapsing. During the big earthquake of 1965, which struck in the middle of a school day, the ceilings and floors rippled with such ferocity that had the quake lasted five seconds more, the entire building, packed with students, would surely have been reduced to a pile of rubble.

But whatever Holy Angels lacked in a physical plant was more than made up for by the incredible spirit there. For the first time in my life, I was encouraged and allowed to pursue any goal I chose. For the first time, my education took place away from the shadow of the boys who had dominated my previous classrooms. It was freeing, even though the rules at Holy Angels were very strict. In many ways, it was the last of the old-style convent schools, run much like a novitiate, with a severe dress code, a rule of silence, and rigorous attention paid to the education of our souls.

Sister Edwina, the principal, ran the school in the manner of a Mother Superior, with an uncanny knack for appearing at the very moment you were misbehaving. She was extremely tough and rarely smiled, although there were occasional flashes of a soft heart. I had the impression that she was fond of me, although exasperated by my natural ebullience and gift for getting into trouble. Obedience was never my strong suit—then or now—and Sister Edwina believed in running a very tight ship. The rituals of her authority may seem benign today, but at the time, we took them quite seriously. The rule of silence was a near impossibility for three hundred teenage girls, but Sister Edwina enforced it strictly, as she did the insistence that our navy blue uniform skirts fall modestly below the knee. Miniskirts were the rage then, and at least some of us tried to circumvent the rule by rolling our skirts at the waist. Often we would be forced to kneel on the cold wood floors of the hallway for a skirt check. (A properly modest skirt would touch the floor when you were in a kneeling position.) Sister Edwina walked along the rows with her ever-present ruler as we hurriedly unrolled the offending skirts. Brown loafers and dark kneesocks were also the look of the moment. But Sister Edwina insisted that we wear ugly brown-and-white saddle shoes with white ankle socks. Perhaps she thought it was better for our souls.

My two closest friends at Holy Angels were Bernadette and Tracy. They were both straight-*A* students, popular, and talented. Tall, thin, dark-haired Bernadette was warm, soft-spoken, and serious. Tracy was as effervescent as champagne, and she had a singing voice so high and sweet that it could bring our music teacher, Sister Carmen, to tears. To this day, I can see Tracy perfectly—a delicately boned girl with an angelic face, pale freckled skin, and long, thick strawberry red hair, who was transformed in song.

I provided a balance to their extremes—at times a serious, solitary writer, and at times bold, outspoken, and mischievous. We were content in our convent-school world, where all the challenges were manageable. But in our final year at Holy Angels, powerful dynamics shifted the solid ground beneath our feet. After graduation, the three of us went our separate ways. Bernadette became a nun. Tracy became a prostitute. I became a lost soul—and a nonbeliever.

My parents were stunned by my defection. It was disappointing enough that I didn't enter a convent, as they had always hoped. But to reject the church out of hand? It was the last thing they'd expected. They had sacrificed so much to make sure I was schooled by the nuns, and the result was a radical feminist nonbeliever. Filled with confusion and despair, they removed their remaining children from Catholic schools. They couldn't know, nor could I, standing on the shifting fault line of the late 1960s, that it was all part of God's mysterious plan. But each Sunday, they knelt in church and struggled to keep their faith steady and their hearts focused on eternal truths as they sang:

> *Faith of our fathers, living still,*
> *In spite of dungeon, fire, and sword . . .*

3

Young Women See Visions

Claire
Atlanta, Georgia

— 1 9 4 2

JESUS CHRIST WAS INSATIABLE—YOU COULD NEVER GIVE enough of yourself to him. Claire learned this from the writings of the great mystic saints. Christ required—no, he demanded—not only your body and soul but every vestige, every nook, every hidden longing of your heart. To be worthy of receiving him, you must empty yourself of the mundane completely—give up all vanity, desire, pleasure—like a vessel drained of its last drop. Even then, you could only hope to be worthy of receiving Jesus Christ, for no amount of mortal sacrifice could ever truly sate his divine hunger.

As Saint Teresa of Lisieux, known as "the Little Flower" because of her pure and childlike devotion to Jesus, wrote with fevered abandonment:

For as long as You wish, I will stay with my eyes on You. I want to be fascinated by Your gaze. I want to be the prey of Your love. I hope that one day You will swoop down on me, carry me off to the furnace of love, and plunge me into its burning depths so that I can be its ecstatic victim for all eternity!

To be Christ's true lover, you must be willing to prove yourself. Beyond all reason, beyond all physical boundaries, it was necessary to walk his path. Even as Simon helped shoulder the burden of Christ's cross, you must take on his suffering. And you must do it joyfully. Claire's parish priest had once given a sermon on the suffering willingly endured by the saints. He had recounted the story of Saint Lawrence, an early church martyr, who had been strapped to a grill and burned to death. As the intense heat slowly roasted his flesh, Lawrence grinned at his torturers and called out, "Turn me over. I'm done on this side." The story made a powerful and lasting impression on Claire. If you truly believed with all of your heart, you could even exhibit high spirits in the face of suffering. She wondered if she could ever achieve such a state of devotion.

Transfixed by the crucifix hanging on her bedroom wall, her head bursting with the tales of brave Christian martyrs, Claire knew in her heart that pain was the key. As it had been the beginning of Christ's transformation, it became the beginning of hers; the sacrifice of her pain was a way to draw nearer to her God.

There was a patch of land behind her family's home where roses grew wild in heavily thorned and tangled bushes. The deep pink flowers exuded an alluring scent, filling the entire backyard with their rich fragrance. When she was a young child, Claire's mother showed her how to carefully pluck the petals when they were at the height of their bloom. She would then add them to rainwater, and store them in empty jam jars. After a month of steeping, she would have sweet-smelling rose water to splash on after a bath.

But Claire had transcended her love for the beauty or the fragrance of the roses; her love was only for Jesus. Now her interest in the wild pink roses lay in their thorns. She wanted to emulate Saint Rose of Lima, who had worn a crown of roses studded with sixty-nine spikes that pierced her forehead. Claire knew she'd be unable to get away with something so obvious. She soon discovered that there were other ways to emulate the holy.

With a pair of pruning shears, Claire snipped off several robust new shoots growing from the wild rosebushes. She chose only the longest—those with the largest purple thorns. She took them to her room, braided them together, bound them with heavy string, and fashioned a girdle of thorns. She then secured the girdle snugly around her waist, concealing its presence under a loose-fitting sweater. The girdle of thorns became her private penance, her constant reminder of the presence of Jesus Christ in her life. She wore the girdle every day, and she thrilled at the deep pricks of pain that sometimes caused her to gasp out loud. The thorns didn't do any real damage, but they left red scratches and ugly welts on her back, her stomach, and her sides. Sometimes she would remove the girdle, rearrange the branches, and use the newly exposed thorns to flagellate herself. She would raise her arm over her head and slap the makeshift whip down hard against her skin until she bled—just as she had read of the saints doing.

Eager to test herself, Claire would experiment with other penances. In attempting to emulate Christ's suffering on the cross, she knelt for hours at night on the hardwood of her bedroom floor, her arms outstretched, until her neck, shoulders, and knees ached with excruciating pain. Rose of Lima had slept on a pile of bricks; Claire placed a rough board under her top sheet and slept on it until her mother discovered it and forbade the practice. "Do you want to grow up deformed?" she screamed at Claire in alarm. "What's wrong with you?"

At sixteen, Claire was a shy, awkward girl with a heavy face and prominent features. She would never be considered pretty; nor did she have a talent for music, or a way with words. Around young people her own age, she usually felt invisible; there was little about her to attract attention. Boys didn't seem interested in her—nor did she care anything for them. They bored her with their silliness. Was she the only one who was aware of the dire state of the world? Had no one else heard the message of Fatima?

In 1917, the Blessed Virgin Mary had appeared six times to three young peasant children in the small Portuguese village of Fatima. She had chosen Lucia de Santos and her two young cousins, Jacinta and Francisco, as emissaries to the church and the world. Our Lady often sent her messages through children instead of appealing directly to church and world leaders. This annoyed the hierarchy in Rome no end.

During one of her apparitions at Fatima, Our Lady revealed a three-part secret to the children, which they kept to themselves. They indicated that it was very grim news indeed. No amount of pressure by church leaders could compel the children to reveal the secret. The younger children, the cousins Jacinta and Francisco, died soon after the apparitions, revealing nothing.

Lucia de Santos entered a cloistered convent, where she continued to receive visitations from Our Lady. In 1941, she finally revealed the first two parts of the secret.

The first part was a vision of hell so terrible that it was beyond human power to describe.

The second part was a message from Our Lady to the church, a message that seemed so urgent, one wonders why Lucia waited twenty-four years to make it public.

The Virgin Mary told her:

> God wishes to establish in the world devotion to my Immaculate Heart. If what I say to you is done, many souls will be saved and there will be peace. The war is going to end; but if people do not cease offending God, a worse one will break out. To prevent this, I ask for the consecration of Russia to my Immaculate Heart, and the Communion of reparation on the first Saturday of

each month. If my requests are heeded, Russia will be converted, and there will be peace; if not, she will spread her sinfulness throughout the world, causing wars and persecutions of the Church. The good will be martyred; the Holy Father will have much to suffer; entire nations will be annihilated.

The third part of the secret—the most terrifying—remained with Lucia. Claire shuddered when she considered what it might be. She envisioned a fiery apocalypse that would consume millions of souls. She wanted to make sure she was in a proper state of grace when this occurred, so every day she said a prayer to Our Lady of Fatima.

With the war brewing in Europe, Our Lady's predictions seemed to be coming true. As always, Claire prayed with fervor, hoping against all hope that she herself might be worthy of receiving a vision.

Late at night, when Claire knelt in her room, closed her eyes, and gave herself over in prayer, any clumsiness she may have experienced would fall away from her. She felt herself as slender as a willow reed, as delicate as a wisp of dandelion fluff blown into the wind. She longed to rise out of her flesh, to feel holy ecstasy, to hear a single sweet whisper from her Lord Jesus. It was her sole obsession.

Claire's secret dream was to become a nun. Perhaps she would join the Poor Clares, the cloistered order founded by her patron saint, Clare of Assisi. The contemplative life was her desire—if that is what Jesus wanted. She prayed and waited for a sign.

By the time Claire finished high school, World War II was well under way. Death and suffering filled the world; the blood of innocents flowed in rivers—just as Our Lady had predicted. Claire's father, an electrical engineer, announced to the family that he had taken an important new job at Boeing, a company in Seattle, Washington, that manufactured aircraft. They would be leaving

Atlanta and moving to a part of the country that Claire assumed was like the Wild West she had seen in the movies. Before she left, her parish priest gave her a gift to take with her—a relic. It was a tiny square of cloth, only an inch in diameter, taken from a habit worn by Saint Teresa of Lisieux, the Little Flower.

Claire's mother was a practical woman. She sensed that her daughter might never marry, and she believed her religious ardor would cool with maturity. She convinced Claire to put off her thoughts of convent life until after the war, and meanwhile to get an education and learn a skill. Claire decided to train to be a nurse; she was attracted to the idea of ministering to God's suffering people. When she was eighteen, Claire entered nursing school at Providence Hospital in Seattle, and she received her nursing degree two years later. She showed herself to be so highly skilled and intelligent that eventually she was chosen to be one of the instructors at the nursing school. Much to her surprise, Claire discovered that she enjoyed teaching almost as much as she did nursing, and she went on to earn a degree in education.

In 1946, with much of Europe laying in smoldering ruins, and the carnage of World War II finally ending, Lucia de Santos wrote down the third part of the message given to her by Our Lady of Fatima. She sent it to the Pope in a sealed envelope, with the admonition that her letter should not be opened until 1960. When Claire heard of this, she was convinced that the letter held a message for her—that she must fast, pray, and devote herself to God's work.

During this period, Claire became familiar with the Sisters of Saint Dominic of the Holy Cross, who had established two major hospitals and many schools in Washington State. The order's joint mission of nursing and teaching appealed to Claire; she saw her introduction to them as a sign from God.

In 1954, she was accepted as a postulant with the Dominican Sisters of the Holy Cross. At twenty-eight, she was a good ten years older than the other postulants, but her ardor was every bit as intense. The order was delighted to have an entrant who was already schooled as both a nurse and a teacher. She had so much to offer them.

Carmen
Seattle, Washington—1954

Carmen had wanted to be a nun since the fourth grade, when she was nine years old. There was a wonderful quality to nuns; such a mystique surrounded them. She couldn't articulate the attraction at the time, but later she came to realize that the religious life was a bastion of order and serenity, and her home was just the opposite. Carmen was the only child of hard-drinking, abusive parents. The family barely managed to stay above the poverty line, living in a squalid little house on the far side of Chehalis, Washington. Carmen's daily life was seeded with domestic violence, and she responded to the battering by developing a hard shell. Deep down, she came to believe she was worthless. She'd certainly been told so often enough.

Carmen envied those friends whose families were large and warm. She fantasized about what it would be like to have a mother who sang as she baked bread and cookies, or a father who was loving and devoted.

However, there was one area where Carmen's parents exhibited some semblance of responsibility, and that was their daughter's Catholic upbringing. This concession to the church was not as strange as it seemed. In the tight-knit Irish community, religious devotion mingled easily with nights spent drinking at the local saloon. The line between the secular and the church was often blurred with booze, as the liturgy and drunken songfests frequently came on the heels of each other. The local priest was as likely as not to join his parishioners—including Carmen's parents and their friends—for a night of drink and song, then end up back at their house after the bars had closed. As she tossed and turned in her small bed, Carmen would hear the priest's sorrowful baritone rising up from the living room below—the homesick tones of "Galway Bay" sounding above her fitful sleep:

> *. . . And if there is going to be a life hereafter,*
> *And somehow I am sure there's going to be.*
> *I will ask my God to let me make my heaven*
> *In that dear land across the Irish Sea.*

When Carmen was thirteen, her parents announced that she was to be sent to boarding school with the nuns—whichever school would take her on scholarship. With an intercession from their priest to the Irish pastor of Saint Alphonsus Church in Seattle, Carmen was offered a scholarship to Holy Angels Academy.

Carmen would bask in her first experience of a benevolent family life. The Dominican Sisters were both her teachers and her guardians. They were also her inspiration.

From the time she was a small child, Carmen had been drawn to music; perhaps it was all those evenings listening to the priest sing; maybe it was the Irish in her. But music infused her with joy and gave her an avenue for expressing her high spirits. It was her greatest comfort, her escape. At Holy Angels, she was encouraged to become immersed in her passion. Music was valued there. The music teacher, Sister Imelda, was a very gentle, gifted nun, who first nurtured Carmen's musical abilities and later her interest in the convent. Carmen had come to adore Sister Imelda for her kindness and guidance. It took no persuasion for Carmen to enter a life where such women existed. Under Sister Imelda's loving tutelage, Carmen finally began gaining a sense of self-esteem. She surprised herself when a thrilling and unfamiliar thought popped into her head: I can do this. I can really be somebody.

Carmen's best friend at boarding school was a local Seattle girl named Michelle. They formed an instantaneous bond, having both come from hard-drinking, abusive families. Michelle, though, wasn't an only child like Carmen. She was part of a large Swedish family headed by an angry, frustrated mother and a controlling, remote father. For Michelle, boarding school was pure heaven compared to the chaos she faced at home. At school, there was structure. There were rules and a schedule. Nobody yelled at her. Everything was clean. There were regular meals. And most important of all, there was an abundant amount of love and tenderness.

For Carmen and Michelle, Holy Angels was both a cocoon and a source of inspiration. They were shielded from the normal teenage experiences of going to dances and movies and having dates, but in exchange they were exposed to literature, music, and the world of ideas. As the two friends approached their senior year, they both knew that they didn't want to leave. They decided to extend their stay indefinitely. They applied for entrance into the order.

Armed with a fierce emotional certainty, their hearts pounding, the girls appeared for their arranged visit with Mother Frances, the prioress of the order. They were accompanied by Sister Imelda, who was overjoyed to have snagged two fine aspirants. This was to be Carmen and Michelle's formal interview, and they were both scared to death. Nevertheless, they had prepared resolutely. They pressed their uniforms carefully and polished their shoes, scrubbed their faces, and curled their hair. Finally, moments before their interview, they stood shaking together outside the convent's parlor door, waiting to take their turns with Mother. They did their best to give each other courage, squeezing each other's sweaty hands tightly.

Michelle was first. She entered the room and stood shyly before Mother Frances. Mother Frances was a large, busty German woman of sixty, her face creased with a light web of lines. She welcomed Michelle with a smile and tried to put her at ease, asking questions about her family and her interests. Finally, she asked, "Now, tell me, dear, why do you want to enter the convent?"

Michelle opened her mouth to speak, but no words came out.

"I . . . I just feel . . ." Michelle stammered helplessly.

At which point, Mother Frances rescued her. "There are so

many reasons, my dear. I understand. Is it because you love God and you want to serve him?" she prodded gently.

"Yes." Michelle nodded eagerly. "I do."

Mother Frances beamed approvingly. "There is no higher ambition." Michelle breathed a sigh of relief. She'd passed the test.

Carmen wasn't accustomed to being speechless, but when it was her turn, she found it hard to get the words out. When Mother Frances asked her if she had any deep-seated fears, she blurted out, "Spiders," and cringed because it was such a stupid answer. Nevertheless, she was approved.

After graduation, Carmen and Michelle entered the order, arriving on the doorstep with one trunk, two large handbags, one small handbag, and a briefcase. These were filled with the only possessions they would be allowed to consider their own. Each of the postulants had been given a list of precisely what she was to bring with her.

In the years before the property that would become Rosary Heights was purchased, the Dominican motherhouse resided in a modest building in Everett, Washington, about an hour's drive north of Seattle. It was a square, flat structure that gave no hint to the outside world of its extraordinary purpose. Other than the small brass plaque next to the front door, no one would have thought it a convent.

Carmen and Michelle could barely contain their excitement as they were ushered inside. It was exciting to don the humble garb of postulants—black veils, with the barest hint of hair showing in the front, ankle-length black dresses of heavy wool, a black cape for outdoors, and black lace-up shoes, especially made, Carmen joked, "for old ladies and nuns."

There were just two others in the group with Carmen and Michelle. Barbara was a somewhat nervous, delicate young woman of breathtaking beauty, tall and statuesque, with turquoise eyes and long blond hair. She had come all the way from Portland, Oregon, delivered by her parents, who seemed very unhappy to see their only daughter—their beautiful child—swallowed up by the convent. Although they were devout Catholics, Barbara's parents nevertheless agonized over the loss of their daughter. There would be no wedding bells, no babies, no nighttime chats around the kitchen table. Their daughter would never belong to them again.

The fourth new postulant was Claire, an older woman of twenty-eight, who was already trained as both a nurse and a teacher. Claire was a large matronly-looking woman with an ample bosom and heavily lidded eyes. Being older, she stayed somewhat removed from the rest, but her pious, holier-than-thou behavior made them all profoundly uncomfortable. There was something about Claire that they just didn't get. Carmen kept telling Michelle that it was because of the age difference, but neither of them really believed that. She was just strange.

Before they had entered the order, they'd been told very little about what to expect from life in the convent. Now the instructions came in waves. The first two years of religious life were designed to be particularly rigorous. The goal was to mold young girls into religious women. It was vital to separate the wheat from the chaff, much like basic training in the military. For their nine-month postulancy and the first year of their novitiate, they would have limited contact with the outside world—or even with the professed sisters in their own order. During their postulancy, every moment would be scheduled, and they would not be allowed to leave the convent except for a medical emergency. Their days would be spent in prayer—Mass and the Little Office (a less rigorous form of the Divine Office, used by active communities)—communal tasks, studying theology, and being coached in the meaning of their vows. Visits from family and friends would be severely restricted, to avoid distraction by outside influences. There would be no newspapers and no radio. Correspondence would be limited, and all letters, incoming and outgoing, would be slit open and read.

Although they were Dominicans, they followed the Rule of Saint Augustine. Most orders followed one of two model rules—

that of Saint Augustine or the Rule of Saint Benedict. There weren't that many differences between the two, although the Benedictine Rule was supposedly somewhat less rigid.

The Rule of Saint Augustine, written in the fifth century, focused on the maintenance of humble, inconspicuous, and quiet behavior. Followers of this rule were required to keep silent except during the half-hour recreation, during the recitation of the Divine Office, and when conversation was necessary to perform a task. Casual remarks, of the type that ordinary humans make all the time—"How are you?" "Look at that snow," or "You have a piece of spinach caught in your teeth"—were strictly forbidden. The postulants were instructed to walk "in a way becoming a religious"—light, even steps, hands folded together out of view, face and eyes cast down. Keeping "custody of the eyes" was essential for a proper religious demeanor. A religious woman was prayerful; she didn't look around. A religious woman didn't let herself become distracted by her environment, or by the people in it. For Carmen, keeping custody of the eyes was one of the most difficult of the rules to follow. Carmen's face was alive with feeling and curiosity. She delighted in observing the world around her. When she would pass Michelle in the hallway, it was almost impossible not to look at her, to share some small confidence—a smile, a grimace, a word. When she heard a noise or sensed that another person had entered a room, it took almost supernatural power to prevent her from glancing up. She fought the temptations, but she didn't always succeed.

There were so many rules to learn. There were rules about everything. Some of them seemed purposely silly tests of obedience. For example, they were allowed to cut their hair only eight times a year—on Easter, Pentecost, the feasts of the apostles Peter and Paul, the feast of Mary Magdalen, the Nativity of the Blessed Virgin Mary, All Saints' Day, and Christmas. They were not allowed to look out the convent windows. They could eat no fruit on Saturdays, in honor of the Blessed Virgin Mary.

Claire, who was a terrible stickler for all the rules, came across old Sister Brigid sitting in the garden eating a juicy Washington State Delicious apple on a Saturday afternoon. She was so disturbed by this that she broke the rule of silence to exclaim, "Sister! You're eating an apple."

Sister Brigid smiled with satisfaction. "Why, yes, I am. And it's a wonderful apple." She took another bite of the crisp fruit, letting a trickle of juice dribble down her chin. Then Sister Brigid got up and walked away, leaving Claire gaping behind her.

Carmen's greatest struggle was the rule of silence. She loved to talk, and no one had ever stopped her before. She'd always sung out loud while she worked, and sometimes she had to bite her tongue to keep the notes from flowing past her lips. Usually, she only discovered she was humming out loud when one of the other sisters frowned in her direction. Once Sister Karen caught her singing "The Tennessee Waltz" while she mopped the kitchen floor. One moment Carmen had been entirely alone, swishing the mop on the floor while executing a dance step—"I remember the night, and the Tennessee Waltz, and I know just how much I have lost"— and the next moment Sister Karen was storming into the room, breathing fire.

On another occasion, Carmen and Michelle were lining the garbage cans with newspapers, and in spite of the edict not to look at the papers, Carmen lost custody of her eyes for the split second it took to see the headline: JAMES DEAN DIES IN FIERY CRASH. The shock took over. She shrieked. Michelle looked at the headline. *She* shrieked. Sister Karen found them on the floor five minutes later, surrounded by opened garbage bags, pouring over the details of the crash. Their penance was to recite an extended rosary with their arms outstretched for the entire time. Carmen's arms ached for weeks.

There was ample opportunity to confess their transgressions. Once a week, there was the Chapter of Faults, based on the stipulation in the rule that "admonishment and correction of the unruly is one of the spiritual works of mercy."

The Chapter of Faults was a public confession of breaches of religious deportment. It was not the same as confessing one's sins in a confessional. Matters of sin were strictly between a penitent and her priest. Rather, the Chapter of Faults included failures to keep the rule—violations of silence, carelessness, waste, not keeping custody of the eyes and the like.

The Chapter of Faults was exquisitely ritualized. The sisters would walk in a procession to the chapter room in order of age, the youngest first. One by one, they would go to the center of the room, kneel, and bow their heads before the Mother Superior.

"Reverend Mother, I humbly confess my fault that I have not rightly observed our holy rule and constitution, but have in many ways transgressed them. In particular, I accuse myself of . . ."

This would be followed by a catalog of failures:

"I looked at Michelle when I was walking down the hall.

"I broke profound silence when I dropped a plate in the refectory.

"My veil was crooked during Divine Office.

"I neglected to make the sign of the cross over my food.

"I laughed when Sister's rosary broke and scattered beads on the floor of the chapel. . . ."

Sometimes the Chapter of Faults dragged on endlessly. Carmen noticed that it was always the holiest, most obedient sisters who seemed to have the longest lists of faults. For example, Claire, who never did anything wrong, as far as she could tell, would go on for a full five minutes or more.

Early Dominicans had endured serious penances for their transgressions. "Six strokes with the scourge"—a whipping—had not been that uncommon, along with other forms of corporal punishment. Thankfully, the custom had long since been discontinued. Still, there were certain penances that Carmen found equally distasteful, if not humiliating. The penance she hated the most was called the floor dish, which required you to eat your meals in the middle of the refectory, crouched on a twelve-inch stool in front of a twelve-inch table. At least she was short! This penance was even worse for the long-legged sisters.

Carmen thought that the other postulants were much more adept at religious behavior than she was; most of the time, she felt hopeless. When would she ever learn? Barbara was helped immeasurably by being naturally shy and quiet, and Michelle got into trouble only when she was around Carmen. Claire was completely different from the other three. As a matter of fact, she was something else entirely—obtusely mystical, self-righteous, and obedient to a fault—as if she were already practicing for sainthood. In class, whenever the conversation turned to the relationship of a religious woman with Jesus Christ, Claire would begin discussing her relationship with the Savior. She would almost transform, her heavy face coming alive with feeling. Once they were talking about the stigmata, a dubious blessing Christ had bestowed upon a chosen few in the history of the church. Descriptions of the stigmata were always vivid and gory. A devout person—usually a woman— would be afflicted with huge bleeding wounds in the palms of her hands and feet, duplicating the wounds Jesus endured when he was nailed to the cross. When these wounds appeared, the afflicted person experienced the same agony that Jesus had suffered—a pain so excruciating, it was impossible to imagine being able to endure it without perishing.

The idea of the stigmata had always made Carmen a little squeamish. The thought of it was unsettling to her; she was afraid she wouldn't be able to stand having something so horrible happen to her. But Claire seemed undaunted. One day, during a discussion, she spoke up, her eyes glistening with real interest.

"What do you think you'd have to do to be chosen for such a gift? How does one become worthy of such a wonderful experience?" she asked their instructor, a crusty old nun named Sister Imogene. Sister Imogene frowned at Claire over her smudged bifocals. "That is for Jesus to decide," she said bluntly, eyeing Claire suspiciously. "But I think practicing humility would be a good way to start."

.   .   .

Even though the four women spent every waking hour together, they were often reminded to maintain an emotional distance from one another. Sister Karen told them again and again that this wasn't a college dormitory. They were repeatedly warned about the dangers of forming "particular friendships." This was a real problem for Carmen and Michelle. The very idea was hard for them to grasp. They had been the best of friends since they were thirteen, and they had always relied upon each other for care and support. Neither of them was sure she'd be in the convent today if it hadn't been for the other. What was so dangerous about that?

One day, Sister Karen drew them aside after prayers. She gave them her sternest look and said, "You've been sitting together and talking during recreation."

They were puzzled. It was okay to talk during recreation. What was the problem?

"I'm sorry, Sister, but I don't understand," Carmen responded. "We're allowed to speak to the others during recreation, aren't we?"

"You abuse the privilege," Sister Karen said sharply. "You do not sit with the others. You talk only to each other. I feel a duty to prevent the appearance of a particular friendship. You have only two commitments in this life—to God and to the community. Believe me when I tell you that terrible sins have been committed in the name of friendship."

They waited for Sister Karen to elaborate, but she said nothing more. After that, Carmen and Michelle tried to be more circumspect. They were careful around the others; they didn't wish to do anything that might jeopardize their religious lives. Still, they hadn't the slightest clue what kind of sin Sister Karen might be talking about. They were unworldly, naïve girls—innocents. They were unfamiliar with sexual matters of any kind. So the underlying fear of lesbianism contained in the concept of a "particular friendship" completely eluded them.

The seemingly robust Claire was having problems of a different nature. After she fainted one morning during the Divine Office, she was taken for an examination. The doctors were shocked to discover that she was covered with cuts, scratches, welts, and bruises. The novice mistress found a scourge in Claire's room. The scourge was a leather rope with metal studs. Claire had apparently been using it to flagellate herself.

Mother Frances was quite disturbed by this. She waited until Claire was released from the hospital, then called her to her office and confronted her with what had been found.

"Our order does not allow this practice," she told Claire in no uncertain terms. "It's archaic. It's harmful, and it does nothing to aid our mission. We are dedicated to teaching others, and nursing the ill. We need all the strength we can muster. We can't fritter away our lives suffering and in pain. Our purpose—*your* purpose, Sister—is to ready yourself for the work of the order. Do you understand me? There'll be no more of this. Tell me you understand."

"I do, Mother. I understand," Claire replied quietly, eyes downcast. Even with all their rules, the Dominicans were practical women, suspicious of those who were extreme in their practice of virtue. Excessive piety was a form of arrogance. It could also be dangerous.

By sheer grit and the grace of God, all four women survived their postulancy. Carmen found that she was growing stronger in her vocation. She didn't rail against the rules quite as much. She began to see how truly wonderful and special it was to be a part of this community. There was a joy here—a happy sisterhood. On April 29, the feast of Saint Catherine of Siena, she was delighted to find the chapel filled with spring flowers. Everyone was in a celebratory mood. When she walked into recreation, there were tables laid out with shortcakes, baskets of fresh strawberries, and big bowls of freshly whipped cream. She didn't think to ask why there was strawberry shortcake on the feast of Saint Catherine. She just piled her plate high. As it turned out, it was a long-standing tradition among the Edmonds Dominicans, complete with heart-shaped plates, tablecloths, and napkins. No one knew why the tradition had begun. No matter, the treat always spurred a spirited discussion of Catherine of Siena. Perhaps strawberry shortcake had been her favorite dessert!

As they prepared to take the habit, the postulants turned their thoughts to the matter of names. During the clothing ceremony, when they would receive the white habits of novices, each sister would be given a name—symbolic of a "new baptism." It was the name she would be known by for the rest of her life. Some of the lucky sisters were allowed to keep their given names; others were given lovely or inspirational names—such as Therese, Cecilia, or Pauline; or names that connoted strength, such as John, Paul, or Joan. But then there were the dreaded names, such as Ingrid, Bonaventure, Alcantara, or Romualda. One day, Carmen came across a poem, entitled "A Postulant's Prayer," that said it all:

> *What's in a name? Well, not too much—*
> *But still enough that terrors clutch*
> *My anxious heart whene'er I see*
> *The Roman Martyrology.*
> *I do revere those holy souls*
> *On the celestial honor rolls*
> *But please, Lord, if it's all the same*
> *Preserve me from the curious name.*
> *Thortgyd and Gundekar I know*
> *Were very holy long ago*
> *And so were Botwid and Pelagious.*
> *I fear I am not so courageous.*
> *I hope no one will think me rude*
> *If I eschew Saint Aggletrud*
> *And say a hearty De Profundis*
> *That I be not named Baldegundis.*
> *O, all ye heavenly hosts attend—*

Now is the time I need a friend!
A name folks can pronounce—as well,
Something my Mom and Dad can spell.

As Carmen read that poem, she laughed so hard that tears streamed from her eyes. What would her name be? At the Chapter of Faults, she had to confess that she had once again broken profound silence.

Elizabeth
Seattle, Washington—1946

Elizabeth was first told that the Catholic church was evil when she was five years old. In the carefree moments before her innocence was shattered, she had been playing a game of tag with her next-door neighbor Martha. The two girls were racing among the apple and cherry trees on the landscaped expanse of Elizabeth's grandmother's backyard. It was spring, and a light wind had scattered the white and pink cherry blossoms like a decoration on the carpet of lush green lawn.

Suddenly, Elizabeth's grandmother appeared at the back door. "Elizabeth, come inside," she ordered sharply. Elizabeth halted in midstride and turned toward the voice. Her friend Martha panted breathlessly beside her. "I have to go." Elizabeth shrugged. The two girls parted, and Elizabeth ran to her grandmother, who was waiting at the back door.

Although her grandmother was physically frail and walked with a cane, she was nonetheless formidable. Her stiff patrician bearing and humorless manner brooked no resistance. She had no tolerance for nonsense or whimsy. Within that framework, she was kind in her way, but she was hardly a sympathetic guardian for a spirited young girl. Elizabeth had lived with her grandmother since the age of three, when her parents had been killed in a car accident. The sprawling property near Ravenna Park was beautiful, with two acres sloping down to a creek—the neat rows of apple and cherry trees creating a shaded arbor dappled with color, the imposing peak of Mount Rainier rising white-capped in the distance. The house was a three-storied mansion of tightly constructed native stone and red brick, impeccably furnished with the stately artifacts of her grandmother's family. Heavy damask curtains shielded the richly wooded interior from light, making it feel a cold, dark, and sober place.

"Come into the parlor," her grandmother commanded, leading the way slowly across the vast Persian carpet.

"What's wrong, Grandmother?" Elizabeth asked plaintively. She recognized the tone of voice, the ominous tightening of her grandmother's jawline, the narrowing of her eyes. What had she done now? She didn't always remember all of the rules; there were so many of them.

"You are not to play with that girl anymore," her grandmother said sharply. Her eyes were blazing with a fearful intensity.

"But why not? I like Martha."

"The girl is a Roman Catholic," her grandmother replied. Then she sat down across from Elizabeth. "She's an evil child." She began to educate Elizabeth about the strange, occult practices of the Church of Rome. Their satanic powers were strong, she warned; they could steal your soul if you let them. Roman Catholics only pretended to be loyal citizens, her grandmother revealed; the sinister truth was that they were engaged in a secret plot to take over the United States. Their leader lived in a palace called the Vatican in Rome, and he controlled the workings of his satanic minions from far across the ocean. Catholics could not be trusted.

In the coming years, Elizabeth learned more from her grandmother about Roman Catholics, and the details were so shocking that they made her a true believer. The mere sight of a priest or nun on the street sent Elizabeth into paroxysms of fear. She often recalled that her grandmother once told her that priests and nuns only pretended to be chaste and holy. They had secret tunnels that ran between the convent and the rectory. They would meet at night and do unspeakable things with one another. It was beyond Elizabeth's ability to imagine what those unspeakable things might be, but the trembling horror in her grandmother's voice was enough to give her nightmares. In some of Elizabeth's dreams, she was a prisoner in some dimly lit cell deep under the ground, a place that smelled of dirt and rotting things. It was smoky and foul, with the stench of pungent incense. Dark shapes in enveloping robes hovered over her, whispering chants and incantations, trying to turn her into one of them. Elizabeth's imagination was fertile enough to manufacture images so dark and horrifying, so detailed and terrible, that, to her mind, they resembled hell.

Such extreme anti-Catholic sentiments had a lengthy tradition in the Pacific Northwest. When white settlers were still struggling for a foothold against defiant Native American tribes, Catholic missionaries were more often than not on the side of the Indians—many of whom became Catholic converts. Catholic missionaries had traveled across North and South America since the fifteenth century. They arrived with the original Spanish, French, and Portuguese explorers. Many Native American tribes had long traditions as practicing Catholics. The biases against Catholics were further fueled by the influx of Protestants from the East Coast, who brought their antipapist views with them.

Being Freemasons, Elizabeth's grandmother's family had an especially virulent hatred of Catholics. The feud between Freemasons and Catholics had a history that stretched back more than two centuries. They were sworn enemies. Most Catholics believed—not entirely without merit—that the Freemasons were engaged in a subversive international plot to destroy the church. The Freemasons planned to replace the Catholic beliefs with their own deity-free secularism, they thought. There was talk that the Freemasons engaged in activities that included secret rituals. Catholics were forbidden, under pain of immediate excommunication, from joining Masonic lodges.

Elizabeth was a bright and curious child, so it was inevitable that she would eventually find reasons to question her grandmother's stories. There were several Catholic girls in her class at school, and they seemed perfectly normal—as incapable as she herself of manufacturing dark plots. She sometimes jumped rope with them at recess, but she knew better than to take any of them home.

Because her grandmother was sickly, she always had live-in help, and one of the maids was a young Irish girl, barely out of her teens, named Mary. Elizabeth liked Mary, and she didn't understand the palpable tension that existed between the girl and her grandmother. It never occurred to her that Mary was Catholic, but one day when Elizabeth was fourteen, she found Mary sobbing in the laundry room. "I'm leaving," she declared. "I can't abide the hatred in this house any longer." The next day, she was gone. "Good riddance to her. She was black Irish, that girl," Elizabeth's grandmother said with disgust. "A Roman Catholic."

Soon after Mary left, Elizabeth came across her small prayer book, forgotten on a shelf in the laundry room. She reached up and took the book, caressing the soft leather cover with her fingers. It was small but thick. The well-worn dark brown cover had a gold insignia inscribed on it that resembled a large looped *P*, with an *X* through it. The words *The Daily Missal* were also inscribed in gold. The thin parchment pages crackled to the touch. The edge of each page was lightly etched in gold. Elizabeth was instantly fascinated. She liked the feel of it; she wanted to read it. She slipped the book into the pocket of her sweater and hid it in her room. She'd never done anything so dangerous in her life, and her heart was pounding in her chest. What if her grandmother found out? But Elizabeth's curiosity was stronger than her fear.

Later that night, alone in her room, she took out the prayer book. A small card fluttered to the floor. On the card was a portrait of a beautiful young woman wearing a robe the color of the sky and a long white veil. She was so pretty. Her face seemed to radiate grace and kindness. She was standing barefoot on a cloud, her eyes drawn upward toward a brilliant light. Winged cherubs surrounded her. On the back of the card, an inscription read:

Mary, the Mother of God,
Is Taken into Heaven

Blessed art thou among women,
and blessed is the fruit of thy womb, Jesus.
Holy Mary, Mother of God,
pray for us sinners,
now and at the hour of our death.

Elizabeth was riveted by the card. Catholics knew who the mother of God was? God had a mother? What else did Catholics know? She shivered with a combination of dread and anticipation. She opened the Daily Missal and began to read.

She kept the book hidden under her bed, so she couldn't imagine how her invalid grandmother found it. Nevertheless, she did. One day, Elizabeth came home from school, to find her grandmother in a fearsome fury, with the Daily Missal in her arthritic hand. She waved the prayer book in Elizabeth's face. "Explain this."

Elizabeth had never seen her grandmother so angry. She stammered, "I found it. . . . Mary left it. . . . I was curious."

"The truth, Elizabeth. Tell me the truth, or so help me God— have you been consorting with these people?"

"No . . . oh, no, Grandmother. I would never."

"I will not have such betrayal in my home."

Elizabeth did not tell her grandmother that she knew Roman Catholics at school. She wouldn't call it "consorting." She promised that it would never happen again. But Elizabeth was in high school now. She was developing a mind of her own, and she was beginning to think that her grandmother might have overstated things a bit. Besides, it was too late. The mysteries of Catholicism had taken hold of her—just as her grandmother had always feared. She had to know more. After school, she would go to the library, on the pretense of doing research for school projects, and instead sit for hours reading *The Lives of the Saints*. She was particularly captivated by the stories of the young women, martyrs and mystics no older than herself, who had given their lives for their beliefs. She was starting to appreciate why Catholicism felt so dangerous. She began to realize that it wasn't only her grandmother who felt threatened by Roman Catholics.

Elizabeth had seen the Dominican nuns at Blessed Sacrament, the beautiful church with the dramatic spire a few blocks from her grandmother's house. The convent at Blessed Sacrament was an old wooden building with a wide front porch. On hot summer days, the nuns sat on the porch in a neat white row, drinking tea and mending garments.

One afternoon, she mustered enough courage to walk up the front steps and ring the doorbell. The door opened, and there she was, inches away from a real nun. She stared. The woman standing before her wore a floor-length white robe of heavy serge, topped by a full scapular. Her robe was belted at the waist, and a string of beads with a silver cross fell at her side. Elizabeth knew this was the rosary she had read about in Mary's prayer book. But the most curious thing about the nun was her headdress, which rose above her head at least eight inches and formed a square platform. The woman truly didn't seem human, but Elizabeth wasn't afraid of her. She was a vision—inexplicably wonderful. Beatific. And age-less in a way that ordinary women were not. She might have been thirty or fifty; Elizabeth couldn't tell. The woman's face was dom-inated by her large, dark, probing eyes, which she fixed on Eliza-beth. "Hello. I'm Sister Dorothy," she said in a kindly voice. "May I help you, dear?"

"Hello, Sister. I'm Elizabeth," she stammered. "I have some questions."

Before Elizabeth could catch her breath, Sister Dorothy was holding the door open, inviting her in. She stepped inside, thinking, I'm crossing over; I can't turn back now. The nun's long skirts rustled and the beads jangled at her side as she led Elizabeth into a small sunny parlor. Sister Dorothy motioned Elizabeth to sit on the plump-cushioned settee. She gathered her voluminous skirts behind her, as Elizabeth had seen women in films do, and sat down next to her. Uncomfortably close. "Now. What can I help you with?"

Elizabeth blurted out, "I want to be a nun." Her eyes locked with Sister Dorothy's. Then she seemed to realize what she'd said. Her hand flew to her mouth. "No, that isn't what I meant to say. I'm sorry." Her cheeks were flushed scarlet; they felt as if they were burning. "I'm not even a Catholic."

Sister Dorothy nodded, unperturbed. "That's all right. You'd like to know more about the Catholic Church?"

Elizabeth nodded. "Yes, that's it. I want to know." Her shoulders slumped, and a look of misery washed over her face. "But my grandmother—she's very anti-Catholic. I know it's not right for me to be here." Elizabeth stood up. "Maybe I'd better go."

"That's fine. Whatever you'd like. But knowledge is never dangerous," Sister Dorothy said. "Why don't I give you some books to read, and you can decide for yourself. It can't hurt, can it?"

Without waiting for a reply, the nun got up and disappeared through a door. She was gone only a short time, but the minutes crawled. Elizabeth became aware of the scent of lemon polish and flowers. Everything gleamed; the windows glistened. There wasn't a speck of dust in the little parlor.

Sister Dorothy returned, carrying four books. "These will give you the basics," she said. "Read them, and then come back to me when you have questions. Oh, and take this, too." She held out a small rosary with carved brown beads as smooth as polished stones. Elizabeth was speechless. She extended her hand, and Sister Dorothy poured the crucifix and beads into it. Elizabeth's heart was pounding furiously; she felt the weight of it in her hand. She had never touched a rosary before.

"It was blessed by the Holy Father in Rome," Sister Dorothy quietly said, a small smile on her lips. Elizabeth's fingers caressed the beads. They felt good between her fingers. What was she getting into?

By the next day, Elizabeth had come to her senses. There was no way she could keep the books or the rosary. It was a deception of monumental proportions. She simply could not do this in her grandmother's house. She found some brown paper and wrapped everything in a package, addressing a note to Sister Dorothy. She thanked her but said she had decided to put off learning about the Roman Catholic church for now. She was too busy with her studies. She planned to ask a Catholic girl at school to return the package to Sister Dorothy.

Elizabeth hid the package behind the coats at the back of the hall closet until she could arrange to have it returned. The closet was rarely used, except when there were guests. She'd forgotten that her aunt was scheduled to visit from San Francisco. Her grandmother had asked the maid to clear the closet to make room for her aunt's things, and the package was exposed. Elizabeth walked in from school on the first day of her aunt's visit and found the women sitting in the parlor. Her grandmother's face was deathly still. Her aunt stared at her lap in dismay. It took only a second for Elizabeth to see the torn brown wrapper, the books scattered on the table, the rosary, her incriminating note to Sister Dorothy.

She had never heard her grandmother's voice so cold, or seen her eyes so full of derision. She might have been judging a stranger, not a granddaughter. "I took you in and raised you when your dear parents were killed," she said. "I would expect gratitude from you. Instead, you go behind my back and involve yourself with these people. There is nothing—*nothing*—you could have done that could sever our relationship more completely. I'm offering you a choice. Once and for all. Will you live here with me in this house or will you go with them? If you insist on defying me in this matter, you will leave this house today, and we will never speak again."

Elizabeth stood frozen in the doorway. She couldn't believe what she was hearing. She was barely seventeen. Where would she go? "Grandmother, I promise I'll send these things back. I'm sorry." She felt physically sick with the knowledge that her grandmother meant what she'd said. Her love was so fragile, so dependent on Elizabeth's obedience. The ultimatum was unfair, the demand that she fall into line, that she sublimate who she was, and instead become a person in her grandmother's image—it was too much to comprehend.

Every day, she planned to take the books and rosary back to Sister Dorothy, but weeks and months went by. She still hadn't done it.

Finally, she knew she could put it off no longer. With deep apprehension, she walked down the front path and up the steps to the convent. The old wooden boards of the porch creaked beneath her feet. When the door opened and Sister Dorothy appeared, the nun's face lit up. She greeted Elizabeth like a long-lost friend. "Come in," she urged, but Elizabeth shook her head and stared downward. "I can't," she mumbled. "I only came to return these." Elizabeth awkwardly extended the books and rosary and placed them in the sister's hands.

Sister Dorothy had an unerring ability to read the hearts of troubled young girls. She cradled the books in one hand and, with the other, reached out and put a hand on Elizabeth's shoulder. "That isn't the only reason you came, is it? Isn't there something you'd like to tell me? Come in, Elizabeth. It's all right."

Elizabeth looked into Sister Dorothy's kind eyes and felt her resolve draining out of her. She slowly walked past Sister Dorothy and through the open door. Then Sister Dorothy put an arm around her shoulder and led her inside to the parlor. They talked for hours.

The Dominican Motherhouse
—June 1955

> *All creatures of our God and King,*
> *Lift up your voice and with us sing,*
> *Alleluia, alleluia!*
> *Thou burning sun with golden beam,*

Thou silver moon with softer gleam:
O praise Him, O praise Him,
Alleluia, alleluia, alleluia!

The joyful sound of over one hundred voices filled the chapel with song as the nuptial procession slowly made its way down the aisle. Four brides of Christ, dressed in wedding gowns of satin and lace, with fragrant wreaths of roses covering their white veils, were presenting themselves to the order for investiture: Barbara, whose natural beauty seemed magnified a thousand times; Claire, her plump cheeks flushed with happiness, her black eyes deep pools of fervor; Michelle, thin as a rail in an oversized dress, smiling happily; Carmen, small, with childlike features, looking sweet and nervous. A brilliant June sun filled the chapel with scattered beams of dappled sunlight as the procession approached. Thomas Connelly, the Archbishop of Seattle, stood regally in front of the altar in rich vestments of white and gold.

Out of the corner of her eye, Carmen glimpsed her parents, who looked uncomfortable and out of place in this haven of sobriety. Her mother's satin wedding gown, yellowed from years in an attic chest, hung on Carmen's small frame like a funeral shroud. She couldn't resist the thought that this gown had not portended happiness for her mother—whose marriage had deteriorated almost from the start, fueled by the joint demons of bitterness and booze.

As she knelt before the altar, Carmen fought off the butterflies dancing in her stomach. The wedding gown, the veil, and the nuptial ceremony were designed to celebrate the personal relationship between a nun and her Divine Bridegroom. But Carmen had never felt the personal longing for Jesus of which the great mystics spoke; she hadn't heard his voice, clear as a clarion in her heart, calling her. Her vocation seemed more of a matter of wanting this life than it did of God wanting *her*. She had nothing of Claire's piety, or Barbara's dignity, or Michelle's faith.

The evening before, as the four of them were ironing the

white habits they would don after the ceremony and putting last-minute touches on their wedding apparel, Carmen, Michelle, and Barbara had been almost giddy. Claire, on the other hand, was so lost in thought at the ironing board that Carmen called out, "You'll burn a hole in your habit if you're not careful."

Claire looked up with a small smile. "Thank you, Carmen. I suppose I can be forgiven if I'm a bit distracted the evening before my wedding night."

Carmen glanced at Michelle, who was kneeling on the floor, battling with a mess of netting for her bridal veil. The two women shared a smile. Claire was always talking this way. She was so holy. Secretly, Carmen felt jealous of Claire's fervor. Sometimes, during the morning office, while Carmen could only dream of being back in her warm bed, she would look over at Claire and study her face, which was transformed by prayer. At those times, Carmen would think to herself, Her soul is on fire.

A few months earlier, the approaching ceremony heavy on her mind, she had asked Sister Karen, "How do I really know if I'm called?" Sister Karen had regarded her with a womanly twinkle in her eye. "Oh, Carmen, how does any young girl know when she has been proposed to? If the Lord has asked for your hand, you'll feel it in your heart, and if you are meant to be his bride—if you truly desire to be his bride—you'll know."

But Carmen did not know what this feeling was supposed to be—this flooding with love. She had never been out alone with a young man, had never been kissed or experienced the racing of her heart. She could only imagine it from stories and movies. And perhaps barely grasp the meaning if she compared it to music. Music was Carmen's way to God—her way out of herself, at any rate. When she sat at the piano or organ and played, let the uplifting notes flow, she experienced a sensation of herself as out of her body, away from the everyday problems and drudgery of the world. Music was the only way she knew to meditate. The timbre of sound spoke of the faith that her thoughts were unable to capture.

Archbishop Connelly's lyrical Irish voice cut through Carmen's musings:

"The Bridegroom is here; go out and welcome him."

Carmen joined the others in responding, "Blessed are those who are called to the wedding feast of the Lamb."

The Archbishop prayed, "Listen, O daughter, give ear to my words; forget your own people and your father's house. So will the King desire your beauty; he is your Lord; pay homage to him."

Archbishop Connelly moved across the altar, his vestments rustling as he approached and stood in front of Carmen.

"What do you desire?"

With trembling voice, Carmen replied, "The mercy of God and yours, and the holy habit of Saint Dominic."

He leaned over and gently removed the wreath of roses from Carmen's head. He then replaced it with a small crown of tightly woven thorns. "Receive the crown of thorns, as a sign that you will take on the suffering of the world, even as the Lord himself chose to do." Then the Archbishop handed her a lily and a long-stemmed rose. "Accept these gifts, a lily and a rose. The lily is the token of virginal purity; the rose of love. May you become sweet perfume in the garden of God."

He blessed her. "In the world, you were known as Carmen. In the order, your name will be Sister Mary Carmen of the Holy Cross. Go now and robe yourself in the garb of your order—the white habit symbolizing truth, zeal for God's glory, and joy."

Carmen rose and walked slowly toward the room where she would remove the wedding dress and put on the white novice's habit. Sister Mary Carmen, she thought. She felt a strange new sensation cradling her heart, and she realized that for the first time ever, she was really *somebody.* She was a bride of Christ.

4

The Calling

Piermont, New York

— F E B R U A R Y   1 9 9 6

EARLY IN 1996, I RECEIVED A CALL FROM MY LITERARY AGENT, Jane Dystel. She had an interesting proposition—a book about nuns. The timing seemed right because suddenly nuns had been receiving a lot of press attention. *Dead Man Walking*, a film starring Sean Penn as a death-row convict and Susan Sarandon as a Roman Catholic nun who is his spiritual adviser, was a big hit. The movie was based on the true story of Sister Helen Prejean, a member of the Sisters of Saint Joseph of Medaille, Louisiana. Everyone seemed fascinated by Sister Helen Prejean, a heroine and activist against the death penalty. But perhaps it was the actress Susan Sarandon's *version* of a modern nun that had people talking. The *real* Sister Helen was certainly far less glamorous, and her experiences on death row were somewhat more chilling than those in the film version. Still, the film had piqued the public's interest and unleashed a flurry of magazine articles about the "new nun."

At around the same time, Sister Wendy, a bucktoothed, wonderfully acute British nun—living monastically in an old trailer and dressed in full habit—was captivating PBS audiences with her brilliant and wry analyses of classic Renaissance art. For all her saintly demeanor, Sister Wendy didn't mince words, or shy away from observing and commenting on the eroticism of the art she discussed.

But I sensed that the revival of interest in Catholic nuns—be they in cloisters or out in the world—wasn't merely due to these two remarkable women. I saw it in a broader context, as the natural outcome of a nation of baby boomers searching for an inner Holy Grail.

I had seen that same searching all around me—had felt it in myself. Our generation had rebelled against more than the Vietnam War. We had rebelled against the stricture of the old and staid, the established and known. The Age of Aquarius—love, peace, and happiness—also launched a wholesale abandonment of organized religion. We rejected what seemed to be rigid and irrelevant dogmatism. And we rejected the false love that was preached from the pulpits. For all their talk of loving thy neighbor, our religious leaders seemed to have lent themselves to the policies of war, genocide, and racism that the Establishment represented.

But on the path to enlightenment, we had stumbled across painfully inadequate gods. Our measures had become too lenient; we were loose in the practice of deification. We were self-absorbed in our spiritual quest. We embraced what pleased our fancy and labeled it a spiritual revelation. Gurus, healers, psychics, channelers, New Age ministers—all offered their differently flavored versions of faith and religion. Our spiritual cravings led us along some strange paths, and still continue to do so. Millions of people swore by *The Celestine Prophecy* and waited impatiently for James Redfield's next revelation, perhaps forgetting that he was writing fiction. Others pronounced themselves forever changed by the teachings of Marianne Williamson, a flashy, telegenic New Age preacher, whose pronouncement "We must love each other" was hardly original—and, to judge by the skyrocketing divorce rate among her Hollywood followers, not exactly effective. Millions of others were finding their guardian angels, or speaking to the dead. New Age spirituality had become a massive stew of unfulfilled longings, snatches of other culture's beliefs, and scented candles promising tranquillity.

Many of these paths led in circles, or flared up like bright flames in the dark void of our spiritual emptiness. They all eventually seemed to flicker and then peter out, as if consumed by themselves. And many people had sensed that the search for spirituality could become a hollow pursuit if it was solely an inward quest. There was more to be found in the wonder of the dark night skies than could be found inside of us. There was more to be discovered in sharing faith than in holding it as a separate personal treasure.

A generation who had dismissed organized religion finally began to turn and look at what had always been. There was a renewed realization that there were profound mysteries that lay at the heart of the few religions that had managed to survive for more than a millennium. That was part of the current fascination with nuns. Women like Sister Helen Prejean were not locked in an inner struggle, confined to a cloistered convent. They were out there in the world. And their mission, their choice, straddled the fence between the church and the secular. They were both ordinary and extraordinary.

Reluctant to explore my own memories of nuns, I was nevertheless intrigued by the idea. What had changed since I'd been a young girl? What exactly *was* going on with the nuns these days? Jane's idea of writing a book about nuns struck a chord. I promised her that I'd give a book about nuns some thought. Once we'd said good-bye, I sat for a while just staring out the window.

My home office, cluttered with books, papers, computer

equipment, and the various tools of my work, was a cozy room on the top floor of an old house overlooking a wide expanse of the Hudson River. Its walls were covered with pictures of my twenty-one-year-old son, Paul, a smiling redhead with shining, curious blue eyes, who was studying art at Pratt Institute in Brooklyn, New York. Two Colonial-style musket windows faced the backyard, a sloping parklike expanse of trees and lawn covered with a fresh blanket of snow. My two cats, Osborne and Inkwell, were curled on the window seat atop a steaming radiator, snoring lightly. It was an idyllic scene.

I had lived in this house for several years with my partner, also named Paul, a smart, charismatic man with curly silver hair and magnetic eyes that registered sharp intelligence and a wicked sense of humor. We had often talked about our different backgrounds. Paul was Jewish, born and raised in Boston. As a Jew in a famously Irish Catholic town, Paul had received an early impression of the church from parochial school kids who lived next door to him when he was a little boy. They may have thought of themselves as soldiers in Christ's army, but they were, in fact, bullies, who rained punches on the little Jewish kid next door while taunting, "The Jews killed Jesus. . . . You killed Jesus."

Not being up on church doctrine at that time, Paul was unable to dispute their claims. As he later described it, "As far as I knew, my family *had* killed Christ and was, to quote the old Lenny Bruce routine, hiding him in the basement. It didn't seem fair that I was the one who was getting beaten up, though. I was only five years old."

What Paul really resented was confession. It wasn't fair that each week his tormentors could go to church and be forgiven for beating him up. It just didn't seem right that their religion provided them a way to unburden themselves of all their sins on a weekly basis! He did remember, however, a time when he was seven or eight, going into a Catholic church with his best friend, Ronnie. Ronnie was a devout French-Canadian Roman Catholic who went to church at least three times each week. He had told Paul about the statues of the saints that lined the aisles, and Paul wanted to see them for himself. He got a lot more than he bargained for. Ronnie hadn't told him about the flickering votive candles in the ruby red containers; the sumptuous gold crucifix that dominated the front altar of the high-beamed church, or the faint smell of incense that lingered like a heady perfume in the still air.

Paul loved all the statues, as well—he thought they were noble and kind-looking, especially the Virgin Mary. He imitated everything that Ronnie did when they entered and left the church. He dipped his fingers in the holy water and crossed himself. He bowed when Ronnie bowed, knelt when Ronnie knelt. Paul really enjoyed it. He consciously ignored the fact that his tormentors— the bullies next door—enjoyed the protection and forgiveness of the very same church. Paul already understood hypocrisy; he just didn't know what it was called. His only mistake had been to tell his mother enthusiastically about the wonderful time he'd had at Saint Raphael's! Needless to say, he was forbidden from repeating his adventure into alternative religions.

When I told Paul about Jane's suggestion that I write a book about nuns, he was as intrigued as I had been. He teased me, "So, what goes around comes around. You're going back to the convent."

Oh, dear! I thought. Was I going back? If so, it would be a long journey. I was forty-five, and I hadn't been in the church for twenty-five years.

When I was a girl in school, the nuns used to say, "You can leave the church, but the church never leaves you." We were taught that God had a vicelike grip. He didn't let you go so easily.

I wondered, though, looking back, if it were not the nuns themselves who had the vicelike grip. In the twenty-five years between the time I left the church and the time I began to write this book, the voices of the Dominicans of my youth pealed in my ears like ever-sounding bells. It would be melodramatic to say that they were a haunting presence, but they had lingered—undeniably.

A certain phenomenon had occurred again and again during my adult life. If I happened to be with a group of people and mentioned that I'd gone to parochial school, someone invariably shared a story of his or her own. Before you knew it, we'd be chatting away in the codified language of former Catholic schoolchildren. Chillingly, whether we'd been educated in Maine, Minnesota, Georgia, or Washington State, the stories were all the same. We were all still held in that vicelike grip. Still members of the special society.

When I came to the East Coast in the mid-seventies as a married mother of a four-year-old son, the first new friend I made was a former Catholic schoolgirl. Her experience had been a mirror to my own. Lynn and I formed an immediate bond that has endured over time and distance. I found it remarkable that Lynn, who grew up in Philadelphia, Pennsylvania, some two thousand miles and a century of cultural influences away from the Pacific Northwest, had heard the same stories and performed the same rituals as I had. Across a continent, and before we even knew each other, we were sharing major elements of the same life.

The cities of the East Coast seemed to be populated almost entirely with former Catholic schoolchildren, still held in thrall by the spell of nuns. Clever con artists found this a useful thing. In the subway stations, one often came across devout-looking women dressed in realistic but phony nun's garb from days gone by. It was said that "subway nuns" could collect upwards of five hundred dollars a day—even when commuters knew they weren't actual nuns. Some people were simply incapable of passing the visage of a nun without dropping coins or dollar bills into the box. They were conditioned that well. They were that guilty.

Lynn and I loved to compare notes:

Did you learn it was a sin to place another book on top of the Holy Bible?
Did you have to capitalize pronouns that refer to God?

Write the initials J.M.J. (Jesus-Mary-Joseph) at the top of every
*   assignment? (Actually, for me, D. was added, for Dominic.)*
Sit on the left side of your chair to make room for your guardian
*   angel?*
Make the sign of the cross when you heard an ambulance siren?
Were you told it was a sin to wash off the black soot that was
*   rubbed on your forehead on Ash Wednesday?*
Did the bishop slap you in the face (to symbolize the suffering of
*   Christians) when you were confirmed?*

Lynn and I found that we had been tutored with the same cautionary tales—about evil Russians who tortured six-year-old Catholic children because they refused to denounce the church; or the boy who stole a candy bar from a grocery store, only to be struck by a car and killed moments later, caught in a state of everlasting sin.

We learned about Limbo, where unbaptized babies floated for eternity in an embryonic haze. Those poor babies! They had died prematurely, before a priest could splash them with the requisite holy water. Their eternal lot was not painful, but it was hardly comparable to the fabulous time being had in heaven. I had always thought the idea of Limbo was cruel. If God was so loving, why wouldn't he bend the rules and let those innocent babies into heaven? Apparently, the church came around to the same view, because Limbo has now disappeared from the catechism.

I remember sitting in a bar with Lynn sometime in the early eighties. We were by now two hardened lapsed Catholics, with a portfolio of sins between us that had never been formally purged through confession. We always had some of our most creative conversations in bars, drinking scotch, smoking cigarettes—as if we were still trying to be those defiant teenaged Catholic schoolgirls. It hadn't escaped my notice—or been disproven by my experiences—that very often the Catholic girls of our generation had grown into women almost obsessed with rebellion, with pushing the envelope. It was as if we were still trying to "show them." But

I was always conscious of that interior voice that whispered Shakespeare's "The lady doth protest too much, methinks." The unvarnished truth was that I had always been too much of a "nice girl" to be a very convincing rebel—and so had Lynn.

On this particular night out, Lynn and I were talking about life in Catholic schools. I was recalling that we would always begin each day with two rituals. The first was the Pledge of Allegiance. Every classroom had a United States flag in the corner, and we turned to face it, hands over our hearts, and said the words— including, without reservation, the phrase that later became so controversial: "One Nation under God." The nuns taught us to dip our heads in reverence when we said "under God."

The second ritual was the recitation of the Apostles' Creed. The Apostles' Creed was the Catholic's way of stating who was *really* boss. It was a rousing chant when recited in sync by thirty schoolchildren.

"I think I can still recite the Apostles' Creed," Lynn said, grinning at me through a haze of smoke. "Can you?"

I closed my eyes for a second, and the memory of the words popped into my head, as if I had pulled a file from a dusty cabinet. I opened my eyes. "Yep."

And so, with heavy-metal music blaring in the background, we leaned in close to each other and recited, in perfect rhythm, words that neither of us had spoken since we were seventeen years old:

> I believe in God, the Father Almighty, creator of heaven and earth; and in Jesus Christ, His only Son, our Lord, who was conceived by the Holy Spirit, born of the Virgin Mary, suffered under Pontius Pilate, was crucified, died, and was buried. He descended into hell. The third day He rose again from the dead, according to the Scripture. He ascended into heaven, and sitteth at the right hand of God, the Father Almighty. From thence He shall come again to judge the quick and the dead. I believe in the Holy Spirit, the Holy Catholic Church,

the Communion of Saints, the forgiveness of sins, the resurrection of the body, and the life everlasting. Amen.

"I never knew who the quick were," Lynn said.

"The quick are the living," I said. I knew that much.

Lynn laughed. "I always believed it. I just didn't understand it."

But understanding was never the point anyway. *Faith* was. The Apostles' Creed outlined the basics that you had to believe in order to be a Catholic. I mean *really* believe. It's almost impossible to articulate, in this age of loose interpretation, the otherworldly nature of true belief.

The mystery of faith, as it was spelled out to us, was exactly that: a mystery. It was not a feeling. It was not a knowledge. It was certainly not proof. In fact, faith was most powerfully present when your heart was dark and hopeless, when you didn't feel the spirit. When you faced unthinkable tragedy and disappointment, when you thought, I can't bear this—that was precisely the moment when you were capable of the greatest faith. As Jesus had said, "Father, into thy hands I commend my spirit."

In retrospect, the concept was probably too complex for young minds, as we knew very little of true suffering. But the idea of faith remained with me in adulthood. I had been fortunate; I had little experience of personal tragedy. Whenever I had seen it overtake others, I wondered, By what grace would it be possible to go on in the face of this?

"I have a question for you," Lynn said. "Did the Pope ever reveal what the letter from Fatima said?"

"I don't think so."

"Hmmm . . . the nuns always said that if the Pope didn't tell us what was in the letter, it was because it was so horrible, we'd die from fear."

"Yeah, they told us that, too." The nuns were the Catholic version of the seer Nostradamus—always hinting at the coming apocalypse.

. . .

As I immersed myself in research, I soon found that it was impossible to talk about nuns without addressing the extraordinary nature of their effect on generations of youth. Whenever I mentioned that I was writing a book about nuns, the floodgates opened. I began to receive phone calls, letters from people I didn't even know who had heard about my book. Every time I was in a social situation, within minutes the conversation would turn to the subject of nuns and stay there. Everyone had a story.

But what was most peculiar about this was the sense that these stories—and the deep emotions that accompanied them—had been closeted for years, buried deep in a remote corner of consciousness, longing to be told. It was like a vast secret breaking loose, the kind of thing one might see in a repressed-memory support group. I began to suspect that if I published a book of letters and stories about adult memories of nuns, it would rival anything Nancy Friday could conceive. Strange but true, people would rather talk about nuns than sex.

But I also realized that the real interest in the religious and common life of nuns was not a voyeuristic curiosity about a weird or anachronistic lifestyle. To the contrary, the fascination with nuns seemed to be much more about today than about yesterday. Who were these women who maintained a mysterious aura even though they were no longer cloaked in the garb of old? What would draw a woman to such a sacrificial life? What possible gratification could come from taking vows of poverty, chastity, and obedience? How could a modern woman, especially a well-educated and enlightened one, align herself with such a misogynistic church?

Nuns have always been full of contradictions. Looking at the history of their religious orders, it's easy to imagine them as the first true feminists—fierce rebels, brave and independent, secure in their calling. And yet the stories told of the early nunneries are replete with torment, shame, and betrayal. One wonders, Were

they heroines or victims? The early convents withstood all manner of abuse—not only from the church's enemies but also from
its own priests and bishops. Locked in their cloisters, the nuns
were prey for unholy men. There is documented evidence of torture, rape, and conditions that amounted to slavery. Yet, even
mired in the hypocrisy of the medieval church, the women's
orders survived and even thrived. Once filled with uneducated
peasant girls, by the twentieth century, the convents housed some
of the most well-educated women in the world—women who
held advanced degrees in an era when the average girl was lucky
to reach high school. Whatever their secret, Catholic nuns had
survived the test of time to become highly respected and influen-
tial. It was a mystery.

Several days before his death, my father called me in New York.
He and I had developed an extremely close relationship over the
years. It often struck me how alike we were, and I was always quite
proud of that fact, because my father, even in a frail state of health,
was high-spirited and full of good humor. His specialty was corny
jokes, and he had one for me that day.

"I have a name for your book!" he announced, and I grinned,
waiting for the punch line.

"And then there were *nun.*" He laughed, delighted with himself, and I laughed along with him because in the end it was not
far from what I expected to find. "That's a good one, Dad," I said
appreciatively. "I'll pass it along to my editor."

It thrilled my father that I was writing a book about religious
orders of women. He never said so, but I'm sure he viewed it as
my return to the fold. I was back where he had always wanted me
to be—with the nuns. It had nearly broken his heart when I ended
my romance with the Catholic Church, although we had rarely
spoken about it. At the time, I hadn't understood it myself, and I
closed the door so tightly that I was able to avoid reflecting about
it. All I knew consciously was that in the year after I left Holy
Angels, everything in my world changed, and the light of my faith

was extinguished. I simply stopped believing. Faith is neither feeling nor idea; it is a driving force that either exists or doesn't. Without that driving force, everything turned gray. Rituals grew devoid of meaning, and I stopped attending Mass—a mortal sin that would have driven me to the bottom rung of Sister Loretta's ladder. Such threats mattered little to me anymore. The church seemed suddenly fanatical. I had grown tired of all the rules, and the threats of punishment and damnation. Even the idea of faith seemed like a clever sleight of hand. How convenient to use faith to explain away all of the things that made absolutely no sense.

I did make one final stab at redemption. I went to confession. In the dark little booth, I whispered through the screen to Father Christopher, "I've stopped believing in God." To my amazement, he didn't try to counsel me; he sounded disgusted. "Don't be so melodramatic," he sneered. "Say five Hail Marys and make a good act of contrition." It only reinforced my despair, but apparently Father Christopher was having problems of his own. Several weeks later, he had a nervous breakdown in the middle of saying Mass, and they had to carry him out of the church screaming.

Ultimately, I convinced myself that my loss of faith was the legitimate result of waking up to the political realities of the church. As an ardent feminist, I began to see the Catholic Church as a two-thousand-year-old drive to subjugate women. It was a church of men in black robes who had been given great power, and who knew or cared little for the plight of ordinary people. The bishops lived in mansions, surrounded by silver and gold; they built lavish churches to the glory of God, while the poor around them perished; they strode arrogantly across the backs of women, kept barefoot and pregnant by edict of the church. They contrived ridiculous explanations for adherence to outdated traditions. Did people really believe that Christ meant only men to be priests because he chose only men to be his apostles? Imagine the uproar that would have occurred in that time had he called women to leave their homes and families to wander the land with a group of men. The Catholic Church was also adept at rewriting history—

or simply ignoring what didn't suit its purpose. The fact that priests were married for centuries—before the church deemed it too inconvenient and expensive—didn't stop the Vatican from pronouncing the celibate priesthood a divine law.

I regarded the Catholic Church as a vast anachronistic body, whose hierarchy of aged, change-resistant men had been responsible for great human suffering over the span of centuries—and today was still responsible for the continued suffering among many women in some of the most impoverished countries on earth. It seemed immeasurably heartless for the Pope to bless a crowd of half-starving Indian women with the charge, "Be fruitful and multiply."

I built my case against the Catholic Church brick by brick, but it was the men who received the brunt of my wrath. My feminism was somewhat simplistic in this regard. I believed that Catholic women—and especially nuns—were not to blame. If anything, they were victims of the papal dictates. They were desperately trying to survive in spite of the church, not because of it.

In 1988, Pope John Paul II wrote an apostolic letter, "On the Dignity and Vocation of Women." The letter was hailed as the first papal recognition of the importance of women to the life of the church. In it, the Pope stressed that the fulfillment of the female personality is found in two dimensions—motherhood and virginity. Both roles exist in the service of a bridegroom, either the mortal husband, through Jesus Christ, or in chastity to Christ himself. Little mention was made of single laywomen, although they were expected to remain celibate and to serve God—rather like nuns, but without any of the perks. The Pope's pronouncement reinforced my suspicion that the women who remained in religious orders were intended to be submissive Marthas, obedient and faithful to the increasingly controlling church hierarchy and its rigid stands on women's issues. They were also, along with lay Catholic women, the real workers who kept the church going.

I thought I had it all figured out, even though I'd had virtually nothing to do with nuns as an adult—and never even considered sending my own son to a Catholic school in New York. I didn't want his head to be filled with meaningless dogma and ladders that led to hell. I thought he should know about religion without being forced to believe in it. Occasionally, over the years, I heard from my friend Bernadette, who was a missionary with the Sisters of Social Service—first in Africa, then in Mexico. I never once asked her what her vocation meant to her or why she was a member of this order. I assumed—how arrogant of me!—that she was lonely and struggling out there in the jungles.

In the mid-1980s, when I became involved in a Catholic charity drive to open a homeless shelter for women in New York City, I had my first real contact with a nun in years. The project, under the aegis of the Catholic archdiocese and a local parish, was to convert an abandoned building into a shelter. The leader of the drive was the parish priest, an engaging Irishman named Father Malley. He was assisted by Sister Constance, a fifty-something bundle of energy in ill-fitting suits and sensible shoes. As I grew involved in the charity drive, I began to sense that things were not as they seemed. Father Malley loved to talk, tell stories about the old country, sing Irish folk songs (he could do a piercing rendition of "My Wild Irish Rose"), play golf with the big contributors, and drink whiskey. Sister Constance was the workhorse. It was she who battled with the intractable city agencies to secure the necessary permits. It was she who consulted with the architects and who traveled to Albany to gain the support of the legislature. It was she who organized the fund drives and supervised the details of the charity dinners—right down to setting up the chairs and tables.

Sister Constance seemed oddly protective of Father Malley, hovering around him like a concerned wife, reminding him about church business, or coaxing him to visit his sick parishioners. I eventually saw the truth. Father Malley was an alcoholic, and Sister Constance was the classic enabler—his protector. She made sure everything worked, so that nobody would know about his drinking. I admired Sister Constance for her unflagging faith and energy, but she also made me sad. Was this her ultimate religious vocation—to prop up a priest with a drinking problem? And then I realized: Sister Constance had been called. Maybe she had been called to take care of Father Malley. Maybe she felt that she could get more done *with* him than without him. And maybe she just loved him. And it was as simple—and as complex—as that.

I do remember one conversation we had. It stayed with me. I wanted to know what kept her going day after day. From my perspective, her life was painfully sacrificial, to little avail.

She eyed me thoughtfully. She knew I was a lapsed Catholic. I'd been honest about that—a bit proud and defiant about it, too, as if daring her to challenge me. She never had. Now she said simply, "Faith keeps me going." I wonder if she saw the brief flash of regret in my face. I didn't even know what it meant anymore to have faith.

I found myself intrigued once again by the mystery that surrounded religious women. It wasn't at all like the old mystery that had provoked my romantic fantasies as a child. As a young girl, I had never wondered *why* women chose to follow such a calling. That question was answered for me by the simple elegance of their habits, the strength of the faith radiating from their eyes, the bell-like jingle of their rosary beads, and the magical life of their communities. Now, things had changed—and *I* had changed. What would draw a woman today to take solemn vows of poverty, chastity, and obedience and join a religious order? Lacking the visible distinction of a habit, lacking even the daily rituals of community, how could a woman keep faith in the sanctity of her mission? There were many secular women dedicated to selfless ministries, women who had no need of an avowed commitment to a religious order. What was so different about a nun?

As I began to gather my thoughts about how I would approach the subject of religious orders in my book, I saw it as a grand journalistic pursuit. I would dig beneath the piety and the pretense, and provide an eye-opening account of the lives of unsung, extraordinary women like Sister Constance. I was confident in my quest. And I thought I already knew what I would find.

When my father asked me, in our last telephone conversation, whether I was planning to get in touch with the sisters at Rosary Heights, his question took me by surprise. Frankly, it hadn't occurred to me. In fact, I wasn't even aware that Rosary Heights was still owned by the Dominicans. I figured that most of the nuns had left the order and that others were living in regular apartments.

"Oh, no," Dad assured me, "there's a group of them out there. I'm sure they'd love to see you."

I demurred. "Maybe if I get out to Seattle in the next few months, I'll see about it."

Three days after his phone call, my father died quietly in his sleep. I got on an airplane and flew west to Seattle. I was going to say good-bye to my father and help prepare for the funeral Mass.

In the Catholic Church, death is not the end of life, and the funeral ritual is not so much a personal event as it is a sacramental send-off. I hadn't expected to be so overwhelmed with the spirit of the requiem, or so moved by the blessings the priest made over Dad's coffin, dousing it with holy water as he prayed. The altar boys, dressed in white cassocks, stood behind him, occasionally swinging their golden incense pots to emit the familiar heavenly fumes into the air, sparking a sense memory of the past. The ceremony was worthy of a king, and exactly what Dad deserved. I found that my grief was eased somewhat as I repeated the prayers of the Mass, which had renewed meaning that day. I think that every person, even the most hardened nonbeliever, experiences a longing for faith in the face of death. Not just a vague trusting kind of faith, but real hard-core faith that tells you your loved one is some-where—dare I call it heaven?—where you will see him again. Tears spilled from my eyes as the priest intoned the solemn and soothing prayers:

> Receive, Lord, in tranquillity and peace, the soul of your servant Richard, who has departed out of this present life to be with you. Give him the life that knows

no age, the good things that do not pass away. Through
Jesus Christ our Lord. Amen

My brothers carried the coffin out of the church, and we
drove the short distance to Holyrood Cemetery. Just before the
coffin was lowered into the ground, the priest lifted his arms and
his eyes toward heaven and boomed—for our comfort—something for the living to take with them:

> O, lover of souls,
> what Thou givest, Thou takest not away,
> for what is Thine is ours also if we are Thine.
> And life is eternal
> and love is immortal,
> and death is only a horizon.
> And a horizon is nothing save
> the limit of our sight.

After it was over, my brothers, sisters, and I gathered around
the hole and stared down at the box that contained our father.

"Damn!" exclaimed my brother Tom, kicking a bit of earth
into the open grave.

The brutal finality of the earth. The cold earth. We were
putting our beloved father in the ground. It was one of the most
completely desolate moments of my life.

The question flashed again: How does one bear this?

The next day, my mother and I took flowers to the cemetery.
By now, we were both exhausted and our eyes seemed perma-
nently swollen with the aftereffects of our tears. As she arranged
the stems in a vase, my mother sighed heavily. I asked her if she was
going to be all right.

She nodded. "Oh, yes. It's easier for me because I believe in an
afterlife."

She really did. What an enviable thing faith is! What had happened to mine? Was it still in there somewhere, waiting to be

stirred up? I suddenly realized that in dying, my father had managed to confront me head-on with a world that I had long ago abandoned.

The following day, I got into my rental car and drove the half mile from my parents' house, down the long, winding road that led to Rosary Heights. Everything seemed familiar. Was it possible that this valuable stretch of land had not changed at all in twenty-five years?

As I approached a small bridge—more like a burp in the road—I slowed down. Beyond the bridge, to the right, was the entry gate to Rosary Heights. It was easy to miss if you weren't searching for it. The plaque, reading ROSARY HEIGHTS, SISTERS OF SAINT DOMINIC, was barely visible amid the shrubbery. I turned my car onto the path and began driving down the road toward the motherhouse. The evergreens rose up on either side, just as they had always done, and as I approached the circular driveway, the stately brick Tudor appeared, unchanged. I was flooded with memories of the many times I had been here for retreats and picnics during my years at Holy Angels. I stopped the car and got out on the cobblestone walkway. For some strange reason, I didn't feel the least bit like an intruder, although, of course, I was trespassing. I walked through the flowered trellis and into the backyard, taking in the magnificent view, the lush gardens, the simple black cross set against the backdrop of the deep blue sky. The storm that would collapse the hillside was still a few months away.

I thought about the young girl—had it really been me?—who had once meditated on the hidden paths in the shade of the evergreens, who had been transported by the heavy perfume of the flowers and lulled by the hypnotic songs of the birds.

A mystery tugged at my consciousness. Who was that girl? What was it that she found here that made her visits so enriching? What made her leave it all behind? The answers dangled just outside my reach. I couldn't remember. It was too long ago.

Another question entered my head: Wasn't it important to find out what that girl had seen and experienced—and what it revealed about the estrangement between herself and the church? What secrets had I locked away deep inside of me? Without those answers, what secrets could I hope to ferret out of convents and monasteries? At first, I rejected the idea. This book wasn't about *me;* it was about *them.* Wasn't it? I shouldn't have come here, I thought. There are too many ghosts.

Yet even as I denied it, I knew in my heart that all the questions I had about nuns rested here, where long ago I myself had experienced extraordinary things. I had managed successfully, for many years, to bury them so far down in my consciousness that I couldn't even remember my own life-and-death battle of the soul. I shivered at the thought that something was waiting for me here.

I began to walk back toward my car, and as I went through the trellis, I encountered an elderly nun walking slowly across the cobblestones, leaning on a cane. "Well, hello," she said cheerfully, and I had a flash of recognition: Mother Dominick? I mumbled a reply and hurried on, not wanting to be caught. But it was too late. With a heady rush of dread and anticipation, I suddenly realized that I wouldn't be able to write with honesty about the nuns unless I was first honest with myself. And that would mean embarking upon a personal excavation, an anthropological dig into my own heart and soul.

> *Halts by me that footfall:*
> *Is my gloom, after all,*
> *Shade of His hand, outstretched caressingly?*
> *"Ah, fondest, blindest, weakest,*
> *I am He Whom thou seekest!"*

So, at last. The hound of heaven's footsteps were closing in on me.

When I returned to New York, I called Jane. "This book is taking on a life of its own," I said worriedly. "My original plan was to find an interesting convent and use it as a centerpiece. But I keep coming back to the order of nuns who taught me and influenced me when I was growing up. I have to go back there, and I don't know what will happen with this book. It's suddenly uncharted territory. I have to take this journey."

"That sounds great," she said. "What's the problem?"

"Well . . ." I blew out a long breath of air. "My personal story is getting all wrapped up in this. It's not exactly a journalistic pursuit anymore. I've never written anything like this."

"I wouldn't worry about *that,*" she said forcefully. "Just trust your instincts and go where it takes you. Maybe we'll get more than we bargained for."

I had never been one to go with the flow, but it seemed I had no choice. I was, frankly, terrified to open up those old closets and see what was inside. I prayed to the God in whom I had lost faith. Give me a direction. I decided I had to begin where it had begun for me—at Holy Angels.

5

Few Are Chosen

Seattle

— 1 9 6 4

WHEN I ENTERED HOLY ANGELS ACADEMY, IT WAS AS THOUGH I'd passed through a hidden door into a place unlike any I had known before. It was a world composed entirely of women. The other world, on the outside, the regular one dominated by men, seemed a shadowy and distant reality, kept remote by the secure walls of the convent school. Some of my classmates resented being exiled to an all-girls high school. They felt marooned on an island of women, cut off from the source of their nourishment, boys. These were the girls who would race to get out of their blue school uniforms as soon as the last bell of the day sounded. With the aplomb of quick-change artists, they would reappear in miniskirts and low heels, their hair teased improbably high above heavily drawn raccoon eyes and death white lipstick. They were mortified not only by the unfashionable cut of the uniforms but also by the stifling, stigmatizing aura of the convent school. What would boys think if they saw them dressed like the fifth and sixth graders? Those girls forced to stay in their uniforms would roll their skirts at the waistband to shorten the hems considerably, and undo the top three buttons of their starched white blouses. To complete the picture of girlish insouciance, they would stick a cigarette in the corner of their mouths, and then strut down the street like reform school vixens, hoping against hope to be mistaken for anything than what they so obviously were: Holy Angels girls on their way home from school.

Granted, I wasn't a very sexually precocious girl, and for me, being placed in an environment without boys was like being set free on winged flight. I thrived at an all-girls school. Having brothers galore, I grew up surrounded by boys; they held no mystery or thrall for me. It was a glorious relief that teachers were no longer cracking their markers over my head and comparing me unfavorably to my sainted older brother, Greg. No more dull-witted boys lurching to the top of the class by virtue of their masculine birthright. No more lovesick mooning or meaningful stares; no more clumsy courtship rituals, adolescent snickering, and sexual innuendo. At Holy Angels, all was possible. Here I was introduced to the idea of women as powerful and noble. Competition was conducted on a level playing field; intellect and excellence were rewarded equally, and both were nurtured and cherished.

I'd always been fascinated by women who didn't seem to need men. It wasn't that I had anything against the male of the species. My father adored me; my brothers treated me as their equal in our rough-and-tumble world of play. It was more a matter of sensing the satisfaction women found in their independence. I had two very prominent role models in this regard—both of my grandmothers. My father's mother, Veronica Schuler—Grandma Vera to us—had been widowed long before I was born. She rented out the main part of the house where my father had grown up, and she lived in a small, cramped apartment she had cobbled together in the basement. I would walk down a steep hill to visit her on summer days. She'd make fresh-squeezed lemonade with lots of sugar and ice, and we'd sit in her bright little basement apartment surrounded by hundreds of knickknacks, listening to Seattle Rainiers baseball games blaring from her radio. My parents worried about Grandma Vera alone in that basement, but she always made it clear that she wanted it no other way—she loved her independence and privacy.

Living just a few blocks from our house in the opposite direction was my mom's mother, Ruth McArtor—Grandma Ruthie. Even while my grandfather was still alive, she'd been unapologetically independent. She worked all of her life as a seamstress in a big factory that made coats, and she loved being a "working girl." The first in her crowd to bob her hair and shorten her skirts, she threw parties, enjoyed a drink or two, and smoked Salem cigarettes. She was always telling me stories about how she and the other girls would joke, gossip, plot, and scheme.

Her most memorable tales held more than a hint of daring—many of them centered on the creative methods she and her workmates devised for makeshift birth control back in the twenties and thirties. No endless succession of children for her—she was determined that she wouldn't be tied down by a gang of kids. It was always a great source of pride to Grandma Ruthie that she had successfully managed to limit her family to two daughters—just what she had wanted. Initially tolerant of her daughter Janet's conversion to Catholicism, she was nonetheless horrified by the particular religious mandate that kept my mother almost constantly pregnant through the first twenty years of her marriage to my father.

It was Grandma Ruthie who made sure I was well stocked with Nancy Drew books, establishing an early girlhood role model of brains, beauty, sass, and the envied red convertible. It was also Grandma Ruthie who later introduced me to Dorothy Sayers mysteries, which featured the marvelously spirited Harriet Vane—a woman who could not be conquered, even by the romantic hero of these books, Peter Wimsey.

Both of my grandmothers were beautiful, warmhearted women. They made no secret of their love for men. The point was, they had never *needed* men.

In quite a different way, the nuns belonged in that same category. The only man they truly needed was Jesus—and he wasn't going to be there most of the time. It was clear to me from a very young age that women could hold their own ground—and that's the kind of woman I intended to be.

Unfortunately, I may have initially gone overboard in expressing my independence. Michael O'Donnell, my innocent fifth-grade classmate, once shyly asked me if he could carry my books home from school. We sat next to each other in class, and when Sister's eyes were turned, we'd kid around, just as I did with my brothers. Completely missing the point of this attempt at a classic courtship ritual, I snapped, "Is my arm broken? I don't need any help carrying my books." I always felt bad for Michael, especially when I finally realized what he'd been trying to do.

The Sisters of Saint Thomas Aquinas, my teachers in elementary school, were a separate branch of the order from the Dominicans at Holy Angels. Their motherhouse was in Tacoma, and we called them the "rounds," because of their oval headpieces, which distinguished them from the Edmonds "squares." Although both groups were from the same "family tree"—originating in Ratisbon, Germany, in 1233—they operated independently from each other and held different charters.

The many Dominican orders didn't have a central motherhouse or share a common line of authority. Each order determined its own rules of conduct within the broad framework of *the* rule. This was more a matter of practicality than anything. As the order branched out from Europe in the 1800s, it became impossible for the Mother Superiors at individual convents to seek permission across oceans and continents for their operating decisions; for the same reason, it made economic sense for the houses to maintain their own sources of income and make local decisions about expansion and development.

The first outpost of Dominican nuns in the United States was established in 1853 when four young German nuns made the long journey across the Atlantic by ship to Brooklyn, New York. Their purpose was to open a school to teach the children of German immigrants, who already had established a large community in New York. This first group of Dominican nuns, the Congregation of the Holy Cross, attracted many others, and eventually it branched out to Newburgh, New York, sixty miles north of New York City. They formed the Congregation of the Most Holy Rosary in 1869. From Newburgh, a congregation was established in Caldwell, New Jersey, which then sent a group of adventurous Dominican sisters west in 1888 to Tacoma, Washington, in the heart of the great Pacific Northwest. This branch of the Dominicans took root as the Congregation of Saint Thomas Aquinas—known to us as the "rounds." The Sisters of Saint Dominic of the Holy Cross in Edmonds originally came from the Newburgh, New York, order. They arrived two years after the Tacoma Dominicans. Like an armada of invading angels, the Sisters of Saint Dominic built and staffed hospitals and schools all across Washington State, including Holy Angels Academy.

If I felt momentarily homesick for the "rounds" of elementary school, I soon got over it. The Edmonds Dominicans were strong and tender, strict but loving—just the right mix to be caretakers of young women's minds and souls. They were passionate and intense, focused and thoughtful, and they demanded the same level of engagement from their students.

My freshman homeroom teacher was a glowing young nun whose face reflected a constant state of delight. Sister Joanne loved being a nun, and she loved teaching. Her warmth made the initiation into high school less painful, and I missed her when she was sent the following year to teach at Blanchette, the coed Catholic high school on the other side of town.

. . .

The hallways of Holy Angels were lined with framed portraits of the graduating classes from every year since 1907, when the school was opened. The faces were strong and determined, full of spirit and grace. I loved to study the eager young faces from years before and imagine the high spirits that lurked irreverently behind the gleaming, intelligent eyes. Some of the faces were vaguely familiar. We would spend hours trying to pinpoint those of our teachers, many of whom had graduated from Holy Angels Academy.

There was our dignified, no-nonsense principal, Sister Edwina, a 1925 graduate; Sister Cecilia, the unflappable, sweet-tempered sports fan, who made sure there were radios and televisions available during World Series games, graduated in 1929; ancient, stocky Sister Albertina, fearsome and imposing, was one of the earliest students, graduating in 1912; frail, disapproving Sister Marietta graduated the following year. Sister Marietta was the bane of my freshman year at Holy Angels—a stern, unforgiving teacher who believed that those girls who were slow to learn algebra should be placed in the back of the class, next to the hissing radiator. I spent a lot of time there, trying with little luck to make out what was going on at the front of the room. To this day, a hissing steam radiator reminds me of Sister Marietta. Then there were the younger nuns, only a few years older than we were—Sister Carmen, who had graduated in 1951; Sister Mark, a 1955 graduate. Even the current prioress of the order, Mother Dominick, was a graduate—from 1928. Their girlish faces on the walls gave little clue to the true identities that were hidden beneath the boxy head-dresses and the enveloping robes. And whenever we tried to pry into their pasts, we always received the same answer. Life for them began on the day of their profession. It was like a new baptism, erasing from the world the girls they had been.

Holy Angels was originally established as a boarding and day school for primary and secondary students in a new parish called

Saint Alphonsus. It was located in Ballard, a bustling mill community on Salmon Bay, an inlet of Puget Sound, on the near northwest side of Seattle. From its inception, Holy Angels developed a
reputation for academic excellence—which at that time was in
short supply in the rough-and-tumble frontier town of Seattle.
When the Saint Alphonsus parish eventually grew to such an
extent that it needed a separate elementary school, Holy Angels
Academy became exclusively a high school for girls. Catholic parents from all across Washington State were eager to send their
daughters there.

We, the girls of the 1960s, were taught that we had inherited
a fantastic legacy from the women who graced our walls. At
Holy Angels, life was presented to us as a glorious ascent. This
determination was boldly reflected in the crusading tones of our
school song:

> *Holy Angels, up and onward*
> *All for one and one for all!*
> *When we build, we build together;*
> *Rising each time we fall.*
> *We will find a path or make one;*
> *Strive, seek, find, but never yield.*
> *Life lies ahead of us,*
> *Succeed we can, we must;*
> *To our nobler selves be true.*
> *Let us find the will to do!*

I was struck with the notion of the nobler self—becoming
someone of substance and merit. I wanted to make a difference in
the world. I had always known that I wanted more—been greedy
for a greater adventure than simply that of someday becoming a
wife and mother. The women who stirred me were the outsiders,
the pioneers, the revolutionaries. They were the women who took
chances in life. They were the faces on the wall.

. . .

As anyone might suspect, Holy Angels was the main recruiting station for the Sisters of Saint Dominic of the Holy Cross. There we were, good Catholic girls, ripe for plucking in our closely knit little school. We were with the sisters at least seven hours each day, five days each week. Religious vocation was a regular topic of conversation. How could such an intriguing subject not be discussed?

"Look around you," Sister Claire, our religion teacher, used to say, her glittering eyes sweeping the room. "Choose the girls you think are the least likely to have a religious vocation."

We smirked at one another. Wasn't it obvious? Everyone's eyes shifted toward Patty, so cool and worldly. There were rumors that she was actually having sex—something most of us could barely even picture. Helen, in the corner—what a sassy mouth she had on her. And me, because I could never seem to stop talking and would never back down from an argument. Everyone knew that being a nun required a capacity for silence, something I had amply demonstrated I was inherently incapable of having.

Sister Claire dropped her voice and then barely whispered, "Those are the very ones God calls."

We shifted in our seats and turned our eyes downward so as to avoid her piercing glance. Sister Claire was an unlikely seductress, despite her thick, moist lips and generous, swaying hips. She set us on edge with her intimate, almost sexual talk of Jesus—"I am his bride, and he knows me"—and her intense, probing eyes. She had entered the convent at what was then the "advanced age" of twenty-eight, and she loved to tell us what a worldly woman she had been—pursued by an endless stream of ardent "gentleman friends" who had proposed marriage. If we believed that this unsettling woman had ever been pursued by anyone other than God, we kept it to ourselves. Sister Claire loved to describe the moment of her calling, which occurred in the stands of a football stadium where she was seated with her current gentleman friend.

She said that she had shuddered suddenly, as if a strong gust of cold air had swept over her, and at that moment she knew she was called to be a nun. We asked her if it was hard to give up men. "Oh, no," she murmured in her soft Southern accent, as she looked deeply into our eyes, "Jesus was so much better than any of them." The idea of Sister Claire at a football game seemed preposterous.

Sister Claire gave me the creeps, for reasons I didn't quite understand then but which I later realized had been the overtly erotic overtones whenever she discussed her relationship to Jesus. Her odd behavior made no sense to me. It had never occurred to me to fantasize about Jesus in that way. I didn't think *that* was what loving him was meant to be about.

Still, Sister Claire was certainly right about one thing: God's calling was mysterious. Each year, it seemed astounding when the most beautiful and popular seniors graduated from Holy Angels and entered the convent at Rosary Heights. I was particularly impressed when Mary Anne Cullinane, the senior prom queen with her movie-star looks, ended up at Rosary Heights. Who would have guessed? The very fact that God's calling veered so far off type made it more impressive still. How did these girls know they were called? How did the prioress of the order recognize in them the qualities necessary to be accepted into the Dominican family? Sister Claire made it clear that although God's calling might be unpredictable, it was hardly capricious. The order's charter required that new entrants possess four measurable indications of a religious vocation. How were such things measured? First, new entrants must possess a spiritual joy; second, peace of mind; third, facility in executing acts of religion; and fourth, ease in the practice of virtue.

In spite of Sister Claire's insistence that the unlikeliest among us might be called, I despaired of ever demonstrating these measurable indications of a religious vocation. Spiritual joy? Peace of mind? My mind was a churning sea of unfettered thoughts—wild, turbulent, uncertain. The only constant was the intensity of my life force. I burned with life, a torch freshly lit and blazing. I couldn't imagine a state of peace. As for spiritual joy, that belonged in the realm of the saints. I had certainly never experienced it, and I wasn't entirely sure if I'd ever seen it with my own eyes.

Now, my best friend Bernadette—*she* was the type, if there was one. Tall, thin, her silky dark hair falling into milky brown eyes, Bernadette had a face that belonged on a holy card. She could adopt a pose of stillness and serenity that was quite remarkable. Her seeming imperturbability was easily recast as spiritual poise, and so the nuns all admired Bernadette. Only I, her best friend and closest confidante, knew that Bernadette was as still as a raging flood. She hadn't mastered peace of mind at all. She was tormented by a constant and elusive quest for perfection; at that time, she was the most driven person I'd ever known. A grade of *B* on her usually flawless report card was enough to make her physically ill. Once recovered, Bernadette would intensify her program of study until the stubborn grade improved. She would arrive at school exhausted, her eyes swollen and red-rimmed. I couldn't understand Bernadette's compulsion. I couldn't imagine striving so passionately for perfection. You only drew more attention to yourself, especially when you succeeded. You constantly raised the bar until it was at impossible heights. I prided myself on doing just the opposite from my friend Bernadette. I surrounded myself with an aura of imperfection instead. It was the only way I could escape closer scrutiny from the sisters. It was the only way to keep my secrets—my dreams, my desires, my passions—safe from them.

Although I had always bristled against authority, I bluffed my way through school by being intensely verbal and glib. My cheerful, outgoing manner was a disguise I used to mask a completely different character, a keen observer and avid writer with a brooding inner life. My favorite time of day was the evening, when I could finally be alone in my room. It was my only sanctuary in our crowded, noisy house—a square white-walled room with a built-in window seat, where I spent many hours daydreaming or writing. I wrote everything down then. I was compelled to write—not stories, but truth. Even then, writing about what really happened was more interesting to me than inventing fiction—shadows of my future life's work looming.

Alone on my window seat, I spent long hours thinking and writing about my destiny. For as long as I could remember, I felt called, destined, to a special purpose in life; I was going to do something. For a long time, I was unable to say exactly what that purpose was, but I always knew that whatever the path, it would ultimately require a freedom from obedience—to either rule or man. When Sister Claire gazed at me with her fervent missionary eyes and whispered, "Have you asked yourself if God is calling *you,* Catherine?" I felt like a fly twisting helplessly in her holy web, soon to be sacrificed to her righteous religious hunger. I admired the intellect and strength of the Dominicans, but I couldn't imagine a life of obedience. God *was* calling me—but not to that.

There wasn't much of an age difference between the high school girls and the young nuns. We loved to chat with them, play volleyball in the concrete schoolyard outside, and try to learn their secrets. There was much laughter, but often I would catch other looks in their faces—quiet sadness, wariness, a tentativeness that sometimes felt awkward and off-putting. In my naïveté, I assumed that they were subject to dark spiritual crises. It didn't seem at all unpleasant to me. Considering my own state, it only added to their appeal. We especially loved the nuns who seemed the most "normal"—that is, the ones young enough to be most like us. Yet, no matter how much time we spent together, not a one of them ever really let go, put down her guard, and opened up. There was always an impenetrable wall between us. Our contact with them stopped at the door of the convent.

I had no idea what went on behind the walls of that convent— what their life together was like. It never occurred to me that life could be mundane and boring for them, as it was in my own home—or that they might be subjected to pettiness, recriminations, jealousy, or disputes. During all of my years in school, I never once witnessed an argument between two nuns. Not even a cross word.

My friend Tracy laughed at my stupidity. Tracy was wise beyond her years; she was in the know. She had several aunts who were Holy Names sisters, and she told the wildest and most shocking stories of the humiliations and penances they suffered daily. One of her aunts, Tracy said, once refused to eat a stew of yams and beans because she was allergic to yams. The Mother Superior ordered that she be brought a bowl of dirt from the garden. She was forced to eat every bite as a penance while the other sisters sat silently at the table. She vomited three times during the ordeal, but no one moved until she was done. Then she got down on her hands and knees and cleaned up her vomit. Tracy had a grotesque collection of stories like that one. When I heard them, my heart sank, much like it had when a friend told me at the age of four that there was no Santa Claus. There are some things you just don't want to know.

Tracy was a fascinating young woman with a complex character. She had an exceptionally quick, clever mind. Her perfect grades came easily, but there was an edge to her intellect, as well. A cynicism. Sister Claire often shook a warning finger at Tracy and said, "You're too comfortable with defiance, Tracy. You tempt fate." Then Sister Claire would try to pierce Tracy's defiance with her intense eyes. Tracy would toss her thick red mane and return Sister Claire's deep gaze, more defiant than ever. The room would almost crackle with the tension between them. Then Tracy would suddenly smile, and all would be forgiven. Tracy's smile was dazzling in that way, disarming and all-embracing.

Tracy's exceptional singing voice made her a favorite of Sister Carmen, our music teacher. I always envied the ability to sing well. I loved to sing, but I was cursed with a tin ear and a loud voice. No matter how hard I tried, my voice cut through the links of melody like an errant chain saw. In choir, Sister Carmen assigned me to the alto section, perhaps hoping I could channel my unfilterable volume into sonorous depth. But this was wishful thinking on her part. As the choir raised its voice as one, my attempt to blend in raked across each song with dissonant claws. Poor Sister Carmen finally cried out in frustration, "Don't sing, Catherine. Just move your mouth. Please don't sing."

Decades later, when I reminded Sister Carmen of my futile attempts at singing and her order that I keep silent, she was appalled. "I would never have done that!" she protested. But she had! I laughingly forgave her, both for her exasperation and her memory lapse. Those were obviously times that tried nuns' souls.

Our generation had the fortune—or the curse—of living in the time of the *aggiornamento*—the renewal of the church. Set in motion by Pope John XXIII, the twenty-first ecumenical council—popularly known as Vatican II—was a monumental force of change in the church, demolishing rusty traditions that had been in place for centuries. From the convening of the council in 1962, the church was on constantly shifting ground—although the Pacific Northwest, one of the newer settlements in the church's world, was far more open to change than its stodgier ancestors back east and in Europe. The Archbishop of Portland, Oregon, had once dared to celebrate Mass facing the congregation—fully twenty years before the practice was sanctioned by Rome.

Vatican II was a watershed moment for the church. Centuries-old ritual was abandoned. The soaring, ethereal beauty of the Latin chants was replaced with comparatively dull, egalitarian English. The church demanded a new spirit of transformation, a renewed commitment to the concept of love. This caused more trouble than one might expect. For centuries, Catholics had used the word sparingly—usually to depict a posture of charity toward others. Suddenly, everything had changed. When the church said love, it meant *Love*. My father, for one, bridled against the infusion of this "touchy-feely" spirit now loose in the church. Once the love of God had been enough; faith had sufficed. All of our prayers were in Latin, and we were comforted and inspired by the soothing cadences, the liturgical flavor of chants it seemed unnecessary to translate. All of this—the Latin, the incense, the priest's voice, the flickering votive candles—added to God's mystery, his *otherness.*

> *Kyrie eleison*
> *Christe eleison*
> *Lord have mercy . . . Christ have mercy.*

And although Catholics spoke of themselves as being "the community of the faithful," the liturgy was actually a very private affair. We knelt in church and prayed with heads bowed, and tried to make our individual peace with God.

Suddenly, the way of the ages was over. The church wanted us to achieve togetherness. The ritual that my father found one of the most offensive until the day he died was the Passing of the Peace. This occurred at Mass, at which point everyone was asked to clasp the hands of those around them and say, "Peace be with you." My father detested this. As far as he was concerned, this was not only a violation of his space but also an interruption of his purpose for being in church. He was also appalled by what Vatican II did to the music. The new spirit was reflected in it; the songs became mushy and simplistic. He just despised them, especially when they were accompanied by a guitar—an instrument he considered sacrilegious in the church. I still remember how my father would always keep his lips clamped shut—as though in silent protest to God himself—as the congregation sang:

> *God is love*
> *and he who abides in love*
> *abides in God*
> *and God in him.*

Our family lived near the University District, the heart of hippie love and emerging radicalism during the sixties. It was hard to avoid what was happening. Our parish church, Blessed Sacrament—

we had moved there from Assumption in the mid-sixties—was hardly able to rise above the times. Instead, our congregation became a guinea pig for a series of experimental liturgies. Originally, my father had been drawn to the simplicity and piety of the Dominican priests. He felt that they were humble, direct, and honest in their relationship to God. But within a span of five years, it almost seemed as if the three priests at Blessed Sacrament had been exposed to something more powerful than their Communion wine—moondust, perhaps. One was transformed into a "charismatic" and started speaking in tongues; another had a nervous breakdown and landed in an institution; and a third priest ran off and married a pretty young college girl. The congregation tried to remain upbeat as a flock of new priests came swooping in to replace their fallen comrades. They were armed with soothing reassurances that it was all God's will; all would be well.

Vatican II came to a close in 1965 with a call for renewal of religious orders. In 1966, Pope Paul VI sent an apostolic letter, entitled *Perfectae Caritatis*—the Decree on the Adaptation and Renewal of Religious Life—in which he called for the implementation of changes and decreed that all orders should hold special chapters (congregational conferences) no later than 1969 to revamp rules and constitutions.

The Edmonds Dominicans decided to begin their chapter in the summer of 1968. But long before that, the changes were becoming apparent. In the spring of 1967, the nuns in our school suddenly appeared for classes one day *without* the heavy box frame and headdress. It had been replaced by a short, soft black veil with a narrow white band, which allowed some hair to show. Soon after, the long robes disappeared, having been replaced by demure knee-length skirts that revealed black-stockinged legs.

Of course, we were eager to get the nuns to talk about the change in fashion. We were young girls and wanted to know everything. Occasionally, one of the sisters would oblige. Sister Carmen made no secret of her relief at being freed of the big box on her head. "It was a torture chamber," she admitted.

"Especially in warm weather. It was like having your head in an oven." Some of the older nuns—who had been wearing the habit for decades—had permanent ridges that ran the length of their foreheads, as well as deep vertical gashes that had been sliced into their cheeks. Their wimples had literally been carved into their faces over the years.

For the first time, in the midst of these changes, I saw friction among the nuns as they disputed how far to take the modernization. Some of the sisters, such as the pious biology teacher, Sister Erin, refused to give up the traditional habit, and they moved through the hallway like ghosts of a distant past. Others, such as old Sister Albertina, accepted the decision, but with great suffering. Sister Albertina was well into her seventies and built like a tank— as wide as she was tall. For a woman like Albertina, the habit was a godsend; it fully covered her body and allowed her to achieve a dignity she might otherwise have found impossible. I'm told she wept with humiliation at the sight of her legs fully exposed for the first time in fifty years. It must have been too much for her. She died in 1969.

There were other disturbing signals, as well. Our popular history teacher, Sister Barbara, occasionally raced from the classroom in midlecture to throw up in the bathroom. Sister Carmen stayed closeted in her band room in the basement, increasingly edgy and withdrawn. She no longer joked around with us after school. Sister Claire's dark eyes seemed to burn even more fiercely, and her full lips were pursed in barely concealed rage.

Modernization was a deceptive word. Once you started questioning one thing, the carefully woven fabric of centuries began to unravel. This wasn't merely change; this was revolution.

It was both an exhilarating experience and a terrifying alteration for the sisters. Their order found itself in the midst of gale-force hurricanes, no longer under the protection of the heavy serge robes. The old ways were gone forever. Everything was threatening to break loose at any moment. Whatever happened, it would never be the same again.

. . .

It was appropriate, somehow, that Sister Elizabeth would appear on the scene of this chaos to stir the already-roiled waters even further. On the first day of school in my senior year, Sister Elizabeth swept into our English class and introduced herself as our new teacher. She was a slight woman, but she exuded an almost electric energy. Her face beamed with intelligence and animation. In a relaxed, friendly manner, as though we were all just girls talking, she took us into her confidence. She explained that she had spent the past ten years in a Dominican cloister in New England but had been sent out on assignment to teach for a year. We gaped at her in disbelief. This sparkling personality, in her short skirt and sassy little veil, came from a *cloistered monastery*?

Sister Elizabeth was an enigma. She was so exuberant, so full of life. She treasured great works of art, the opera, and the theater. She taught Shakespeare with the reverence and intensity usually reserved for the Scriptures. Everything about the world excited her. I couldn't understand the dichotomy; it baffled me. The sacred and the secular had always been presented as two separate and distinct paths. For weeks, I said nothing about the obvious paradox. Finally, on a day when Sister Elizabeth had been discussing the intensity of the commitment between Romeo and Juliet and their need to have their young love sanctified by God, I found my thoughts elsewhere. All of a sudden, I raised my hand, then blurted out, "Why did you join a cloister? How did you know you were called to that life?"

Sister Elizabeth didn't try to deflect my curiosity. Instead, she took the question seriously. She asked the class if we would prefer to continue discussing *Romeo and Juliet,* or would we rather have her discuss life in the cloister? We slammed our books shut so readily that it sounded like a gunshot going off.

I had been the one who'd started it, so I spoke for the class. "Please, Sister. Tell us."

"Well, it's very difficult to explain how a person feels drawn to the contemplative life," she said thoughtfully. "I never imagined it was for me, and I was drawn to it almost unwillingly. I mean, it wasn't a choice; it was a calling. It was almost as if I were lost in a forest and had to decide which way to go. It was all up to me. No one was offering me directions, suggesting I go one way or the other. My Mother Superior, the priest who counseled me—no one ever tried to make up my mind for me. Not in the least. What happened was that I learned a lot about what I really wanted, and what I needed. Ultimately, I confronted myself. I went it alone— battled with God on my own." She looked suddenly wistful. "I know it seems to all of you that the cloistered life would be suffo- cating and lonely. I thought it would be, too. I thought I'd be cut off from the world. But it wasn't that at all. There was such free- dom, such *spiritual* freedom, within the confines of that cloister. I don't even know how to explain it. It's real freedom, though. Free- dom within yourself. Do you understand?"

"No, I can't imagine that," I said frankly. "How can you be free? You're locked away, aren't you? Can you tell us what it was like?" Amazingly, she did.

Elizabeth's Calling

Once she had followed Sister Dorothy through the convent doors on that uncertain day nineteen years earlier, Elizabeth somehow knew she had made an irrevocable choice. But she didn't yet know the true nature or scope of that choice. She was almost mystically drawn to Catholicism, but she had many questions. After she graduated from high school, and while she was studying literature and music at the University of Washington, Elizabeth continued her quest. Sister Dorothy introduced her to Father Joseph, a quiet, studious young Dominican priest at Blessed Sacra- ment Church, who became her mentor and instructor. She proved to be a difficult student. She felt compelled to question everything, to force Father Joseph to defend every ritual, every obligation.

"The rosary," she said to him one day. "It bothers me. Why do I have to repeat the words over and over again? What's the point?"

Father Joseph nodded. "There's a reason for everything, Elizabeth, but I can understand how you might see it that way." He seemed incapable of taking offense. "Ah, I have an idea. Do you know what a mantra is?"

Elizabeth confessed that she didn't.

"In Buddhism, a mantra is a series of words—sounds, really— that you are given as your own way to reach a higher state. The guru—the teacher—who gives you this mantra chooses a special word or series of words just for you. You are asked to chant the words over and over, creating a sound that will vibrate inside of you and outside of you. Some people say it's another way to reach to heaven. The rosary is just like chanting a mantra. You've got to free your mind before you can soar in prayer. You know what I think, Elizabeth?" Father Joseph leaned in and smiled. "You *think* too much."

Elizabeth found it fascinating that a Catholic priest would offer a Buddhist context for saying the rosary, but Father Joseph's explanation worked for her. She tried to stop thinking so much; she tried to free her mind. At first, it felt like a free *fall,* and she found it frightening. But to her surprise, she found herself growing increasingly comfortable with prayer. She found another, infinite world opening to her—she found herself finally able to soar on the wings of prayer. It was a place she liked to be; it became familiar to her.

Gradually, she found herself being drawn to religious life—not as a teacher but as a contemplative. No one could have been more astounded by the choice than Elizabeth herself. She was a bright, verbal, imaginative woman, and an excellent teacher. She'd always thought that women in monasteries must somehow be dull and simple—or that perhaps they were social misfits, chronically unmarriageable. How else could one bear to live that way? But while reading the works of Saint Teresa of Avila, she discovered how wrong she had been. For one thing, Teresa was not at all the pious automaton that Elizabeth had imagined populated the cloistered convents. The founder of the Discalced Carmelites revealed herself to be flesh and blood. She was brilliant and real. She was a woman capable of biting sarcasm, pointed wit, simple logic, tremendous practicality, and incredible passion. What a formidable person she must have been! Teresa was at once an activist and a contemplative; she transformed the corrupt practices of the old order, returning the Carmelite Sisters to their mandate of poverty. *Discalced* means, literally, "return to poverty." Teresa accomplished this almost single-handedly. Bearing that in mind, perhaps her greatest contribution were her treatises on the way of mental prayer—the striving for spiritual communion with Jesus Christ.

It impressed Elizabeth that Saint Teresa's writings bore no hint of self-conscious piety. To the contrary, her explanations about contemplative prayer seemed self-effacing. "There are souls God knows He must gain for Himself by this means," Teresa explained in *The Way of Perfection*. "Seeing that they are completely lost, He wants to leave no stone unturned to help them. Therefore, even though they are in sad shape and desperately lacking in virtues, He gives them consolations, favors and emotions which begin to move their desires and occasionally bring them to a state of contemplation."

There was a Carmelite monastery of women in the heart of Seattle, and Elizabeth arranged to meet with the superior, Mother Teresa. She was instructed to go to a side door and ring the buzzer. The door clicked open, and she entered a small room. It was chilly inside—underheated; Elizabeth pulled her sweater tightly around her. The room was empty but for a plain silver crucifix on the wall and a single chair placed before a heavy grille that revealed very little of what lay on the other side. Carved out of the wall next to the grille was a large revolving container called a "turn." Gifts of food were placed there by visitors from the outside world. The turn was rotated inside at the press of a button. The Carmelites had long depended on these donations for their sustenance. Elizabeth had brought a basket of fresh fruit, and she placed it on the turn.

After a few minutes, a shadowy figure appeared behind the grille; she was enveloped in a heavy black veil, and her face was a blur. The sister introduced herself as Mother Teresa. She then listened intently as Elizabeth told her story and explained why she had come to see her. When Elizabeth was finished, there was a long silence as Mother Teresa considered what she had just been told. Finally, Mother Teresa quietly said, "I don't think you would be happy in the Carmelites, Elizabeth. Your mind is too active."

Elizabeth didn't know how to react. Whatever could she mean? Teresa of Avila possessed the most active mind that Elizabeth had ever encountered! Her writings on the contemplative life plainly stated that it required mental acuity. She said exactly that to Mother Teresa, and through the grille she could see Mother's head dip down, as if she was considering the point. Suddenly, Mother Teresa rose from her chair and said, "Our life is not for you. Go in peace. God bless you." And she was gone.

Elizabeth was devastated by Mother Teresa's terse rejection. After thinking about it for a few days, however, she became outraged. So, these were the Carmelites! Had they forgotten the message of their foundress? Did they desire only women with empty heads and subservient wills? She had a better chance of being accepted by the Carmelites if her mind was *less* active? She was relieved that she'd found this out before going any further.

The years passed, and Elizabeth quietly continued her spiritual search. She found a position teaching in the Seattle public schools, and she moved out of her grandmother's home and into an apartment. Quietly, and with little fanfare, she was baptized a Catholic. Her grandmother refused to speak to her for an entire year. Even later, when the old woman thawed a bit, their relationship was never the same.

Elizabeth loved teaching, and she found that she had a true gift for it. But there was always the gnawing in her gut, the tickle in the back of her consciousness. Something else was calling her. She couldn't explain it.

Over the years, Elizabeth had met many nuns—all of them in

active orders. She had known a number of young women who entered these orders. Sister Dorothy introduced her to the Edmonds Dominicans, but she was never at ease with them. She always felt like an outsider, searching for the place she truly belonged.

One day, Sister Dorothy called her with some surprising news. She was leaving Seattle, transferring to a Dominican contemplative order back east.

"The Dominicans have a cloister?" This was news to Elizabeth. "I thought the Dominicans were teachers and nurses."

"The Dominicans are all things," Sister Dorothy explained. "In fact, the motto of the Dominican order is 'to give to others the fruits of contemplation.' Those in the cloister provide spiritual support for those in the world. I have come to the conclusion that I am called to take on that role."

Elizabeth went about her busy life and kept in touch with Sister Dorothy after she had gone east. As she would say later, the idea of entering a monastery was like a constantly ringing phone—a phone she refused to answer for fear that she'd hear a voice from heaven saying, "This is God. Where are you?"

When she received a letter from Sister Dorothy asking if she'd like to come for a visit during her winter school break, Elizabeth couldn't refuse. She flew to New York, rented a car, and made the two-hour drive to the monastery.

The Dominican monastery was in the tiny New England town of Guilford, Connecticut, on Long Island Sound. The simple stone buildings were surrounded by seventeen acres of sloping hills and wooded landscape. A constant breeze carried the salty smell of the Atlantic Ocean up from the Sound, and the seagulls shrieked their familiar messages over the roaring of the waves. It reminded Elizabeth of home.

A double black iron grille now separated Elizabeth from her old friend. Sister Dorothy told her of her life in the cloister, and Elizabeth confessed the extent of her own struggle. Sister Dorothy urged her to speak with the Mother Prioress before she left. "You'll have no peace if you don't," she said. Somehow, Sister Dorothy's words resounded deep within her. Elizabeth knew it was the truth.

When Elizabeth faced the Mother Prioress the next day from behind the grille, she remembered her ill-fated visit many years before to the Carmelites. Although hesitant at first, she decided she had to address her rejection head-on. She told the prioress everything. Did she also think that Elizabeth's mind was too active? Would the Dominicans be unhappy with someone like her? Would Elizabeth be unhappy among the Dominicans?

The woman behind the grille leaned as far forward as she could. Elizabeth could almost make out the gentle smile that graced the prioress's lips. She stated with quiet certainty, "You belong here. When can you come?"

Elizabeth met the eyes of the prioress through the cross-hatching of the grille. All doubt disappeared. "I'll be back at the end of the school year," she said.

When she arrived in Guilford to begin her postulancy, Elizabeth was surprised to find that she wasn't the oldest in the group. She'd assumed that the other postulants would be seventeen- and eighteen-year-olds, fresh out of high school. Instead, she found herself among women much like herself. Two others were teachers, another was a former airline stewardess, and the eldest of the group was a forty-year-old former executive secretary. Like her, they also had been irrevocably drawn to this higher calling—compelled to practice the way of the contemplative.

Although Elizabeth struggled with the confinement—the initial psychological downsizing of being contained within four walls—her spirit was alive with freedom. Being a contemplative was an act of pure faith—praying for those who didn't pray. The world they prayed for was a very dim and distant reality. There were no newspapers, no radio or television. They lived in a state of the purest faith.

In Guilford, Elizabeth found the intellectual excitement she had been searching for since reading the works of Saint Teresa of Avila. The work was hard, but every minute was rewarding. She labored in the print shop. She perfected the haunting Gregorian chants and the complex notes of the Divine Office. There was tremendous variety within the uniformity.

Of course, she had her brushes with authority. One of her most prized possessions was her collection of opera recordings, which she had brought with her to the monastery. Elizabeth had always viewed the passionate swells and languid dips of opera as deeply expressive of human longings. They provided her with a sense of elevation, grandeur, and grace. She particularly loved the sumptuous Italian composers. Their passion seemed both secular and divine. One day when she went to look for her opera collection in the library, it was gone. The shelf where her records had sat was empty. Perhaps they'd been moved to another room, or been borrowed by one of the other sisters. As she was considering the possibilities, Sister Fredericka, an older, professed nun, happened to enter the library.

"Looking for your opera records? They've been thrown out," she abruptly announced.

Sister Elizabeth's vow of obedience momentarily deserted her. "Thrown out?" she shrieked. "Why on earth would anyone do that?"

"Silence, Sister," Sister Fredericka ordered. Elizabeth bit her tongue in an effort to contain herself. "Opera," the older sister stated firmly, "is filled with the passions of the world. That is not appropriate here. It is a temptation. It is an indulgence. It is sinful. You will not speak of this again." Sister Fredericka strode from the room.

Tears of fury sprang from Elizabeth's eyes. What a foolish, ignorant woman! Opera a temptation? Sinful? Too worldly? She almost packed her bags at that point. Only the fiercest prayer kept her from leaving.

Elizabeth loved the contemplative life, but she was exhausted by an unrelenting inner struggle. Did she really belong? Should she be teaching? She burrowed deep into her consciousness, attempting to discover her true motivations. The question haunted her: Was this destiny, or was this escape?

When a person lives in silence for a long time, a painful inner journey is inescapable. Elizabeth began to see a lot of things in herself that she didn't like. Her pride, her lack of charity, her petty little jealousies—all were exposed to her like open sores. No matter how hard she strived to attain the unattainable, no matter how sincere her quest for perfection, she had to face herself.

It was humbling. Human failing, original sin—whatever one called it—she shared the imperfections of all people. And this naturally led her to question her choice of place in the world. Was she in the monastery because it satisfied her selfish longings, or was she here on a mission?

She wondered, too, would God have given her such a gift for teaching if he intended her to close herself off from the world? Was she hiding her light under a bushel?

She continued to question her decision right up to the day of her final profession and beyond. She was beginning to wonder if she was fated to live in the hell of her own doubts for the rest of her life, when God intervened.

For some time, Sister Elizabeth had been having trouble sleeping, and she almost always felt exhausted. Even though she tried not to let it interfere with her work and the schedule of prayer, sometimes she found it hard to hold her head up. When she started losing weight—something she could ill afford, given her tiny frame—she was sent to the doctor.

The doctor could find nothing apparently wrong with Sister Elizabeth, but after a full examination, she sat her down and posited a strange theory. "I have been studying the research on sleep cycles," the doctor told her. "Some of the nuns have no trouble getting up in the middle of the night for prayer. They get their deep sleep either earlier or later. But I think it may take you longer to enter the REM state. So just as you're beginning to fall into deep sleep, the bell rings. You're suffering from a severe case of sleep deprivation."

Elizabeth asked her, "How can I change that?"

"I'm not sure you can," the doctor told her frankly. "It's

probably better for you to change your schedule so that you work during the day and sleep through the night."

Sister Elizabeth returned to her cell and burst into tears. She feared that this was God's way of saying, Leave the cloister. Return to teaching.

After much discussion, it was decided that Sister Elizabeth should take a sabbatical. She would be sent on loan to the Edmonds Dominicans to teach at their high school.

As Sister Elizabeth told her story, we sat in rapt attention. It was unusual for a nun to speak so openly. I asked Sister Elizabeth, "What did you finally decide you were doing in the cloister? Were you there to pray for others? Is that the purpose of being cloistered? So that nothing else interferes?"

"No," she admitted. "I think I went about it in a very selfish way. Certainly the contemplative nun prays for those in the world who are unable to pray for themselves. But it was more than that. I longed for a more personal relationship with Jesus Christ. I was on my own spiritual quest. I was trying to find my way to the Infinite."

I pondered her words: "I was trying to find my way to the Infinite." That was it. What could be a greater and more profound journey? But how did one go about it? What was contemplative prayer? I had always struggled with the meaning and practice of prayer. Prayer, I knew, was not confined to *prayers*—the Hail Mary, the Our Father, the Act of Contrition, the Apostles' Creed. Prayer was not captured in words. Saying the words could put one in a state of prayer, but they were not the end in themselves. In the simplest terms, prayer was conversation with God. But which God? As Catholics, we believed in the Holy Trinity—three distinct persons in one God: the Father, who was the God of Abraham; the Son, who was Jesus Christ; and the Holy Spirit, the breath of divine presence in the world. The Holy Spirit was the most enigmatic aspect of the Trinity—the engine that made connection with the Father and Son possible, but who remained somehow distant. Jesus seemed like the most available of the Trinity to pray to. He was only thirty-three years old when he died; he was always depicted as young and charismatic. But how did one really get close to him?

By this time, I had attended thousands of Masses, prayed hundreds of rosaries, walked the Stations of the Cross dozens of times, and still I had not even begun to master the practice of prayer, at least as I understood it.

"True prayer," instructed Sister Claire, "is a state that requires emptying the mind of all thought, of frivolity, of worry, of plans. In this state, the mind, like an open, expectant vessel, waits to be filled with God's grace." I despised those images. Empty vessels? Passive, empty vessels? That's what we were supposed to be? I had trouble believing that.

"Sister," I spoke up. "I don't think God wants us to be empty vessels. Doesn't he want us to be helping the poor and fighting against injustice? Are we supposed to wait around, hoping God will fill us with his grace? If the greatest virtue is charity, doesn't that mean being active?"

"Ah, Catherine, why does silence trouble you so much? Why do you resist it?" Sister Claire's face was alight with pleasure. I had inadvertently offered a juicy morsel for her to chew on. "Let me ask you this," she proposed. "If your boyfriend was in the room with you, would you be distracted? Would you be chattering about nonsense, or thinking about what you were going to do later? Of course not. You would be completely focused on your boyfriend, body and soul. You would love him. He would be the only thing in the world for you, Catherine. He would be your lover. Is that not true?"

My classmates were tittering and shifting all around me. Sister Claire was bearing down on me now, moving in closer. Her ample bosom loomed over me, casting a dark shadow on my desk. I nodded a meek assent in self-defense, although never having had a boyfriend, much less a lover, I couldn't really say.

"*Jesus* is that lover," she rasped. "But you cannot expect him to enter your soul if it is cluttered with other desires."

Across the room, Patty clucked. It was the tiniest noise, but

Sister Claire heard it and whipped around. She began to walk toward Patty, her matronly hips swaying. Every girl in the room was at attention now. Patty moved around in her seat, trying to get comfortable—a difficult proposition, because she was almost seven months pregnant. Although she'd tried to hide it as long as she could, her ample belly strained against the wool fabric of her blue uniform skirt. She was trying desperately not to laugh.

Sister Claire's nostrils flared as she set her sights on the one girl among us who had demonstrable experience with a lover. "Miss Moran, you are amused by something?"

Patty shook her head. "No, Sister," she whispered.

"I suppose you think you know all about it," Sister Claire hissed. "Why don't you tell us, Miss Moran. Tell us the difference between human sex and the presence of Jesus Christ inside of you. Do you even *know*?"

Patty was no longer laughing. Now her face was very red, and she was blinking away tears. She struggled to her feet and pushed Sister Claire aside. Then she stumbled out of the room. She never came back.

Later, I told Sister Elizabeth what had happened. Her eyes flashed with anger or disgust—I couldn't tell which—but she said only, "Well, Sister has her own problems. Don't take it too much to heart."

"But what about what she said?" I asked. "The empty vessel thing. Is that the way to pray? Is that what you did in the cloister?"

"There are two ways of going about meditation," Sister Elizabeth replied. "One is, as Sister Claire said, to empty yourself of everything. But there's another way, too. Would you like to know what it is?" She shot me a tantalizing look.

"Yes, of course."

"Do just the opposite. Fill yourself up. Let everything *in*!"

The backdrop to my spiritual quest was a series of shattering events that took place in my final year at Holy Angels. Everything that had seemed so sure and certain was suddenly ephemeral and

without substance. Palpable tragedy was underscored by the confusion and conflict taking place not only in the world but also in
our personal lives.

Our religious foundation, our comfortable old Mother
Church, was being reconstructed even as the world itself began to
tear at its own edges. Life suddenly seemed mad; the possibility for
violence and annihilation seemed rife; tragedy stalked our presidents, our civil rights leaders, our society. A war escalated slowly far
away, a slow-motion train wreck that would consume thousands
and thousands of young lives and set generations against one
another. We were on the edge of apocalypse, but we had no idea
such a cataclysm was upon us. Everything was changing—drugs,
sex, faith, war, love, peace, and happiness. Everything was becoming irrevocably different. As if to underscore the depth of the crisis, Sister Claire informed us that the two Popes since 1960 had
both read the message from Our Lady of Fatima. Both had considered it too alarming to share with the world. It was said that
when Pope John XXIII read the message, he put his head in his
hands and sobbed with fear.

All of us were going through one kind of a hell or another, but
it seemed that Bernadette was hit the hardest. Within the space of
a year, her father died of throat cancer, her brother killed himself
while cleaning his rifle, and Bernadette herself almost died when
her appendix burst. Tracy's favorite aunt, one of the Holy Names
Sisters, committed suicide. Tracy was devastated by her loss; she was
never the same after that.

My life was no bed of roses, either. My family was in incredible turmoil. My forty-two-year-old mother spent half of that year
in a dangerous pregnancy. Although her doctor had advised against
more children, her priest assured her it was God's will. When my
youngest sister, Joanne, was born, my mother had nine children,
three under the age of five. My brother Jim joined the army and
was shipped off to see the beginning of three tours of combat in
Vietnam. My brother Greg dropped out of the seminary and

joined the navy. The Pacific Northwest was keeping pace with the rest of the country, so my thirteen-year-old brother, Tom, was caught by my parents using drugs. It wasn't pretty. They called the police, and he was remanded to a youth home, a euphemism for a youth prison. The Schuler household was no longer the cheerful, secure place it had once been. My parents were in a state of barely controlled panic. The vortex was spinning more and more wildly out of control. Who would it consume next?

In April of 1968, weeks before graduation, our class went on a final weekend retreat to Rosary Heights. On Saturday afternoon, Bernadette, Tracy, and I sat together on a bench by the edge of the bluff, overlooking Puget Sound. We should have been excited and filled with anticipation. We were three bright young women with our lives ahead of us. Thanks to the mentoring of Sister Lawrence, my brilliant and nurturing journalism teacher, I had been awarded a scholarship to study journalism at the University of Washington. Bernadette had won a scholarship to Seattle University, a Catholic college. Tracy intended to pursue a musical career; she had both the talent and drive for it. But our mood was pensive and guarded that day. We were already beginning to separate, preparing to become strangers. The small window of light that had been our girlhood was closing, leaving us outside in the darkness. Now we were confronted with the need to define ourselves—not just what we would *do* but who we would *be*. And we could not help one another with that.

"Just think," Tracy said unconvincingly, "no more Sister Albertina."

"Yeah," Bernadette and I choroused. Suddenly, it didn't seem like such a great thing to be without Sister Albertina, or any of the rest of the nuns. Life with them was if nothing else safe. Freedom, that indefinable something we had all hoped and longed for, that concept we had spoken endlessly about, was upon us, and it looked to be a bear trap.

Later, I walked by myself in the woods surrounding Rosary

Heights as the last rays of the sun sent beams and shadows dancing among the trees. It was so peaceful and safe here. Maybe I could tie myself to a tree and stay in this sanctuary—if only I could. I pressed my back against a giant evergreen, spreading my hands behind to hold on to the trunk, the better to imagine myself tied to it. I pressed my head against the rough bark and closed my eyes. Could I?

I heard a voice calling my name. It was Bernadette. Time for prayers. Reluctantly, I turned and made my way back through the woods to join the others.

That evening, I found Sister Carmen sitting at the piano in the chapel, leaning against the keys, her head bent. She jumped when I sat beside her and quietly said her name, as if I'd interrupted her from sleep. Her eyes seemed puffy and her face as pale as a ghost. But I knew better than to comment on a sister's possible illness, and so I didn't dare ask her what might be wrong.

"This is such a beautiful place," I said. "You were here for your novitiate, weren't you?"

"Yes. Ours was the first group to have our novitiate here." Sister Carmen closed the piano lid and sat back on the bench.

"Have any of your friends left?" I asked.

"Yes, we've all had friends leave."

"That must be hard."

"It is." Sister Carmen's eyes glistened for a moment, and I could see her jaw set.

"I've decided to speak to Mother Dominick about entering the order," I confided to her.

That changed her mood. "Really? You want to join us, Catherine?" She suddenly yawned. "I'm sorry, dear. I'm just so tired." She rose from the bench, then turned and placed a hand on my shoulder, giving it a gentle squeeze. "Good luck, honey."

The next day, we gathered in the chapel for a final prayer service. Tracy stood to sing a solo, with Sister Carmen accompanying her on the piano. Tracy's voice was like a high keening, a wail, as she sang:

Hear, O Lord, the sound of my call;
Hear, O Lord, and have mercy.
My soul is longing for the glory of You.
O hear, O Lord, and answer me.

Every night before I sleep I pray my soul to take,
Or else I pray that loneliness is gone when I awake.
Why do I no longer feel like I've a place to stay?
O take me where someone will care, so fear will go away.

Hear, O Lord, the sound of my call;
Hear, O Lord, and have mercy.
My soul is longing for the glory of You.
O hear, O Lord, and answer me.

It was a strange hymn to choose, I thought, full of despair, longing, and loneliness. Odd that Sister Carmen would decide to include it in our final service. Perhaps she was sensing the turbulence we were experiencing. Or perhaps she was feeling it herself.

My appointment with Mother Dominick was set for 10:30 Saturday morning at Rosary Heights. My father agreed to drive me to Edmonds and wait in the car. My parents were delighted by my choice, almost giddy beyond all reason. I was their shining star, their firstborn daughter. How proud they were! My father, great lover of nuns that he was, could think of nothing finer than to have one in his very own family. His joy was mixed with a palpable sense of relief. One of his children was escaping the vortex, being rescued by the church.

As we drove up the winding path to the circular driveway in front of Rosary Heights, the dew shimmered and dripped off the bushes like falling tears. I felt infused with grace and excitement. What a crazy, wonderful thing I was doing!

I was admitted into the house and told to wait in the library. I sat there taking in the details. I'd never been in this handsome book-lined room before, but someone had once told me that there were hidden panels in the walls. If you pressed against certain spots, the wall would open, revealing secret passages and rooms. I wondered where you had to press.

Mother Dominick entered with a soft rustle of skirt and a scent of lemon and soap. She was a beautiful woman with a stately bearing and large, attentive eyes. Her smile was warm and welcoming. She sat in a chair across from me and said, "So, tell me, Catherine, why do you think it is right for you to join our order?"

I realized I had prepared no response to this question. What could I say? I was called; just as I had always been told it would happen. It was a feeling, a knowledge, a conviction. What more could I say about it?

"This is the right thing for me, Mother. I have a vocation," I said. "I'm sure this is the life I want."

Mother Dominick settled back into her chair and regarded me thoughtfully. "That may be true. I came to the Dominicans forty-three years ago, and I can remember it as if it were yesterday. The way I felt. How sure I was of my vocation." She paused and looked past me out the window. "So much is changing now."

I couldn't tell if she thought that was a good thing. For once in my life, I kept silent.

"Our own order is changing," she went on. "Not just the habit has changed but the way we work, as well. Once, our order thrived by taking young girls and molding them, educating them, and directing their lives. But today's religious vocation requires more. It requires a certain level of maturity. The point is, Catherine, I think you may make a fine nun someday, but I'm going to ask you to wait. It's not time for you yet."

I felt my face and throat burning. What was she saying to me?

"Go to the university. Become a journalist. Grow up. Then, if you still feel that you're called, come back."

I could barely speak. I rose, thanked Mother Dominick, and stumbled from the library. I don't remember how I made it out the front door and to the car. I don't recall what I told my father. I was stunned. Empty. Robbed. Mother Dominick had looked into my soul and determined that I wasn't called!

It had never once occurred to me that I might be rejected. The nuns had waged such an intensive twelve-year courtship. Suddenly, every certainty I had ever held, everything I knew about myself and my life, was gone. Who was I now? What was I supposed to do?

I had always believed that the calling to serve God was a great mystery. It had been presented to us as a terrifying possibility. But if you were truly called and chose to answer, a great peace would descend upon you. It would feel right; all doubt would disappear. It was like walking across a swaying rope bridge. You put one foot in front of the other, kept your head up, and stepped very carefully while hanging on to the slippery ropes for dear life. But once you'd made it across, you fell into the arms of your beloved, and there you'd remain—finally safe. I was completely bereft. How could I have been so wrong?

6

Crisis of Faith

Elizabeth
Seattle, Washington

— 1 9 6 8

WERE IT NOT FOR HER JOY AT ONCE AGAIN TEACHING IN THE classroom, Sister Elizabeth would have been completely miserable. Rather than being embraced at Saint Alphonsus Convent as a welcome addition and a *sister*, she was treated by the others as an outsider, an interloper. From the day of her arrival, she had been made to feel distinctly unwelcome. Several of the sisters snubbed her outright; others displayed frigid disdain. There were a few who were openly hostile. Even Mother Dominick, whom Elizabeth had heard so much about and looked so forward to meeting, had greeted her coolly. For some reason she could not fathom, the sisters were suspicious of Elizabeth's motives for leaving her cloistered community to spend a year with them.

Perhaps she'd been foolish to think she could just waltz in and easily become a part of the Saint Alphonsus community. She knew from experience that the dynamics of a religious community were more complex than simply inhabiting a common space and sharing a common rule and mission. True community did not spring full-blown from the earnest desires of a few well-meaning souls; nor was it a spontaneous flowering. It had to be developed, shaped, cultivated. So rather than fleeing Saint Alphonsus and her rough beginnings there, Sister Elizabeth instead prayed for humility and patience, hoping that in time she would be accepted by the other sisters.

Time passed, and the community made no effort to embrace her. In fact, things only got worse. As difficult as it was to accept, the hard truth was that the more the other sisters came to know her, the less they seemed to like her. She felt constantly tested—as if a secret committee had met and found her guilty of the sin of pride. There seemed to be a concerted effort to knock her down a few notches. Perhaps she didn't appear as docile, as humble, as the other sisters imagined a cloistered nun should be. Sisters who'd never been exposed to the cloistered life often had the misconception that monastic nuns were meek little church mice, trained in advanced subservience. Even after all of her years in the cloister, Sister Elizabeth didn't have a subservient bone in her body. That didn't mean that she took her vow of obedience lightly. She had found that many religious hid behind the vow of obedience. It gave them an excuse to take the path of least resistance, to glide through their lives on automatic pilot, confident that someone else would make all of the important decisions for them. There was a saying in religious life: Keep the rule and the rule will keep you. Oh, how wonderful if it were that simple. It never was, of course. Sister Elizabeth understood that obedience was a multilayered virtue. True obedience required far more than simple submission to man-made (or woman-made) rules. You must be obedient to *the* rule—the master rubric that defined the human calling to God. And that required a strength of will, and intellect.

One evening, it was Elizabeth's assignment to set the table for dinner. She had just finished laying out the silverware when a young sister, a temporary professed no older than twenty-one, stormed in from the kitchen and said nastily, "Where do *you* come from? That's not the way we lay out the silver." The young sister swept all of the silver up into a pile. "Now. Do it the correct way."

Elizabeth took a deep breath, sighed, and swallowed her rising rage. "Of course, Sister," she said, with deliberate politeness. The young nun pursed her lips smugly and turned to leave.

"Oh, Sister . . ." Elizabeth called after her in a sweet voice, "One more thing."

The young nun turned back.

"It's good that I've been in the cloister all these years," Elizabeth said calmly, "and have learned as much as I have about love, humility, and self-control. Otherwise, Sister, I would knock your lights out."

The other sister blanched and hurried from the dining room.

On Wednesday afternoons, when she had no classes to teach, Sister Elizabeth made it her habit to take long walks. It gave her time to clear her head, it reinvigorated her, and it gave her a place to put some of her tremendous physical energy. No matter how cold or windy the day, she bundled up and went down to the locks—a man-made passageway that enabled the traverse of fertilized salmon eggs to flow into the sea.

One Wednesday, as she was heading toward the water, she noticed a frail-looking woman huddled on a bench at the bus stop two blocks from the convent. It was a bitter day, and an icy rain was falling. As she drew nearer to the bench, Sister Elizabeth recognized Sister Celestine, an older teacher at Saint Alphonsus grade school. Sister Celestine had always been kind to her, but their paths hadn't crossed that often.

"Sister," Elizabeth exclaimed in surprise. "What are you doing sitting here? It's freezing out. You'll catch your death of cold."

Sister Celestine smiled a welcome. "Hello, Sister Elizabeth.

The bus will be right along. I have to haul myself downtown every Wednesday. Doctor's appointment, regular as clockwork. My old body isn't keeping the right time so well on its own anymore."

That was clear from Celestine's swollen arthritic hands. "Can't someone drive you?" Sister Elizabeth was horrified that this poor, sickly woman was being made to wait out in the cold and rain and was forced to take the bus to get to her doctor's office. "Oh, it's all right, really. It's too much of a bother, and no one is available week after week. I understand. I get on fine."

"Sister, forgive me for saying so, but that's nonsense!" Sister Elizabeth exclaimed. "Listen, I have Wednesday afternoons off. I'll ask Sister Josephine if I can arrange to have the car, and I'll drive you. Would that be all right?"

"Oh, you're very kind, dear, but it's not necessary. Thank you. You're very sweet," Celestine protested. She didn't want to be any trouble.

Elizabeth was beside herself with indignation for Sister Celestine. Was she the only one who found this kind of behavior outrageous? What was going on in this community? Didn't they care about one another? This wasn't how she believed a community of religious women should behave.

When she arrived back at the convent, Elizabeth went immediately to the superior. "Sister Josephine," she said, "I came upon Sister Celestine at the bus stop. She was on her way to her weekly doctor's appointment. If the car is free, I would be perfectly happy to drive Sister Celestine there and wait to drive her back to the convent. I always have a briefcase full of papers to correct, and I can correct them anywhere. I want to drive the sister. Please."

So Sister Elizabeth took on the task of driving Sister Celestine, and she received far more than she had bargained for. In spite of her chronic health problems, Celestine was delightfully spirited, at the same time caustic and kind. She had a gift for piercing through bravado and getting at the heart of the matter. And she could be trusted with secrets. Celestine didn't hold vocational struggles against you.

Sister Elizabeth had also found a friend in Sister Carmen, thanks to their shared love of music. Sometimes in the evening, the two women would go next door to the school auditorium. Carmen would play the piano, and Elizabeth would raise her lush contralto in song. For hours, they would go from religious, to classical, and finally to popular music, filling the entire auditorium with wonderful sounds.

Carmen was sick again. Burning with fever. It was the third time this winter. Elizabeth carried a tray down the hall and tapped at the door. "It's Elizabeth. I have some soup for you. May I come in?"

Carmen pulled herself into a sitting position. It took almost all of her effort; she felt so tired, so weak.

"Elizabeth. Come in, please." Elizabeth gently placed the tray on Carmen's lap. "Can you stay and visit for a few minutes?"

"Of course." Elizabeth grinned wickedly. "Let 'em talk."

Carmen tried to bring a spoon of the hot soup to her lips, but she didn't feel in the least bit hungry. She could feel her lips begin to tremble. She felt like crying. "It's my birthday next week, you know," she quietly said. "I know we don't celebrate birthdays—but I'm going to be thirty-two years old. Thirty-two." She set down her spoon and leaned back against the pillow. "I always thought that by the time I was in my thirties, I'd know exactly how my life was; I was so sure I'd be secure." Carmen's eyes filled with tears. "Oh, Elizabeth, look at me! I'm a mess." She sniffed and then blew her nose. "I remember—there was this nun, Sister Lucy. She was my idol. I asked our novice mistress once why Sister Lucy was so serene. She told me, 'Sister Lucy is serene because she has her vows.' I thought something magical would happen when I was professed." A huge tear plopped into the soup. Then another. Carmen put her hands over her eyes. "But here I am. I don't even know who I am. Oh, Elizabeth, I want to be my own person. I want to be myself. I don't want to be Sister Carmen anymore. I don't want to just be some image. I want to go out there and see what's really going on. Sometimes I feel like I'm not even living in this century."

Sister Elizabeth felt great compassion for her friend. She had felt the same things herself, been there when all of her long-held convictions deserted her, when she wanted to run for the door and never stop running. Surely this was what John of the Cross meant when he spoke of "the dark night of the soul."

Carmen spoke. "I keep thinking about being alone. I mean, we're ultimately all alone anyway, but . . . I've never even been with a man. That contact, that feeling, I don't know. Sometimes I wonder what it would be like to be really important to somebody—do you know what I mean? Maybe be the most important person in somebody's life. And then I think, God forgive me, do I really want to die a virgin?"

This last remark struck Elizabeth's funny bone. She unleashed peals of laughter, and soon Carmen was joining her.

When she caught her breath, she said, "Oh, dear. I always blurt out the wrong thing."

"Oh, I don't know," Elizabeth said with a wink. "It seems like a pretty good question to me. Why don't you rest now."

Juggling the empty soup bowl and teacup, Sister Elizabeth pulled Carmen's door closed behind her and began walking down the hallway toward the kitchen. Sister Claire suddenly appeared and blocked Elizabeth's way.

"What were you doing in Sister Carmen's room?"

"I was bringing her some soup and tea. She's still quite ill, I think."

Sister Claire was furious. "I think that is for me to do. You seem to forget, Sister, that I am a nurse. I will decide what Sister Carmen needs, and I will provide it." She regarded Elizabeth through narrowed eyes. "You think you're special, don't you? You don't have to follow any rules, do you? I heard the two of you laughing in there. I know what's going on."

Sister Elizabeth didn't want to have this confrontation. She tried to continue her trip to the kitchen by edging around Claire's large body. Claire shifted her weight and kept her almost pinned to the wall. Her face was only inches from Elizabeth's. "You're just manipulating Sister Carmen for your own ends. You're bewitching her."

"Bewitching her? What are you implying?" Elizabeth asked. She couldn't believe this!

"Oh, don't play the innocent with me." Sister Claire sniffed. She stepped aside and let Elizabeth continue her journey to the kitchen.

As the school year was drawing to a close, Mother Dominick informed Sister Elizabeth that she and Sister Celestine had been selected to be part of an experimental program in northwest Washington State. In the fall, they would begin training lay teachers to teach religious education in the small towns throughout the area— which included a large Indian reservation. To do so would require the two nuns to set up housekeeping on their own. They would be too far from Saint Alphonsus to continue to live there. They would also be attending a special summer program in Spokane to prepare them for their new mission.

Elizabeth was glad for the opportunity to escape the un-friendly confines of Saint Alphonsus, and happier still to be paired with Sister Celestine. Celestine's health had markedly improved, and the two women looked forward to their adventure. Elizabeth decided that her return to the cloister in Guilford could be put off for another year.

In September, Elizabeth and Celestine settled into a charming little house on a narrow beachfront on Camano Island. The first Sunday after they had moved in, they drove thirty minutes across a small bridge to La Conner, where the Indian reservation stood. There they met the priest who would work with them and super-vise their efforts. After Mass, he invited them to join him for breakfast at the simple rectory in which he lived.

Father Jim Curtis was a shy-looking man with pale blue eyes

and a shock of thick wavy brown hair. He was tall, well over six feet, strongly built, and appeared to be in his early to mid-forties. Although he kept insisting that he was really a simple little country priest, Elizabeth was completely thrown off guard by Father Curtis. She soon discovered that he was a full-fledged theologian—an intellectual of impressive dimensions.

What on earth was he doing on an Indian reservation in northwest Washington State?

He grinned widely when she finally asked him that question. "I'm doing the same thing that you're doing. God's work." His grin was infectious. They both laughed.

Besides, he added, he'd only be serving in this parish for another year. He had been accepted at the University of California at Berkeley for the Ph.D. program in theology. But that was far in the future, he insisted. In the meantime, there was much that needed to be done, and here they were, with the will to do it.

Elizabeth and Celestine threw themselves into the work of the parish, spending twelve-hour days traveling from one far-flung outpost to another. The more they did, the more they were asked to do. Father Curtis placed increasing amounts of responsibility on their shoulders, but they almost never saw him. They never heard from him except when there was some sort of problem. At first, Elizabeth had found Father Curtis to be utterly charming. Now his behavior had become odd and off-putting. He was highly critical and remote. What was wrong with this priest? Had he gotten a report from Saint Alphonsus telling him what a misfit she'd been? Was she being punished for some past sin of which she was unaware? Had she read him wrong?

In late October, on the day he was to hear their confessions, he came to the beach house. "Before we start, I have a few things I'd like to say," Elizabeth bravely began.

Father Curtis's eyebrow arched, and he gave her a questioning smile. "What's that, Sister Elizabeth?"

She was almost unnerved by the strange expression on his face. He wouldn't look directly at her, refusing to meet her eyes.

Nevertheless, she ploughed ahead. "It's just that Sister Celestine and I have been breaking our backs with all of the new projects you've asked us to take on, and yet when we try to get you to sit down and work on some of the plans for these things, you're always busy with a hundred other things. Because of that, we go ahead and decide how we're going to implement all of this stuff by ourselves. Then, when we are finally able to corner you and explain what we're doing, you always behave as though you don't approve of anything we've chosen to do at all. I've written music for you; did you ever say a word to me about it? I've been running the choir, and you've yet to come to a single rehearsal. I've been running the Confraternity of Christian Doctrine classes, I'm trying to set up the Catholic Youth Organization, and I've been doing all of these things without any help from you. All I get from you is criticism—and no advice. If I'm not doing the job you want done, say so. I'm a lot tougher than I look, okay? I would appreciate your telling me where I am falling short, Father, so I can do something about it. Well?" Elizabeth stopped, breathless. She hadn't realized the extent of her fury, and now she felt as if she'd gone too far.

Father Curtis didn't say a word. He just kept looking past her with a strange expression she was unable to read. "Father?" Elizabeth said. "Father? Would you look at me when I'm talking to you?" Father Curtis's pale blue eyes locked with hers. After what seemed an eternity, he finally looked away.

"It's not what you think at all," he murmured quietly. "I *do* approve of what you're doing. I think you've been doing a great job. It's just that I don't think . . ." Father Curtis stopped, placed his hands on the table, and stood up. "Please let me try and explain, Sister Elizabeth. This is very hard for me. I just can't trust myself to get any further involved with you. You've done nothing wrong, Sister. Basically . . . I'm . . . I'm *in love* with you." He looked at her with tortured eyes. "I thought I came here to hear confession, not make one. I'm sorry, Sister. That's *my* confession. I love you."

. . .

Sister Celestine found Elizabeth an hour later, awash in tears. She couldn't stop crying. She choked out the story to Celestine, and the older woman didn't flinch. She went to the cabinet and pulled out a pint of brandy reserved for emergencies and poured two glasses. "Now, let's look at this situation," she said, firmly pressing a glass into Elizabeth's hand.

Elizabeth took a drink of the liquor, then set the glass down and blew her nose. "There's nothing to look at." She sniffed. "I've got to go back to Guilford. I can't handle this. I've made a mess of everything. They're going to have to find somebody else to take the rest of the year. I just can't handle this."

Any other nun might have responded, "I'll drive you to the airport," but Sister Celestine was a thoughtful, perceptive woman. Perhaps she trusted the mysterious workings of the Holy Spirit more than most. "Wait a minute," she said. "You're letting emotion lead you—and fear. Let me ask you this: Do you feel any attraction for him at all?"

"What's that got to do with it? He's a priest. I'm a professed nun."

"Just answer."

Elizabeth stared at the floor and blushed bright red. "Oh, I don't know. . . . Well, yes. He's marvelous. But that's not what I'm thinking of."

Celestine's face softened. "My friend, I think you should stay. Get to know him better. What harm can it do? Consider what God is calling you to do. Maybe the Holy Spirit put this in front of you. Maybe it's why you left the monastery, why you came here."

Elizabeth gazed at Celestine with overflowing eyes. And to think people wondered why she loved this woman!

Celestine drained the last of her brandy and grinned at Elizabeth. "I'll change my name to Sister Chaperone," she said jauntily.

"I will be with you like a shadow so that no one will ever be able to say there was anything improper. And whatever you choose, at least it will be based on something solid."

Elizabeth smiled gratefully. "How did you get to be so wise?"

Celestine cackled loudly. "Wise? I don't know about that. Maybe I'm just old. My sense of propriety has been replaced by something closer to faith. Do you know what I mean?"

Elizabeth nodded thoughtfully. "Yes, I'm starting to think that I do."

In the coming weeks, Sister Elizabeth and Father Curtis began their uneasy courtship. Elizabeth marveled at the novelty of their behavior. This was no hot romance; rather, it was something she could treasure even more. Often, they took long walks along the beach, their passionate conversation reserved for matters of theology, struggles of the soul, and questions of commitment and responsibility.

Ever so slowly, Elizabeth fell in love with this remarkable man. She felt, too, that the possibility presenting itself to them was truly transcendental. The church was changing so fast. Jim was confident in his belief that within five years, priests would be allowed to marry. They would share a ministry—form a community in family for the new era.

In spite of her excitement, however, Elizabeth was troubled by doubts. Everything was happening so fast. She needed time. She longed for the quiet embrace of Guilford, the steady environment of her community. She shared her feelings with Jim late one night as they walked along the stormy shore. "Jim," she said urgently, "I think it would be best if you would just let me go back to Guilford—spend a year thinking and preparing myself for this new life."

He didn't respond at once, just continued to walk in brooding silence.

"Please, Jim," Elizabeth said. "I'm afraid."

Jim stopped short and turned to look into her face. "You're afraid," he said with a trembling voice. He threw up his hands in exasperation. "Oh, I know, Elizabeth. I'm afraid, too. But I believe so deeply—with every fiber of my being, I believe—that this is meant to be. We must act out of faith, not fear."

Elizabeth didn't respond, but she was crying.

"I'm not going to wait," Jim said firmly. "I won't give you an ultimatum. I respect you too much for that. But it's time."

It took Elizabeth two weeks of prayer. One night, she drove over to the rectory and knocked on the door. When Jim answered, she reached out and took his hand. "I'm with you," she said simply.

Jim's face lit up with pure joy. He wanted more than anything on earth to wrap his arms around this wonderful woman, the woman he loved, but he controlled the impulse. They had both agreed that there would be no touching while they were still under obligation to their vows.

The first thing Elizabeth did was write to her prioress in Guilford, stating that she wanted to be freed from her vows so she could marry. She decided not to write to Mother Dominick because she knew there would be a scandal. It was her plan to get permission from Guilford and then depart quietly with Jim to California.

She began to apply for jobs in California. When she was offered a good job with San Leandro High School, she saw it as a sign.

Jim was handling his arrangements in a somewhat different manner. His archbishop already knew he was leaving to study at the University of California at Berkeley at the end of the year. Jim decided to tell him nothing more than that.

Elizabeth was at first alarmed. "What about your dispensation?" she asked.

"I'm not asking for a dispensation," Jim said firmly. "Do you know what happens when a priest gets a dispensation?"

Elizabeth admitted that she didn't.

"You sign a piece of paper saying you're *unfit* to be a priest— *unfit* to be a pastor. I am not unfit, and I won't say that I am. I have a calling to be a priest, and that hasn't changed just because I've chosen to marry. I think it will be only a few years before the church will come around and allow married priests to be pastors. Meanwhile, I'm still a priest—albeit a rebellious one." Jim cocked an eyebrow at Elizabeth and asked, "Why are you bothering to get a dispensation?"

"My situation is different," Elizabeth said.

"Maybe so, but it sounds like you're not up on your canon law. You must know that there is no dispensation in canon law for a solemnly professed."

"I do know that," Elizabeth said. "But I need to go through the formality of extricating myself from the order. I don't want to leave under a cloud."

"Strictly speaking, though, you'll still be a nun and I'll still be a priest."

Elizabeth laughed. "Well, isn't that something?"

Carmen
Rosary Heights — 1969

It was November 22, the feast of Saint Cecilia, the patron saint of musicians. Carmen was in the kitchen doing dishes, staring aimlessly out the window, when Mother Dominick, who had returned to her given name and was now Sister Hilary, walked in and began making tea.

Carmen didn't look up from the sink, but she said, "Mother . . . Sister . . . I've decided to leave." She felt Sister Hilary's eyes boring into her back, and she turned to face her, nervously wiping her soapy hands on her apron. "I'll finish out the school year. I need to do this, Sister, but I won't let you down. I'll take care of my commitments."

"Have you prayed about this?" Sister Hilary asked quietly.

"Oh yes, Mother." Tears sprang to Carmen's eyes.

"Have you been influenced by anyone? You know, Sister, the changes have been happening so fast. Sometimes a person will take it as a sign that she can do what she chooses—break her vows, pursue a sinful direction."

Carmen thought she might be talking about Sister Elizabeth.

Or maybe about Michelle, who had left the previous year. "No one has influenced me," she replied.

Sister Hilary nodded slowly. "I make one request. Remain silent about this for the time being. And keep praying for guidance, Sister."

Carmen managed to stifle the temptation to say anything about her plans. She continued teaching, just as before, but she felt as if a heavy burden had been lifted from her shoulders.

Then one day while she was helping Sister Brigid with the mending, her resistance broke down. Carmen loved old Sister Brigid. She was a real character, with a thick Irish brogue, who, in spite of the vows she'd held for more than fifty years, somehow managed to march to her own drummer. Carmen thought Sister Brigid had the gift of true charity and goodness. She knew she could trust her with the truth.

"I have decided to leave the order at the end of the school year," she said.

Sister Brigid set down her mending and rubbed her arthritic hands together in a gesture of delight. "Well, dear, you're smart," she said. "When I came over here from Ireland, I was only thirteen. They told me they were sending me here for high school. Next thing I knew, I was in the convent. I didn't know why, but it was horrible. Well, you know, dear, this was long before we had sanitary supplies, and when women menstruated, they used cloth diapers. My first job was in the laundry washing bloody linens. I cried myself to sleep every night. I wrote and begged my mother to bring me back. But my family was poor. I finally figured it out that they sent me to the convent because they couldn't afford to keep me." She smiled at Carmen. "Well, that's my silly story. I must say God has provided for me."

Carmen stared at the old woman, openmouthed. She had never heard such a story. Brigid had been trapped in the convent. That explained the strange stories she'd heard about Brigid—how she was always wandering off to do her own thing. There was a story that Brigid had once walked out of the convent on a whim and gone to ride the ferries for a day. Another tale had it that Sister Brigid had once decided to have a little party with the young nuns. She had a bottle of whiskey, but they needed mixer. "Run down to the market, dear," Brigid instructed one of the group. "Get two quarts of 7UP and charge it to the convent. It's okay. You have my permission." Later, when Sister Peter, the house treasurer, discovered the purchase on their monthly statement, she had a fit. But Sister Brigid never got in trouble for her transgressions. Everyone in the order intuitively knew what was going on. Sister Brigid had been a good nun for all these years, but there was a piece of her—the part that believed in *choice*—that rebelled against her forced vocation.

"Now, dearie," Brigid said, "go down in my trunk, and you'll find a nice bottle of Irish whiskey. I think we need a bit of a nip."

Whenever she could, Carmen snuck away from the convent to visit Michelle in her tiny apartment in south Seattle. Michelle had gotten a job teaching in the public schools, and Carmen was hoping that she could do the same. She depended on her close friend for many things that year. Michelle, after all, knew what it was like on the outside. So far, she had survived.

"The hardest thing about it," Michelle told her, "is that people give you a choice about everything. 'Do you want fries with your hamburger?' 'Do you want the plain or the floral design on your checks?' 'Which sweater do you like best—the red one or the blue one?' I spent my whole life never having a choice, and now I have too many choices!"

"I've never had a checkbook or written a check," Carmen confessed. "You'll have to show me how to do it."

Michelle also advised her not to tell people she'd been in a convent. "You wouldn't believe how rude people are. They ask the stupidest and most embarrassing questions. This man at work who's a Baptist, says, 'How many lesbians were there?' I told him that I didn't know anyone who was a lesbian, but he won't leave the subject alone."

Carmen also needed help learning to put on makeup, set her hair, and pick out clothes. She didn't even know how to apply lipstick.

Spring arrived, and Sister Hilary told Carmen she could now tell the other sisters about her decision. Things had changed since the days when Carmen was a young sister. Then, if someone left the convent, they were spirited away in the dead of night. The others wouldn't know about it until they saw the empty place in chapel. It was horrible to have a sister disappear and never have a chance to say good-bye. Thankfully, the order had become more open. It was important to Carmen to be able to say good-bye.

She didn't anticipate how difficult it would be. Barbara burst into tears, and Carmen was shocked because she had never seen the reserved Barbara sob like that. It was just as hard for the older nuns to see the young women leaving. Sister Boniface put her head down on the table and cried. "Oh, dear, I didn't know you were unhappy. I didn't know." She cried and cried. Carmen watched helplessly. She felt like such a rat. She hadn't wanted to make anyone cry.

When Carmen entered the convent, she had provided a dowry, as all entrants were expected to do. Her mother had turned an insurance policy over to the order. Canon law stipulated that when a sister left the order, her dowry would be returned to her. So Carmen received two thousand dollars. With Michelle's help, she bought an ancient, pale blue Datsun for five hundred dollars. She was finally ready to go.

The night of graduation, Carmen went to the church and played the organ for the ceremony. Tears streamed down her cheeks as she watched the seniors, bright and hopeful girls, walking into an exciting future. Now she would be one of them. After the graduation ceremony, she took off her veil and held it against her face for a brief moment before hanging it on Sister Brigid's door. Then she got in her little Datsun and drove away. At the first stoplight, she took a tube of lipstick from her purse, carefully applied some to her lips, and smiled at her reflection in the rearview mirror.

7

Hear, O Lord

Seattle, Washington
— 1 9 6 8

PERHAPS MOTHER DOMINICK POSSESSED SOME MYSTICAL ABIL-
ity—had the means to see beyond the burning eyes and fervent
demeanor of a young girl. In any case, it seemed that Mother was
right about me. I never returned to Rosary Heights, never again
asked to be allowed to join the postulants. Some might argue that
I *did* have a calling, but I closed my heart to God's voice after
Mother rejected my first request. I myself never really knew. Perhaps if Mother had accepted me and I had entered the novitiate
that fall, I would have stayed and been happy there. Maybe I could
have avoided the seismic spiritual upheaval that occurred in my
life, and the unsatisfied quest that followed me throughout my
adulthood.

I realize now that Mother Dominick probably turned me away because she had grown weary of what seemed to be a revolving door at the order. The young, inexperienced girls they had always relied on to restock their ranks no longer made such good nuns. They weren't as pliant as they had been in the past. They chafed at the rules, challenged the vow of obedience, and kept at least one foot firmly planted in the secular world. Some even tried to push the envelope on what was considered appropriate garb. As a result, too many of the young postulants were leaving after a year or two. A sea change had swept across the United States. Enticed by the tremendous new freedoms being explored on the outside, many young women fled Rosary Heights to better taste the times.

When I graduated from Holy Angels in 1968, the world as I had known it was coming apart. Entering the University of Washington in September of 1968 was like stepping into a box that contained all of the right elements to foment either an explosion or a revolution. The new era had actually begun in 1960. The country eased itself out of the conservative fifties with the election of John F. Kennedy to the White House. Camelot, the Cuban missile crisis, the heightening military involvement in Vietnam, the crisis of civil rights in the South—all spun wildly toward his assassination. His death was followed by the ascent of Lyndon Johnson and the escalation of the war in Vietnam, Martin Luther King's murder, Bobby Kennedy's assassination, and finally, catastrophically, Richard Nixon's election as president in 1968.

Nixon may have arranged détente with Communist China, but he declared war on the children of America. The Vietnam War continued its savage pace, snatching young men from the streets of America and sending them to fight in an undersupported quagmire, over a patch of napalmed hell. Of such engagements are heroes made and careers solidified, on the backs of drafted children. Those who protested against more young lives being sacrificed to a meaningless war were branded traitors, punks, lefties, radicals, Commie sympathizers, Commies. There was no middle ground. "Are you part of the solution, or part of the problem?" was the mantra chanted by both sides. Nixon gave permission to Americans to hate anyone with long hair, to hate almost everyone between the ages of seventeen and twenty-three, to hate anyone who dared say no.

Along the tree-shaded pathways and rolling green hills of the University of Washington, the air crackled with danger. Radical leftist movements rose up and collided with anyone who dared disagree with them, and there were many. Newly longhaired antiwar demonstrators battled with pugnacious ROTC cadets and local police. Black Power leaders derided them all as crazy white boys, shouted into bullhorns, demanding "Power to the people," and strutted around the campus with surly reproach, Afros, and dashikis. Meanwhile, SDS, the Students for a Democratic Society, desperately tried to maintain its aura of being the most committed of the radical groups, and it wove a subversive web over the entire university community. There seemed to be a political undercurrent to everything. After only a few weeks of classes, police dressed in heavy riot gear stormed into my normally placid freshman philosophy class and arrested our noble, appropriately philosophical longhaired professor, who grinned and threw us the peace sign before they cuffed him and roughly dragged him away. He was charged, along with six others, of conspiring to overthrow the government of the United States. Our philosophy professor? They were immediately dubbed "the Seattle Seven," in honor of the recently fractious trial of another political group, the then-famous Chicago Seven.

Classes were canceled. Professors refused to teach their subjects, instead dedicating their classes to discussions of the war and the protests. The campus was in turmoil: What side are *you* on? Women's liberation appeared on the horizon: To hell with the boys; what about us? What are we? Coffee-makers? Baby-makers? Comfort toys? *Don't sexualize me. Don't call me baby or honey. Don't look at me that way.*

It was intellectual and emotional overload. I was trying to concentrate on my studies, but too much was going on. Too much information and too many ideas were coming from too many directions at once. All of these passions so searingly expressed only made me more deeply confused. Where did I belong? Whose side was I on? Whom should I join? What was right?

There was little help to be had. With some thirty thousand students on campus, the University of Washington was a crowded, lonely place. The alienating environment seemed to demand that we grow up instantly. No more kind, nurturing teachers. No more relationships or special attention. No more words of encouragement. It was do or die. Even my freshman writing class, the one place I expected to find a safe haven, was cold and unwelcoming. Well over one hundred students filled the audience of a huge theater, the rows angling steeply up to the ceiling. From my high perch, the professor was a distant, modest speck. He never knew me by name or face, only as words on a page—and in his opinion, those words were sadly lacking in quality. Only recently the star of demanding, meticulous Sister Lawrence's journalism class, I shuddered in horror as my papers were returned to me with ugly red *C*'s slashed over the first page, and critical comments in the margins that often bordered on the abusive. In one instance, my professor wrote "Crap!" across the front page of a piece I had thought was quite good. Another time, he scrawled, "You're a bluffer" on an essay. I didn't dismiss his criticisms lightly, but even at eighteen, I knew my writing wasn't *that* bad. I began to feel as though something else was going on there. No matter; I continued to do my best. I soon discovered that whatever I did, it didn't matter. My freshman writing professor hated my work. At Holy Angels, my self-esteem had risen to celestial heights. I thought I could do anything. Suddenly, it seemed as though I could do nothing.

I wasn't a quitter, though. I decided I would be a journalist, no matter what. After all, my tuition was being paid by a scholarship from the *Seattle Times.* Didn't that count for something? I decided to join the campus radio station and learn broadcasting. But the day I was scheduled to begin, SDS took over the radio station and held it hostage for months, spewing radical ideology over the air. I didn't have a chance.

As the months passed, I felt myself becoming more and more disoriented. In early November, I decided to call Sister Elizabeth.

"Catherine!" She was delighted to hear from me. "How's it going at my old alma mater? Do you love it?"

"Not really," I confessed. With Sister Elizabeth's gentle questioning, I soon spilled out the complete story of my failure, humiliation, and misery.

Sister Elizabeth then made a surprising suggestion. "If it wouldn't affect your scholarship, maybe you could take the next quarter off. Get a temporary withdrawal and come stay here for a while. We have the loveliest little house right on this beautiful beach. You can help us with our mission. You can teach the Indian children, and you can spend some time reflecting. It'll be good for you. I promise."

I was desperate for rescue, so I said yes without a moment's hesitation. Maybe if I could just escape all the turmoil going on around me for a little while, everything would be all right. Less than a week later, I was on a train, taking the three-hour local to Arlington, Washington.

Sister Elizabeth met me at the train station, looking bright-eyed and chipper in her little modified habit. She introduced me to Sister Celestine, and I instantly liked her down-to-earth attitude and mother-hen quality, spiced with her dry sense of humor.

The sisters' house was small but cozy, like a ready-made cocoon. It was situated on a rocky beach on Camano Island, across the water from the Indian reservation.

I settled in and was put to work the very next day. There was plenty to do. Our purpose was to teach Confraternity of Christian Doctrine classes to the Native American children, while also training laypeople to take over. Two pleasant older Indian women sat smiling and nodding in the back of the classroom as I led the class in the catechism, watching me pretend to be a teacher. God only

knows what they thought! I approached them after the class, only
to discover they didn't understand a word that I'd been saying.

Everyone on the reservation was very agreeable about calling
themselves Catholic, but the cultural clash between their native
beliefs and Catholic teachings was for the most part unbridgeable.
It was not unusual to hear the children singing songs about Jesus
one moment, only to hear them praying to ancient spirits the next.
Their relationship with the innumerable gods of the natural world,
as well as the ghosts of their ancestors, mingled comfortably with
the rituals of the church and the images of Christian saints.

It bothered me. I suppose it was a combination of the certitude of youth and the certitude of belief, but I had been raised
with the conviction that one chose a single doctrine. How could
one say, "I'm Catholic," and in the next breath talk about spirits
and magic? It made me wonder about the evincing of faith when
I learned that the community gathered regularly in the Great Hall,
a lofty, outsized structure of rough-hewn massive logs, and performed ancient tribal fire ceremonies and other rituals. They
would chant and dance long into the night, bolstered by bottomless jugs of alcohol. The spirits of their native ancestors spoke to
them during these ceremonies, not the voice of Jesus.

I shared my distress with Elizabeth, and she shrugged it off
with a smile. "I have never seen a people of such abiding faith," she
said. "If their beliefs cross a doctrinal line, is it really such a serious
thing? Isn't it more important to open yourself and believe?"

Truthfully, I didn't know. In my childhood, when I had read
stories of the great Catholic missionaries Ignatius Loyola and Francis Xavier, they had always succeeded—or so I'd been led to
believe—in breathtaking feats of total conversion, not this wishy-
washy brand of devotion. Elizabeth's comment gave me something
to think about. "Isn't it more important to open yourself and
believe?"

It was the first time I had been exposed to such enlightened
thinking, and I must admit that I was intrigued. But the really
unconventional mind belonged to Father Curtis. While I was

there, he often came to dinner at the beach house, and we would sit for hours discussing faith and theology.

Father Curtis was a charismatic man—tall and muscular, with enigmatic pale blue eyes. He was also brilliant—like a modern-day Thomas Aquinas—in his command of church doctrine and moral law. Everything was open to question and debate. Father Curtis believed that blind faith was the retreat of the lazy.

He enjoyed tinkering with my certitudes.

"What do you think it means when we say the Pope is infallible?" he asked me one evening.

"It means that the Pope is divinely inspired," I automatically responded. I knew my catechism.

"Do you think that the Holy Spirit comes down and whispers in his ear?" He smiled.

"I don't know," I said. "But we've always been taught that papal infallibility is the cornerstone of Catholicism. It's what differentiates us from the Protestants."

"Why don't you consider this," Father Curtis replied with sparkling eyes. "As church doctrine, the concept of papal infallibility didn't even exist until the thirteenth century. Maybe somebody decided that there were too many 'divinely inspired' types around. I think it was a way of saying, Someone has to be in charge here. At that time, there were so many factions within the church, the Pope may have been feeling a little insecure. What if he's suddenly infallible? Not much you can say to refute the Pope then, is there? Maybe we've been encouraged to take the idea literally because over the centuries it's been a convenient tool to aid the church in silencing potential rebels and heretics."

"Watch out, Jim, you're spouting heresy again." Sister Celestine laughed.

I'd never really known Sister Celestine, although she had taught at Saint Alphonsus while I was at Holy Angels. The grade-school teachers were mere shadows to us—figures we passed in the courtyard or on the stairs. I found her to be very sweet and generous, but she was also very careful about what she said in my presence. I wasn't completely insensitive. On some level, I realized that I was invading a cherished privacy in their neat little house, but Celestine never gave any sign of resentment. Nor did she seem to mind being saddled with an eighteen-year-old girl who was in the midst of what must have appeared to her to be a mundane spiritual crisis. I did sense, however, a certain level of unstated tension, an almost palpable excitement. There were secrets in that house—things I wasn't meant to know. Rather than intruding further, I often took walks along the beach at night and left the sisters alone.

I loved the beach at night, especially in the dead of winter. We were in a secluded corner of the island, and the long, narrow stretch of beach was always empty. I never met another soul during any of my endless walks. I could hear the thunder of the ocean from a long distance away. Huge green-and-white waves came crashing against the shore, spitting foam over the rocks and onto the beach. Unlike the mellower, gentle summer waves, which desultorily lapped the shore, the winter waves were in an almost constant uproar, throwing bits and pieces from both Puget Sound and the Pacific back up—rocks polished to a high shine by the constant frictional press of sand and water, tangled lumps of inky green seaweed with slick bulbous caps, agates as delicate as tiny crystals, broken shells and sharp barnacles that looked like screaming faces. A large piece of driftwood shaped like an arched bow was my favorite resting place on the beach. It reminded me of a log I loved to climb on when I was a five-year-old and my family took summer vacations on Orcas Island. It seemed far more magnificent in my childhood memory than it probably was. I'd climb on top of it and scrunch down, enjoying from a safe perch the wild peacocks that were the island's trademark. I would spend hours watching them as they strutted up and down the beach, fanning their brilliant blue-green iridescent feathers, trumpeting their mating calls, displaying their plumage.

As I sat on the driftwood at Camano Island, my thoughts were hardly as carefree as they'd once been. Like the crashing waves, they were filled with flotsam and jetsam. Yet, maybe because of the clean air, or the silence and the solitude, I was no longer as miserable as I had been. I felt I could face my uncertainties and go on in spite of them. The important thing was to go on, not be frightened off by a few bad experiences. I knew I was capable of that, and more. I still believed in myself. My confidence was restored.

"Would you like to go for a walk, Catherine?" Sister Elizabeth asked one morning shortly before I was scheduled to leave. It was a typical Camano Island winter day—raining, windy, and cold. We bundled up in coats and boots. Her small veil whipped in the wind as we walked along the rocky beach. We talked about my return to the University of Washington, which I was now better prepared to face, and the work at the reservation. I had discovered that I enjoyed the work, and I mentioned that I might come up to visit for a while during the summer to help out.

Elizabeth looked at me thoughtfully. "I'm not going to be here, Catherine."

"You're going back to the cloister?" It was the first thing that came to my mind.

"No, I'm never going to go back to the cloister," she said gently. "Oh, this is harder than I realized. I want you to know how much I think of you, Catherine. I would have told you before, but it's . . . Father Curtis. Jim and I are leaving here together at the end of the month. We're going to be married."

"You and Father Curtis? Oh!" I needed a moment to re-sort the world. Of course! Why not?

"I wouldn't want you to get the wrong idea, Catherine. We've kept our solemn vows. Why, we've never even held hands."

I laughed at that, and so did Sister Elizabeth. Having sat through many evenings of theological debate, it was obvious to me that, for the time being at least, any passions they expressed were directed elsewhere. We continued our walk in the wind and rain, laughing and chatting.

Later that night, I turned the idea over in my mind. I was almost surprised to realize that I didn't think it was a tragedy. It wasn't an affront to the church or its vows. I had learned so much from my time here, from the theological discussions and debates with Father Curtis and the sisters. The church had changed since Vatican II. It was only a matter of time until priests would be allowed to marry. And I had come to admire the two of them so much that I couldn't imagine that their decision was anything but right.

"I'm happy for you," I told Sister Elizabeth the next day. "I think you're both very good people, and very courageous." I knew it would be hard for them. They'd be treated as outcasts. They'd be on their own. I wanted Elizabeth to know, for what it was worth, that I was on her side.

A week later, at the train station, Sister Celestine held me in a warm motherly embrace. "I'll see you back in Seattle, Catherine," she whispered.

Sister Elizabeth hugged me tightly. "You'll be fine. You're a great girl. I have a feeling that you're going to jump into life with both feet flying."

"Thank you for everything, Sister. Good luck," I said as I hugged her back. "Let me know where you are. I'll come and see you. I'll come and hear Jim say Mass."

I boarded the train feeling misty-eyed but resolute and ready to go. I didn't know then that I would never see Sister Celestine again, or that Elizabeth and Jim would vanish. It would be more than twenty-five years before I'd find them again.

When I returned to Seattle, I tried to get in touch with Sister Carmen, but I was told she was gone. There was no forwarding address.

Rosary Heights — 1969

Sister Hilary was so angry, her voice was shaking. "She was planning this all along, wasn't she?" she demanded.

Sister Celestine responded calmly, "No, Sister. Of course not."

"She seduced a priest. She seduced him."

Celestine sighed heavily. "Sister, you speak of Elizabeth as if she were some satanic temptress. She is a good woman."

"I have heard disturbing reports from a number of sources that they have actually been married for a year—that they were married in a Methodist church in Arlington. What do you know about that?" Sister Hilary demanded, challenging Celestine.

"I know it's a lie," Celestine said coldly. "Tell me, who said such a thing? There was nothing the least bit inappropriate about this relationship. I was with Sister Elizabeth every minute. Unless you doubt my word. Do you?"

"Hmmm . . . no." Sister Hilary tightened her jaw. "But tell me. How could you, in good conscience, keep this from me for so long? You had an obligation to tell me that one of our members was breaking her vows and endangering her vocation."

"She broke no vows, Sister," Sister Celestine retorted. "Struggling with one's vocation is not sinful. It was a very difficult decision for her to make. And when she finally did, she wrote to her Mother Superior in Guilford. That is Sister Elizabeth's order. It wasn't my place to say anything to you."

Sister Hilary rose and waved Celestine away. "There's nothing more to discuss. I forbid you to have any contact with them."

Sister Celestine was silent.

"Do you understand?"

"Yes, Sister, I understand."

In her room, Sister Celestine sat at her small desk and wrote a letter to Elizabeth.

> You and Jim are constantly in my prayers. I am eager to know how you're doing, but it would be best not to write to me here. Send any letters for me in care of Carmen. She'll see that I get them. I have faith that God is watching over you, and I wait for the day when I can see you again.
>
> Love, Celestine

Seattle—1970

Tracy had disappeared. I couldn't reach her. Finally, I was able to track down her sister, Nan, and she reluctantly gave me a phone number. "I'm not sure you want to call her," Nan said.

"Why?" I demanded. "What's going on?"

She shrugged. "I don't know. A lot of stuff has gone down. You remember our aunt? Tracy took her death real hard. You know our family—maybe suicide runs in our genes or something. But when our aunt killed herself—wow. Tracy flipped. A nun killing herself, that was bad."

"Nan," I said patiently, "tell me what has happened to Tracy."

It was like pulling teeth, but I managed to get pieces of the story. After graduation, Tracy had tried to earn some easy money so she could go to New York and pursue her singing career. She ended up working in a seedy topless bar in Ballard, and met some people there who turned her on to drugs. After a few months, she was living with some black guy in the rough Cherry Hill area of downtown Seattle. Nan suspected but didn't know for sure if Tracy had been turned out on the street. She was pretty sure that the guy Tracy was with was involved in prostitution.

I knew what I had to do.

"Give me the address," I said. "I'm going to go down there and see her."

She tossed a slip of paper at me. "You're crazy!"

I *was* crazy. I possessed the fearless naïveté and sure innocence of a twenty-year-old. It never even entered my mind that there was any danger involved in my going to Cherry Hill. I was feeling like my old confident self again. Tracy was my friend, and it sounded as if she was in trouble. I had to try to help her.

I found her building on a scummy strip of bars and clubs. The front door was propped open, and I walked into a dark, stinking foyer. I climbed two flights of crumbling stairs that led off into fetid, barely lit hallways. I stepped carefully, trying to avoid pieces of broken glass and other rubbish strewn over the stairs. I tried to walk as quietly as I could, practically tiptoeing so I wouldn't make any noise. I was afraid of unleashing any of the demons that might be lingering behind those doors.

The door to the apartment where Tracy was staying was splashed with graffiti, and the lock looked broken. I took a very deep breath and knocked.

The door flew open, and there was Tracy. She looked almost the same, except for the vacant, almost docile look in her eyes. She was also thinner than she had been, and sadder.

Her eyes opened wide at the sight of me, and for a moment I caught a glimpse of the old energy. Her hand flew to her mouth, and I noticed purple bruises across her knuckles. She put her hand down and smiled at me. Tracy had always had the most radiant smile. Her front tooth was chipped.

"What are you doing here?" she croaked.

In as cheerful a tone as I could muster, I said, "I've come to take you to lunch."

"Oh, wow. Okay. Just a minute. Come on in." She backed into the apartment, and I followed her inside. The tiny living room was crowded and dirty, with an old sofa, a table piled high with unwashed laundry, and stuffed paper bags all over the floor. It smelled like stale fried food, cigarette smoke, and dirt. At first, I thought we were alone. Then I heard voices, and a large black man walked into the room. He was at least six foot three, his hair slicked back in a shiny pompadour. He was wearing a green satin robe, had heavy gold rings on his hands, and was smoking a cigarette. He smiled at me and gave Tracy an amused look.

"Introduce me to your friend, Tracy."

Tracy complied in a shaky voice. "Catherine is my friend from school. She's my old friend. Catherine, this is Anthony."

"Hey, Catherine, what's happening?" Anthony smirked at me.

"I came over to take Tracy to lunch," I told him with a nonchalance I certainly didn't feel.

He smiled in a friendly manner, flashing gold teeth. "How

nice. That's a good idea." He casually walked over to Tracy and slid a ringed finger down her cheek. "Have fun, darling, but try to be back in two hours. Okay?"

The relief on Tracy's face was painful to watch. We hurried out of the apartment and down the stairs. A few blocks away, we found a decent place to eat, and we ordered lunch.

"Tracy," I said when our food had been served, "what's going on? What are you doing here? I don't understand."

She shrugged and took a hungry bite of hamburger. "I grew up, I guess."

"You're kidding, right?" I pointed to her bruises, her chipped tooth. "What is all this? Why are you with this creep? What about your singing career?"

"It'll wait." She tried to give me one of her dazzling grins, but it didn't work anymore.

"Are you a prisoner of that man?"

She shook her head. "Let's just say I'm unable to leave right now."

I leaned across the table and forced her to meet my eyes. "I know one thing. You never have to feel trapped. You can get out of this. I'll help you."

She jumped up. "I've got to get back."

I stood up and grabbed her arm. "Why don't you come with me? Now, Tracy. Don't go back there."

Tracy's eyes suddenly started to take on a glazed look. "It was good to see you. I was hungry. I gotta go now. I'll be in touch." She hurried out of the restaurant and down the street.

I tried to call her the following day, but the phone had been disconnected. I never saw Tracy again. Years later, when I found out that she'd been murdered, I was too stunned to grieve. I locked Tracy's murder away with all of the other loose ends of my life and simply moved on.

What does a good Catholic school girl, a convent aspirant, do when she stops believing in God?

† She adopts a posture of indifference.

† She makes politics her religion.

† She learns to pity the nuns for their naïve obedience.

† She turns her wrath on the men in the cathedrals, calling them "old men in black robes."

† When she hears that Holy Angels Academy has been closed, she thinks, Good riddance to that place.

† She throws her high school yearbooks in the trash, destroys her Sodality of Mary emblem, and burns her award certificates. What good is any of that stuff?

† She breaks as many rules as she can. Since she no longer believes in hell, it doesn't matter.

† She always sits on the far-right side of her chair.

† She marries the son of a Methodist minister who is as sick of the institutional church as she is. They raise their son without religion.

† She moves to New York and hones the cool godlessness of the sophisticated urbanite. She divorces her husband.

† She makes carelessly irreverent remarks about the Pope, enjoying the shock on people's faces when she calls him "evil."

† She stays away from churches, except when she pickets with pro-choice feminists outside of Saint Patrick's Cathedral on Sunday mornings. She chants, along with the others, "Keep your rosaries off our ovaries!"

When a friend discovers that she's a lapsed Catholic and asks her, "Did you ever want to be a nun?" she laughs scornfully and denies the truth. "Nah, not me!"

8

Rebel Brides

Carmen
Seattle, Washington

— 1 9 7 0

ON THE DAY THAT CARMEN LEFT THE ORDER, THE ONLY PEOPLE she knew were female, white, and Catholic. She didn't know any men. She knew no blacks, Asians, or Hispanics. She knew no Protestants or Jews.

Carmen initially felt like a phantom, ethereal and other-worldly. She was completely disconnected from common reality. She had a lot of catching up to do. Her young students at Holy Angels had known more about life than she did. It seemed as if everyone in the world had been involved in a long, convoluted conversation that she'd heard only snippets of, or had missed completely. Carmen had never seen Elvis Presley gyrating on *The Ed*

Sullivan Show, or the Beatles. She'd never seen an episode of *Dr. Kildare, The Man from U.N.C.L.E., Gunsmoke,* or *Star Trek.* She'd heard about *The Flying Nun* but had never seen the show. She hadn't read *On the Road, The Second Sex, The Feminine Mystique,* or *Silent Spring.* She'd never seen a copy of *Cosmopolitan, Glamour,* or *Rolling Stone.* The last movie she'd seen was *The Sound of Music.* (Ironically, the sisters were granted permission to see this movie because it was about nuns. Actually, it was about a nun who left the convent and fell in love with the character played by Christopher Plummer.)

Carmen was a trained musician who'd never been to a folk or rock concert. She'd never heard of the Jefferson Airplane, the Doors, or the Lovin' Spoonful. Her musical taste buds hadn't been exposed to the sounds that framed eras. She had never heard "Return to Sender," or the Kingsmen's raunchy "Louie Louie," or Ray Charles's "What'd I Say?" or even "Ode to Billie Joe."

Carmen went out on her first date when she was thirty-two years old. It was a tremendous act of courage. After spending two days deciding which of her four basic outfits to wear, and how much makeup was appropriate for the evening, her perfectly oblivious date came to pick her up. They went to see *Midnight Cowboy.* Her date thought the movie was brilliant, absorbing, the most meaningful film he'd ever seen. Carmen tried to follow along, but she didn't have a clue. She just didn't get it. Fifteen years in the convent had left her in the dark about the generational metaphors.

The effort to adjust and learn was even tougher than she'd imagined. Most of the time, it felt like an insurmountable climb up a sheer cliff. Hair, clothing, makeup—life was a confusing jumble of choices. She didn't even know what to wear. When she'd gone shopping with Michelle at the clothing outlets, she had been attracted to the racks bearing the most garish colors—like a child whose eyes are drawn to shiny objects. Deprived of the sensory bath of color for so long, Carmen's postconvent wardrobe quickly became a mix of chartreuse, orange, and hot pink. The air bathing her legs was a startling new experience, and she chose skirts as short as she dared. At times, she would catch a glimpse of herself and do a double take. She'd think, Wow! Is that really me?

She furnished her apartment with a burnt orange beanbag chair, a discarded wire spool for a table, and a fake fur rug of deep electric blue. In the morning, the sun would catch the colors and throw pastel tendrils against the white walls. She sometimes consciously softened the focus of her eyes and let the vibrant colors dance and blur together.

During her first year out of the convent, Carmen was forced to face the realities of the secular life. She found herself missing the comforts of Rosary Heights far more than she had imagined. In the convent, she hadn't had to worry about her next meal, and she hadn't had to worry about paying the bills. There were no taxes to pay. She hadn't been forced to scrape together money to buy a secondhand winter coat. Living on the $6,200 a year she was being paid to teach music at a Catholic elementary school, Carmen was barely making ends meet. Her tiny apartment—a one-room studio—was on the second floor of an old house in the University District of Seattle. The floors were so badly warped, it gave her vertigo whenever she looked down. The two ground-floor apartments were occupied by other ex-nuns who taught in the same Catholic school. There were fewer nuns teaching in the local Catholic schools than ever before. The sudden shortage had opened up positions that had never gone unfilled. Suddenly, there was a need for lay teachers, or Carmen and the other ex-nuns might not have had jobs. Carmen observed that they were poorer living as seculars than they'd been when they lived under the vow of poverty. On payday, the three women would pool their money and buy a pint of gin and a quart of grapefruit juice for a celebratory drink or two. On some Friday nights, they would scrape together enough money to go to the movies. When Carmen saw *They Shoot Horses, Don't They?* she found it so unrelenting and daring that it made her eyes burn. The images, the performances, and the music were searing and unforgettable. The three women started going to the movies as often as they could. For Carmen, it was a shortcut to learning the ways of the world—a visual version of foreign-language tapes.

Occasionally, the three lay teachers were invited to parties at the convent attached to the school where they taught. Although Carmen was sure of her decision, being back in the atmosphere of a convent set loose a sadness and longing in her. She *had* loved her vocation. But she didn't intend to return to religious life. No, her mind was made up. There was no going back. However, the comforts of the convent weren't lost on her. The *food* was so good. There was so *much* of it. Carmen would surreptitiously put a little bit of food in her scarf and take it home for later. She was living on a subsistence diet.

This particular convent had several young nuns fresh over from Ireland who hadn't had their spirits squelched by years of convent life. One night, the Irish sisters invited the three lay teachers to join them at an Irish pub. Carmen and her friends were so poor that they quietly nursed their beers for hours, while the nuns drank everything they could get their hands on. Drunk as lords, the sisters then brought down the house with a rollicking night of song. Well, Carmen brooded as she shepherded her sodden charges home at 2:30 in the morning, it was necessary that *someone* stayed sober.

Michelle was going to be married. She had met a man and fallen in love. Carmen was happy for her, but she viewed Michelle's fiancé with somewhat skeptical eyes. Ken was too handsome and slick for Carmen's tastes. And he was a smooth talker, too. He claimed he was a big real estate agent. Michelle was marrying a real estate agent? Carmen tried to judge her feelings carefully. She just wanted to make sure that Michelle was doing the right thing, making the right decision. And she approached the matter cautiously— or so she thought.

"Michelle," she asked, for what must have been the hundredth time, "are you sure he's the one?"

Michelle had long since grown exasperated by Carmen's questions. "How should I know?" she snapped. "What do I know about men?"

"Exactly. Maybe you should just wait a while, spend some more time adjusting to living on your own," Carmen suggested.

"Look," Michelle replied. "I don't want to wait anymore, okay? I just want to be a normal person. And Ken loves me."

Carmen didn't know how to respond to that. "He loves me." What could she say? He's too good-looking? He's too smooth? Michelle didn't want to hear her opinions. Carmen imagined that it would be nice to have a man tell you he loved you, to have him whisper sweet nothings in your ear.

Michelle became pregnant within months after her marriage to Ken. She'd hardly had time to experience being a wife, and now she was going to be a mother, as well. Carmen couldn't keep her eyes off her friend's belly as it expanded. Michelle glowed with contentment as her pregnancy proceeded smoothly. She had always loved children so much. Now, at last, she'd have her very own.

"Carmen," she said one day near the end of her pregnancy, "do you remember when we were in the Sodality of Mary and we used to take care of those little kids during Mass?"

"Oh, yes." Carmen remembered all right. She had hated it. All those bawling, drooling kids.

"I loved being with the children," Michelle said dreamily. "I never dared hope to have any of my own. I knew I was going into the convent. I knew I would never have children. It hurt so much, but I offered it as a sacrifice. Everything that's happened, I never expected, and now this. I've never been so happy."

That night, Michelle gave birth to a beautiful little baby girl with thick black hair and enormous dark eyes, luminous as phosphorescent pools. Carmen was with her in the delivery room. Ken couldn't make it. He apparently had a midnight real estate meeting. Ken had begun showing his true colors a few short months into the pregnancy, and Michelle hadn't seemed to care.

Michelle didn't care now, that was for sure. She beamed with pleasure and poured tears of joy as rivulets of sweat dripped down her forehead. She had her child, her baby, her precious Kathleen. What more would she ever need now?

It was almost three in the morning when Carmen finally left the hospital. She came out into the cool early-morning air exhausted, her pink blouse matted to her body, almost transparent with sweat and tears. Now she was Aunt Carmen. Imagine that. Michelle was a mother. And she was Kathleen's aunt. Aunt Carmen!

Carmen's own forays and skirmishes into the world of men were less successful. She quickly discovered that she was the perfect fool for every fast-talking "nice guy" in the world. It was as though she had a sign over her head: GULLIBLE EX-NUN. PLEASE LINE UP. She may as well have gone to bars in her old habit. Some men had an almost unerring instinct for detecting women who had absolutely no experience in life.

One night, she went out to a bar with a friend who was a nun. Sister Anne was young and fun-loving. That night, she was dressed in jeans and a blouse. Her short hair was blown into a cloud of gold, and she had a splash of pink on her lips. No one would ever have guessed that she was a nun.

In the course of the evening, the waiter poured them fresh drinks and gestured to the end of the bar. "The gentlemen send their compliments," he said. Carmen and Anne glanced over and the two men saluted them.

"Oh, damn," Carmen said, conscious of the fact that she was out drinking with a nun. "What do we do now?"

Sister Anne laughed. She was enjoying herself. "We just smile and say thank you," she said.

They lifted their drinks and mouthed silent thanks to their benefactors. The two men came over and pulled up stools next to them. They told Carmen and Anne that they were in town for a Kiwanis convention. Carmen was so naïve that this revelation sent up no caution signals.

The more loquacious of the two was a tall rakish character named Ben. Carmen's mouth dropped when he told her that he spent a lot of time with the dead; he was a grave digger. What a profession, Carmen thought to herself. In the course of the next couple of hours, it became clear that Ben liked Carmen. As they parted, he asked her to go out with him the next night.

"Go for it," Sister Anne cheerfully encouraged her. "He seems like a perfectly nice guy." So Carmen accepted his invitation, and they had a great time. At a late-night piano bar, Carmen loosened up enough to play the piano and sing for the first time since she'd been out of the order.

Ben was dazzled by her playing and her voice. "I'm in love. I think I want to marry you," he said. His eyes shone with a light that sent shivers down Carmen's spine and made her knees weak. She couldn't believe it. No one had ever said those words to her before. Ben probably could have done anything he wanted with her that night, but he behaved like a gentleman. He took her back to her apartment, gave her a chaste kiss, and handed her a card. "This is my number at the cemetery," he said. "Call me there, not at home. I live in a house with my mother, a widow lady, and her son. It's too complicated to explain."

"Who's the widow lady?" Carmen asked.

"Oh, some friend of my mother's. An old bag," he replied.

Ben and Carmen continued to see each other. When she needed to talk to him, she would call him at the cemetery. Carmen had never felt like this before. It was beginning to look as if Ben was really in love with her. He kept talking about marriage. Carmen was starting to get serious, too. She thought that she loved Ben.

Then a week went by without his calling. Carmen tried to reach him at the number he'd given her for the cemetery, but to no avail. She was alarmed. Something was wrong. Maybe Ben was sick or had been in an accident. She debated for a long time before calling Ben's home.

A young man answered the phone. "Is Ben Wagner there?" she asked.

He said, "Do you want Ben *G.* Wagner or Ben *H.* Wagner—because if you want Ben *G.* Wagner, that's my dad. He's not here right now. I'm Ben H."

"Thank you, no. I'll try later," Carmen said, and she hung up the phone quickly. Ben G. Wagner? Ben H. Wagner? All of those years in the convent must have addled her brain, she thought many years later, because she *still* didn't get it. What had the boy said? ". . . if you want Ben *G.* Wagner, that's my dad." My dad? Ben has a boy?

Ben finally called the next day, and she told him what had happened.

"Oh," he said quickly, "that was the widow lady's son. He doesn't have a father, of course, and he really likes me a lot. So he takes my name. It's cute, isn't it?"

Carmen was still gullible enough to buy Ben's explanation! It took another month for her to find out that Ben was married. The pitiable thing was, she wasn't able to figure it out herself. Michelle finally had to explain it to her. Michelle, who'd only been out of the convent a year longer than Carmen, had become a woman of the world—comparatively speaking. Carmen imagined that being trapped in a rotten marriage could do that to you.

Carmen didn't give up trying, though. She was a little behind the curve, but she'd catch up. She just had to stay in there swinging—metaphorically, that is.

"Have you ever been married?" a man asked her one night, pressing drunkenly against her in a dark corner of a smoky bar's faded banquette.

Carmen automatically started to say no, then hesitated. She thought of the day she'd gone down the aisle with the other brides of Christ, remembered the feel of the wedding dress against her body, the veil wreathed with roses, how beautiful the day had been.

"Yes," she answered, staring at the table. "I was. A long time ago. Once." Then she added, "I wore my mother's wedding dress."

The Sisters of Saint Dominic of the Holy Cross abandoned the practice of wearing wedding gowns and veils for profession in the late 1950s. Uniting a professed religious with her Divine Bride-groom in these spiritual weddings had been designed as a powerful message to the brides—give yourself over to him completely. Their marriage to Christ was meant to fulfill their deepest needs, and it was extolled as being far superior to the physical intimacies offered by marriage. Their minds, bodies, and souls belonged to him.

But times changed, and religious women changed, as well. Many religious felt that the symbolic marriage to Christ was elit-ist. They no longer wanted to have their vows referred to as a "higher calling." It isolated them from those they wished to serve—the ill, the poor, and the needy. They didn't want to be seen as otherworldly.

For much of its history, the church had elevated the choice of a religious life above any secular calling. "One should come chaste to the gods," the ancient Roman philosopher Cicero proclaimed. The Roman Catholic church took this sentiment to heart. Sex and marriage became twin concepts fraught with sin and evil. How could one serve God when defiled by sex? How could a man give himself to Christ with a wife and bawling children pulling at him?

The church's real problem had always been sex. The human animal craved it, so temptations of the flesh were condemned with a special ferocity. This inevitably led to a retreat from the church's original position, which had allowed for married priests in the early centuries.

Women were obviously the problem. It became clear that they were the temptresses—even a *wife* could be a temptress. In the fourth century, the Spanish Synod of Elvira proclaimed that "all clerics . . . are commanded to abstain from conjugal relations with their wives and not beget any more children. Those who violate this order will be expelled from the priesthood." This order was the first in a tightening circle of repression that over the centuries sought to eradicate tens of thousands of priests' marriages. Pope Gregory I ordered his seventh-century priests to "love your wives as if they were sisters and beware of them as if they were enemies." In the eleventh century, Pope Gregory VII wrote of "sundering the commerce between the clergy and women through [proclaiming] an eternal anathema." The Roman Catholic church's obsession with celibacy was yet another reason for the schism that separated the church of the West from the church of the East.

Considering how purity was valued, it should come as no shock that virginity was held up as a great and shining prize. This was demonstrated by the frequent appearance of virgin martyrs in church history. Young women died rather than give up their maidenheads, some of these martyrs refusing to relinquish their chastity even in their marriage beds. As a result of their struggle, many of these virgin martyrs achieved sainthood. A contemporary feminist interpretation might be that these women died rather than cede control over their own bodies—but that wasn't how the church wanted such sacrifices to be viewed.

The most recent officially declared virgin martyr was Maria Goretti, a twelve-year-old Italian girl raped by a neighbor. As her attacker defiled her, Maria is reported to have cried, "Death before sin!" Obligingly, her attacker produced a knife and stabbed her to death. It was always unclear, as with other virgin martyrs, whether her attacker actually succeeded in taking her virginity. Maria's canonization in 1950 was somewhat suspect, since Pope Pius XII chose that moment to launch an antismut campaign, denouncing the increasingly open sexuality of women as portrayed in the media and in film.

Theologians have always highlighted Mary's purity, her virginity, as the shining exemplar of female spirituality. Because she was not defiled in the process of conception, Jesus was able to be born in a state of absolute purity, devoid of original sin. This phenomenon came to be known as the Immaculate Conception. Mary then remained ever virgin, forever the Perfect Mother to the Perfect Son. No one seems to have much cared about poor, long-suffering Joseph.

Saint Augustine of Hippo and Saint Thomas Aquinas are the two men most responsible for crafting church philosophy and doctrine concerning sexual matters. Each was absolutely obsessed with sex. Augustine, who lived in the declining Roman Empire between A.D. 354 and 430, was an uninhibited sexual marauder who gloried in his conquests. He spent his youth filling his every appetite, reveling in the sins of the flesh. Then there came an epiphany, and he converted to Christianity. In the process, he abandoned his current mistress and their child—not an especially charitable or compassionate act for a man who would be anointed to sainthood. Augustine's epiphany also came with a slight twist. Rather than seeking forgiveness for his own sins, Augustine instead blamed the women with whom he had sinned. They were temptresses; they had powers so great that men were forced to become sinners. No one needed a lot of convincing on this matter. Since primitive times, men had been in awe of women's sexual capacities and so had arranged taboos and restrictions meant to harness, dampen, and forbid their ascendence. So Augustine's idea really caught on. It wasn't *us;* it was *them*. He once wrote that his vision of hell was "the burning of lust." He also came up with the idea that the original sin Adam and Eve committed had nothing to do with eating forbidden fruit. Their disobedience to God, fomented by Eve, was about lust, desire, passion, sex. According to Augustine, Adam and Eve could have done anything they wanted in the Garden of Eden. It was when they decided to find pleasure in each other, rather than in the abundance God had given them, that the trouble began. Sex was dirty, evil, ungodly. It got you thrown out of paradise.

Thomas Aquinas, a thirteenth-century scholar, was also fixated on the place of women in relation to God. In his *Summa Theologia*—roughly, the final word on Catholic doctrine—Thomas wrote, "Nothing drags the mind of man down from its elevation so much as the caresses of woman." He never mentioned what man's mind was elevated to before his defilement at the hands of woman. He never suggested the possibility that an elevated man might be able to resist the caresses of a woman. This curious tidbit is also revealed: "Because there is a higher water content in women, they are more easily seduced by sexual pleasure."

Thanks to Augustine, Thomas Aquinas, and a handful of others, the subject of intimate relations between man and wife has occupied some of the greatest minds of the church over the centuries. The argument—which still goes on in some circles today— was whether there was any way for married couples to fulfill the mandate to procreate without experiencing sexual pleasure. At various times in church history, there have been attempts to ban sexual relations among couples who were unable to bear children, when a woman was pregnant, and after the onset of menopause. Before medical science proved it a fallacy, the belief that birth defects and grotesque deformities were caused by sex during pregnancy was widespread.

The theologians argued that since God hadn't provided a way to avoid pleasure in the act of procreation—for men, anyway— that it was vital to focus on defining the levels of pleasure and the levels of sin. Many an aging celibate spent years engaged in "theological" discussions about the minutiae of sex. Was it more sinful to have intercourse with a beautiful woman than an ugly woman? The pleasure with a beautiful woman was greater, was it not? But what if the uglier woman were more adept at the act? What then? Which was the greater sin?

By choosing to refer to each nun as a bride of Christ, the church set her on a pristine sexual pedestal. Her chastity, like that of the Holy Mother and the virgin martyrs, made her superior to all other women. The direct implication was that women, no matter how good or how religious, were defiled when they submitted to sex. The nuns rebelled against the bride of Christ label because it kept them always holier than thou, forever apart from the very people they wished to be with and to serve.

There was another reason why so many of the sisters found the pretense of a bridal ceremony embarrassing. It was somehow demeaning to march down the aisle wearing the cast-off, ill-fitting wedding gowns of mothers, sisters, and friends—as if to say, This isn't a real wedding, of course, but every girl should get to wear a wedding dress at least once. Of course, there'll be no bridal night, no champagne, no wedding cake with matching bride and groom, no honeymoon. But enjoy!

Weren't there more powerful metaphors for this great calling? The disciples who followed Christ were not all men. There were women, too, and they were never considered his brides or his concubines. Scandalous as it was at the time, wealthy married women were among his benefactors. He was a true friend to women, and women were drawn to him for that reason. As it is today among the Orthodox Jews, it was considered disturbing and provocative that a rabbi should be so open and free with women, but it was Christ's way. Why should nuns be considered any differently from his disciples?

Soon after the wedding gowns disappeared, the postulant garb was also changed—again to the delight of many. They used to call postulants "the Black Crows," because that's what they looked like in the long black dresses, veils, and capes. Within ten years, the religious habit itself was severely modified, and it finally disappeared. This was a controversial decision; when a group of Edmonds Dominicans, among the first to modify their habits drastically, attended a conference in San Francisco in 1968, they were snubbed by sisters from other orders. Some sisters admitted privately that they missed the special cache of the habit—the respect they received on the street, the free ferry rides, cups of coffee, and other perks. Others said they welcomed the privacy of anonymity. "Every stranger, every passing drunk feels comfortable telling you his troubles when you're in your habit," one sister mumbled.

Many devout Catholics were shaken by the change. They felt robbed of their most powerful separatist symbol. But the frequent complaint "If nuns look just like ordinary women, how will anyone know they're religious?" was met with good-natured aplomb by religious women. They pointed out that originally religious habits were not meant to be indelible signs of Catholicism. Early religious orders made it a point to adopt the peasant dress of the times. It was donned to signify each nun's affinity with the most humble, the poorest. To continue dressing as twelfth-century peasant women in the twentieth century no longer suited the needs or desires of the orders.

A treacly but popular religious folk song of the late 1960s gave the best answer to the question "How will people know?"

> *They'll know we are Christians by our love, by our love.*
> *Yes, they'll know we are Christians by our love.*

For many in the church, the modernization of the religious orders was disturbing—signaling a move away from tradition, a diminishment of spiritual ardor, and a caving in to the secularism of the times. Perhaps as a consequence of the narrow parochialism of the 1940s and 1950s, many Catholics felt the comforting mantle of the True Church slipping from their shoulders. They felt suddenly bare without the practices and symbols that had defined their own spiritual experience. Conservative movements rose up in reaction, with a cry to "take back the church." Theologic reactionaries theorized dark conspiracies and suggested that religious orders had been infested with *feminists* intent on bringing the True Church to its knees. The catastrophic decline in enrollments at seminaries and convents was blamed on the modernization that took place after Vatican II, and perhaps that was partially true. But the orders were no longer interested in recruiting young men and women attracted by the habit, the rigidity of the ways, the surety of custom and ritual. It was a new world, and certainly the convents wanted new women: thinking women, educated, experienced, and, most of all, secure about their vocations.

The romantic vision of the religious life was to a great extent an invention of the last half of this century. Until then, religious vocation was an unexamined, unremarked-upon fact of life. But with the advent of widely disseminated books and films, nuns became the focus of much interest. With books and films such as *The Nun's Story; The Bells of St. Mary's; Come to the Stable; Heaven Knows, Mr. Allison; Lilies of the Field;* and the musical *The Sound of Music,* the peak of curiosity and fervor was reached in the decades preceding and following World War II. Good nuns, troubled nuns, dying nuns, singing nuns—nuns were everywhere. The women in religious orders now proclaimed, "We're not somebody's idea of a romantic vision!"

Catholic nuns also fueled the flames of controversy when they broke their silence to denounce church decrees that affected the lives of women. They discovered, to their alarm, that the church had a simple attitude toward rebel nuns: If they made trouble, they were expendable. In 1984, Geraldine Ferraro, the first women candidate for the vice presidency, and a devout Catholic, announced that she was pro-choice on abortion. This brought threats from several bishops that not only Ferraro but also Catholics who supported her were in danger of excommunication. It was a stunning blow to church-state separation. Excommunication was the most terrible punishment the church could inflict. It not only meant that you were thrown out of the church and denied the sacraments but that you were most surely damned to hell.

A defiant group, called Catholics for Free Choice, bought a thirty-thousand-dollar full-page ad in the *New York Times,* challenging church doctrine on abortion. Among the ninety-seven signers were twenty-four nuns, representing various orders. Within days, the mighty weight of the church hierarchy was pressing down on the rebel nuns. Pressure was exerted on their orders to force them to make a public retraction or be expelled. At first, the sisters refused. But they were no match for the church in this cruel arm wrestle. Donna Quinn, a Dominican sister living in Chicago, and one of the leaders of the group, couldn't believe the church hierarchy would refuse them a hearing. When she heard that Jean Jerome Cardinal Hamer, the Belgian Dominican prefect of the Vatican's Congregation for Religious and Secular Institutes, was speaking at Chicago's Holy Name Cathedral, she went to hear him speak. Afterward, she joined the line of people who were waiting to meet him. When she stood before him, the cardinal recognized her immediately and glared angrily at her. When she asked him, in a quiet voice, "Will you dialogue with the signers?" his face turned red with rage and he screamed, "I'll *give you* dialogue! You come to Rome. You'll *get* dialogue!"

Sister Donna turned away, feeling as if she'd just been threatened by a Vatican hit man.

The Edmonds Dominicans faced the same uphill battles. Somehow they managed to remain steady in the eye of the hurricane. They had always been unembarrassed about their pro-woman stand. They abided by the declaration made at the order's chapter in 1978: "As women religious who have made the commitment to justice, we have a special obligation to be models of justice, equality, and presence for other women."

As the debates raged on, and as they watched their numbers dwindle, they kept their eyes focused on the tabernacle. They stood in its shadow—defiant, determined, and full of faith.

Guilford, Connecticut
—December 1984

Elizabeth stepped inside the door of the cloister, holding fast to eight-year-old Faith's hand. There was Sister Miriam smiling at her, tears sparkling in her eyes.

"Welcome home," she cried, wrapping Elizabeth in an enveloping embrace. "We've missed you so much."

Elizabeth found that she could not restrain her own tears. She had been dreaming of this homecoming for years. And she had never once doubted that she would be welcomed as a sister.

Finally, the two women drew apart. Sister Miriam wiped her eyes and turned to Faith, who was silently chewing on a braid and staring at Miriam with wide, curious eyes. "Well, you're a finelooking young woman," she observed. She held out a hand. "Welcome to our community," she said solemnly as Faith wrapped her tiny hand inside the satiny gnarled fingers.

Elizabeth was overcome with a new emotion as she watched her daughter being welcomed into her community. This was the way it should be.

Later, as they visited in the parlor with three of the sisters, Faith sang a simple nursery rhyme in her lilting, broken little girl's voice and Elizabeth observed how delighted the sisters were. They found excuses to draw her to them, and they caressed her dark brown hair. Elizabeth would catch an occasional glimmer in the eye of one of the sisters. A moment not exactly of regret, but of wonder. The presence of a child triggered a natural maternal instinct in these women, who had long ago given up the choice of motherhood.

On the second day, Elizabeth sat in a parlor chair, waiting for Sister Miriam and gazing reflectively out of a large window that gave a breathtaking view of the hills and valleys that stretched behind the substantial property. She remembered that when she'd first arrived at the cloister, she had brought her skis. She didn't know whether it was contemplative to be skiing in the mountains, but she loved to ski. She was surprised when her superiors didn't have a problem with the idea of a contemplative nun skiing. They were, however, doubtful that their meager hills would sustain a skier.

The first time Elizabeth tried it, an anxious group of nuns peered out the window. They thought she was going to kill herself. She knew better. Elizabeth was an adept skier. It was an intense, meditative experience for her, an exhilarating dance with the infinite. As she sped down the hills, she tried to make it interesting for the nuns who were staring out the window with open-mouthed horror. She dodged in and out of the fir trees, swirled, and dipped. While her fellow nuns were moaning and crossing themselves, Elizabeth was flying. She was consumed with joy.

Suddenly, Faith raced into the room and broke her reverie. "Mommy," she announced with an important air, "I've been invited to the parlor, where Sister is decorating for Christmas." Elizabeth smiled with delight.

Just then, Sister Miriam appeared at the door, carrying a tray. "I understand your daughter has volunteered to help Sister. She's needed now, I believe," she said with a wink. "Perhaps you and I could have tea while Faith is busy."

Faith sped off to keep her date, and Elizabeth sat down with Sister Miriam.

"It's so good to have you here," Miriam said softly. "You will always be a part of our family. And your dear daughter will be welcome here, as well."

Elizabeth nodded gratefully.

Miriam examined Elizabeth closely. "You seem happy."

"Life is good for us," Elizabeth replied sincerely. "But things haven't been easy. Sister, it has been fourteen years." She paused, struggling. "We've had to face some bitter truths."

"What kind of truths? Tell me."

"When Jim and I first decided to leave our lives, to marry, we had a sense of mission. A certitude that we weren't that far from the path. I knew I could never go back to being a nun, but neither of us doubted that Jim would be a pastor again. We hoped that someday we'd still be able to serve the church. We're finally facing the fact that it may not ever happen. This Pope—he seems so rigid. It breaks my heart."

Elizabeth paused, but Miriam remained silent. By long practice, she had learned that silence was the best way to enable someone to speak.

"We were married by a judge in Reno. Can you believe that?" Elizabeth shook her head, still amazed by the irony. "I don't really know how to explain this, but we still considered ourselves a religious couple. We loved the church. Jim believed, with every fiber of his being, that he would be a pastor again within a few short years. I believed it, too. We weren't prepared for the hatred—for the way we would be shut out."

It had started immediately. Shortly after they were married, Elizabeth and Jim attended Mass in a church near where he had grown up. The Mass had just begun. The parish priest raised his arms over the congregation. "The Lord be with you. . . ."

Then his eyes lit on Jim and Elizabeth. Slowly, he brought his arms down and gripped the edges of the altar. His face turned white, as if he had seen a ghost—or a devil. Then he was moving—purposefully striding in front of the altar and down the carpeted steps toward the congregation. He stopped at the row where Jim and Elizabeth were sitting and glared at them. His face was red now, beaded with perspiration. He extended his arm and pointed an angry finger at them. "You!" he shouted. "How dare you come here? Get out!"

For a moment, Elizabeth thought her husband was going to leap from the pew and strike the priest down, but he did nothing of the sort. Instead, Jim held his emotions in check. He smiled at the priest, stood, took Elizabeth's hand, and they walked slowly down the aisle and out of the church. They stood in the bright sunlight outside, holding hands, trying to be strong. But Elizabeth couldn't stop crying for the rest of the day.

She dabbed at her nose with a tissue. "I'm sorry. I get so worked up. I know God doesn't care about this kind of junk, but it gets me." She sniffed. "There was this Jesuit priest, Jim's best friend from seminary. When he heard that Jim and I had gotten married, he told people that if they came to our house, if they were friendly to us, they weren't welcome to come to his house or his church. He'd turn them away. Like we were dirty and unclean, somehow; tainted. We know we've done the right thing, but no one seems to want us. It's so lonely out there. Where do we go? Where do we pray?"

Sister Miriam set down her teacup. She reached over and pressed her lined hand against Elizabeth's heart. "Here," she whispered. "You pray here."

9

The Labyrinthine Ways

Seattle, Washington

—JANUARY 1997

THE RECORD-BREAKING STORM THAT LEFT ROSARY HEIGHTS dangling on the edge of a precipice was a catastrophic event. Since late December, two feet of snow had fallen on Seattle, followed by sheets of ice and torrential rains. All of the Schuler family agreed that it was a shame Dad wasn't alive for this. He loved the weather.

Dad would have been mesmerized by this bizarre climatic shift. He'd always been an avid follower of weather patterns, perhaps because he spent so many years driving for Foremost Dairy. Thanks to Dad's obsession, my parents' house contained every conceivable meteorological device—thermometers, barometers, weather vanes, even a dedicated shortwave radio that blared out constant reports. When we were little children, a wooden cuckoo clock in the shape of a sharply gabled house sat in a place of honor on our mantel-piece. It not only kept perfect time but also doubled as a barome-ter. At the stroke of each hour, a tiny little door popped open. If the weather forecast was fair, two smiling blond children came twirling out. But if the forecast was ominous, an ugly old witch with a black wart on her nose emerged. My father loved that clock, especially the ugly witch. One of the first lessons I remember him teaching us was the ancient mariner's rhyme: "Red sky at night, sailors delight; red sky in the morning, sailors take warning." It was too bad that Dad had to miss this show. He would have been out in the backyard taking measurements, fiddling with his weather vanes, and keeping the bird feeders fully stocked.

On the East Coast, January 1997 brought oddly mild weather. I kept close track of the storm patterns pounding Seattle, and I worried about my family's safety. I talked to my mother every day. She had begun feeling a bit stir-crazy—nervous about the sound of ice-laden branches from the trees that surrounded the house snapping and falling, and the wind whistling through the cracks in the roof. She reported that our old family cat, Pepsi, a great lover of the outdoors, was in a state of deep gloom. He sat in his favorite chair and watched the bullets of icy rain pelt against the sliding glass doors. The tundralike backyard began to lose its old appeal. Across town, my sister Mary's basement flooded. This was a stun-ning feat of nature, since Mary and her family lived on top of one of Seattle's many hills.

My mother called me one day to report a sad event. "Some-thing shocking happened. It's been all over the TV and the papers. They had a major landslide at Rosary Heights last night, almost an avalanche. The nuns were forced to abandon the property in the middle of the night. It looks pretty bad."

This *was* shocking news. "Is it . . . gone?" I asked, barely in a whisper.

"No, the motherhouse is standing, so Rosary Heights is still holding on. But they don't know for how long. Most of the bluff just tore away, from what I saw on TV. Another big storm . . ." her voice faded out. "Weren't you going to talk to some of the nuns there, for your book?"

"Yes. That's what I'd planned on doing anyway."

"Well, they may not be there by the time you get around to it," she said ominously.

I silently cursed myself as we hung up the phone. What had I been waiting for? It had never occurred to me that Rosary Heights could just *disappear*. I felt entangled in a web of my own design. Or maybe it wasn't that at all; perhaps the old hound of heaven's footsteps were finally catching up with me, just as Sister Martina always knew they would. In any case, it was clear to me that I would have to pay a visit to Rosary Heights—and quickly, before the very land that had kept it so majestically placed for all of these years was swept into Puget Sound and lost forever.

Whom could I get in touch with? Whom could I call? I didn't have a single contact anymore. I knew many of the sisters had left the order, and others had died. And worst of all, I didn't even know their names. The women of the order had relinquished their religious names and returned to their baptismal names many years ago. The nuns I knew then might be called something else now. It made my head throb. Would it even be possible to get a list of the sisters' former and current names?

And then the answer came to me. Of course. I needed to call Bernadette.

Bernadette and I had never lost touch over the years. We remained for each other the same as we'd always been, ever since Holy Angels. There are some people who wouldn't call what we had a friendship. We had taken different paths, and our contact was sporadic. But the bond between us was deep, labyrinthine, and complex, like the roots of an old tree. It was more than simple friendship. We had a connection that allowed us to pick up where we'd left off, no matter how many months or years had passed.

Each of us had led a very different life from the others. We arrived at our beliefs about the meaning of feminism from opposite directions. When she was twenty-five, Bernadette had joined the Sisters of Social Service, whose motherhouse was in Southern California. From there, she'd been sent on missions across the world. She'd spent many years in Africa, then in Mexico. Bernadette was a grass-roots activist and nurse, on the forefront of the new peace and justice movement that had become central to the mission of many Catholic religious orders. Working in the heartlands of famine, poverty, ignorance, and disease, Bernadette gave of herself selflessly, marshaling every local resource in an attempt to better the plight of those she served.

Late one night in August 1992, in the midst of yet another brutal summer heat wave, the phone rang in my apartment. I was still living in New York City then, in a one-hundred-year-old sixth-floor walk-up in the heart of Greenwich Village. The voice on the phone was instantly recognizable to me, although Bernadette and I hadn't actually spoken for nineteen years, since 1973. She was calling to tell me that she had decided to leave the order and was going to establish her own nurse-midwifery mission in California. We asked each other the usual questions, quickly trying to catch up on our lives. She was forty-two years old—we both were—and she had been in the order for seventeen years.

Frankly, I didn't know what to say about her decision to leave the Sisters of Social Service. Was this good news? Sad news? Was she bitter, burned-out, or just tired? I suspected that her decision had something to do with her recent work in California. She had been ministering to people with AIDS—primarily gay men. Her mission was not a popular one with many Catholics, including members of her own order. It infuriated her when she heard people in the church—Christians!—actually refer to AIDS as God's punishment for a sinful lifestyle. Her experience had shown otherwise. She felt humbled by the courage and goodness these men displayed every day. They faced their deaths with more faith than most of their detractors ever hoped to possess. She believed there was a special place in heaven for people who suffered so deeply and sacrificed so much. *Her* God was a compassionate, loving God. He would not forsake them.

Of course, Bernadette's position on this and other aspects of the peace and justice ministry placed her in dramatic contrast to the dogma and attitudes of the church. She became more and more frustrated by the behavior of the hierarchy, and even by the directives of her own order. Her calling to serve the poor and other outcast members of society remained intact. But she felt she could no longer fulfill her mission under the banner of the hierarchy.

After that conversation, we continued as we always had, maintaining our usual sporadic contact. Now I was phoning her for advice. Although she had spent much of her adult life in foreign lands, Bernadette always knew what was going on in Seattle. She kept up-to-date on which sisters had left the order at Rosary Heights and which sisters had stayed.

"Why don't you get in touch with Sister Joanne?" Bernadette suggested. "She's still at Rosary Heights."

Sister Joanne. I started rifling through my mental filing cabinet, flipping back through the years, until I saw myself sitting in Sister Joanne's classroom when I was a fourteen-year-old freshman at Holy Angels. I came up with a picture of the smiling young nun who had been my homeroom teacher. She'd been wonderful. I wasn't surprised to hear that she was still in the order. I'd rarely met anyone who radiated such joy and received so much pleasure from being a religious. Without hesitating, I wrote to her, reintroduced myself, and asked if she wouldn't mind my paying her a visit. She responded immediately and warmly, and a month later I was standing at the familiar front entrance of Rosary Heights and ringing the bell.

A woman—who I correctly sensed was a lay secretary, not a member of the order—greeted me and ushered me into a bright, comfortable room. She invited me to take a seat in one of the simple Victorian-style wing-back chairs. She then left me to tell Sister Joanne I was waiting. This might have been the same room I'd sat in when I'd come to speak with Mother Dominick twenty-eight years ago. I couldn't remember. My memories of the rooms on either side of the cool, dark main passageway of this imposing house had faded with time. I was left with only the blur of impressions—like a whiff of lemon polish and Murphy's Oil Soap. Now, as I waited for Sister Joanne, I looked around with a more critical eye. The room was generously proportioned, with a row of bay windows facing out onto gardens. There were built-in bookcases along the walls, containing countless volumes dedicated to religion, psychology, and education. A small chandelier cast a soft glow on the mustard carpet. I leaned against the back of the chair. It felt so strange to be here. Had anyone asked me even a year before if I could imagine ever sitting in a room at Rosary Heights again, I would have said they were delusional or mistaken.

I began to feel a bit tense, listening for the sound of footsteps. In the old days, the faint jangle of rosary beads sent advance warning of an approaching sister, but those days were gone. Now they could just sneak up on you silently.

Sister Joanne burst into the room like a shell going off—an attractive woman of enormous energy who looked to be in her mid-fifties. As I was registering the fact that this woman was completely familiar to me, as if I'd seen her just yesterday, she threw up her hands in a gesture of amazement. "Catherine!" she exclaimed, her face beaming with a broad, welcoming smile. "I'd know you anywhere. You haven't changed a bit. You're exactly the same as you were! Let me give you a hug."

Sister Joanne's smile was sincere; it completely disarmed me and sucked the chill right out of the air. Her silver hair was tousled and cut short, and she was wearing a well-cut crimson suit.

"I can hardly believe you remember me." I laughed. "The last time you saw me, I was a little freshman in high school, and you were still in full habit."

"Yes, that's right," she said, her eyes twinkling, "but I found you hard to forget. You were a memorable young lady. You were always on the go. And you were *always* talking. I remember that I couldn't shut you up." She sat down across from me. "Now, Catherine, tell me everything."

"*Everything* is a pretty tall order, Sister." So I gave her the abbreviated version.

"I live in New York, and I'm a writer. As I told you in the letter I sent a few weeks ago, right now I'm working on a book about the lives of women in religious orders."

"So, you write books. Sister Lawrence was always going on about you. She spoke of you quite often, in fact. You were one of her favorite girls when she taught you. She said you were a comer. What a shame she couldn't be here to see this. She was always saying you'd be a writer, and here you are. She died two years ago, you know."

I nodded dumbly. I wanted to yell, Stop it! You're messing with my head! Why would Sister Lawrence talk about me? I was a nondescript little journalism student who wrote insipid articles for the school paper, *The Clarion.* The most memorable thing I ever did was accidentally break an expensive backlit table in the layout room. Then I graduated and dropped out of sight for almost thirty years. I wasn't even memorable to myself; I could barely recall what sort of person I'd been all those years ago. But I soon discovered a surreal and unnerving truth: The sisters never forgot. You couldn't get lost if you tried.

I thought it was a fluke, but again and again, I would meet nuns and former nuns who had inhabited brief moments of my young life. *In every instance,* they related to me as if our separation had been recent, rather than decades old. They regaled me with stories about myself that *I* didn't remember at all. I began to feel that it wasn't just that I had been so memorable. It was as if I, along with each of the thousands of young girls who had come under their tutelage, had been locked inside their hearts, minds, and souls forever. It seemed we were never out of their thoughts or their prayers.

Sister Joanne looked so happy sitting there, so full of life. It wasn't what I'd expected. To be perfectly honest, I had dreaded this moment. I was afraid that the strong, safe sanctuary of the

Dominican order of my youth lay in shambles—an idea I suddenly discovered myself unable to bear after all these years. I knew that many of the sisters had left, and there were very few new postulants who had arrived to restore their depleted ranks. I feared seeing the signs of age, sadness, and despair on the faces of women who had once been my role models. I'm certain it's one of the reasons I resisted visiting Rosary Heights for so long. It seemed much easier to seek out strangers in unfamiliar orders—those in which I had not invested a piece of myself.

But that was finally the point of my being here. I was forcing myself to edge to the precipice of my own life and leave the dispassionate journalist behind. I decided to ask Joanne if I could return to Rosary Heights in May, to live the life and get a feel for their mission. She thought that was a great idea.

Sister Joanne and I talked about so many things that first afternoon together. She asked after Bernadette. Remarkably, she remembered that we'd been best friends in 1964. She also asked about other classmates, whose names, I was ashamed to say, I had long since forgotten.

"We were all so sorry to hear about your father's death," she said with genuine feeling. "He was always so nice to us. We said a prayer for him here." I appreciated that. My father, lover of nuns.

She asked if I'd be interested in seeing the wounded bluff, which was still cordoned off with bright orange barriers. We stood up and stretched. "This is such a beautiful house," I said.

Joanne smiled conspiratorily. "Did you know there were secret panels in some of these walls?"

"You read my mind," I exclaimed. "Someone told me that once, and I've always wanted to see them, but I thought it would be rude to ask."

Joanne led me next door to a dining room with a large sturdy table in the center and a sideboard against one wall. She walked over to a polished oak wall and pressed gently with the palm of her hand. The wall disappeared and there was a small kitchen. "This used to be a wet bar," Sister Joanne told me. "Imagine that." She walked across the room and pressed another spot. "A china cabinet." Then another. "Look. A full closet."

"Well, my curiosity is certainly sated," I said with a grin. "You can't imagine the stories we used to tell about your hidden passageways."

"Oh, I think I can," she said over her shoulder as she led me down the hallway to the back door.

It was a clear day, but the grass was damp and the wind off the Sound was strong and steady. As we walked through the archway and toward the back of the house, I almost did a double take. Where once there had been a band of stately evergreens, there was now a breathtaking and unimpeded view across Puget Sound to the Olympic Mountains. We got to the edge of the bluff and looked over. I could see only a mess of stone and brush below, with more barricades. The angle was so steep, it prevented a full view to the very bottom, where the buried train tracks had been cleared and repaired.

"My mother was quite upset that the press made such a big deal about the tennis court and swimming pool," I said. "She thought they were trying to make it look as if you were living in the lap of luxury—like, 'Oh, the poor sisters. They lost their swimming pool.'"

Joanne laughed. "Don't you wish! That swimming pool was more trouble than it was worth. Frankly, we'd rather have had the money." She turned serious. "It's just ridiculous the ideas people have. I'd never realized it before the mud slide, but most people— I mean even most Catholics—think we're supported by the archdiocese and that we never have to worry about a thing."

This was news to me, too. I stood there looking at the distant mountain range, trying to find a place to put that vital piece of new information. "You're not supported by the archdiocese? I think everyone has always just assumed that the church takes care of the sisters."

"Not at all. We've always been self-supporting. Even when we staffed the Catholic schools, we were paid ridiculously low salaries, something like eighty dollars a week, and we'd pool our money and have to live off that. We raised the money ourselves to pay for this property."

"I didn't know any of this," I said.

"Of course, we're struggling more now because the average age of our sisters is older," Sister Joanne said frankly. "A lot of our elderly need support, and we try to provide it."

"Wait a minute," I said, remembering an article I'd read in the *Catholic Northwest Progress,* the Seattle religious weekly. "What about the archdiocese's fund-raising drive for retired priests and nuns? They collect money in all of the churches. Doesn't that money go to support the elderly religious?"

"Yes, but it's not very much by the time it gets distributed," she said. "Let me put it this way. If I had to, I'd take a job as a salesclerk at Nordstrom's. We have to take care of ourselves just like everyone else."

I was dumbfounded by the idea of Sister Joanne working as a salesclerk at Nordstrom's. What was the world coming to?

Back inside the motherhouse, we wiped the wet grass off the soles of our shoes and headed into the kitchen for tea. The kitchen was actually two large rooms filled with dozens of cupboards and sweeping food-preparation areas. It was hard to believe that this massive kitchen had originally been built for a private family.

An elderly woman sat at a built-in table along the wall in the first room. "Sister Hilary," Joanne said brightly, "this is Catherine Schuler—well, she's Whitney now. Catherine is one of our girls. She's writing a book about religious orders."

Sister Hilary beamed at me. I wasn't going to mention that we had met each other before, when she'd still been known as Mother Dominick. She had told me to wait, had turned me away from the order in this very house, twenty-eight years ago.

I would learn during the coming months that someone saying, "Catherine is one of our girls" would always bring smiles of delight, hugs, and knowing nods. Apparently, attendance at Holy Angels gave one a lifetime membership in the society of those who belong. To think—all those years I had been "one of them," and I didn't even know it.

Before I left, Sister Joanne pressed a heavy book into my hand. "Hot off the press," she said. I looked down at the cover. A picture of the bluff, the cross, a tree that no longer stood there. *Evergreen Land: A History of the Dominican Sisters of Edmonds, Washington.*

"The story of our order is such an inspiration. I know that people like to talk; they think the religious orders are dying. But we've never felt so inspired, so invigorated by our mission. Everyone's fixated on the visible signs. I know a lot of people would prefer if we were still encased in our old habits. They see that we look like everyone else, so they assume we *are* like everyone else. I think they miss the point. We've closed some of the convents now, and our sisters are living more on their own, in apartments. And now this property is in jeopardy. But I think we should look at it this way: What is passing away is the settled, stable way we lived for a few decades. But our order, our founders, were not the least bit staid and stable. They were itinerants—which is, of course, the Dominican way. The women who founded our branch of the Dominicans were pioneers, just as we are today. Read this book. You'll see."

On the long flight back to New York, that's just what I did.

New York City
— 1853

It was a hot, humid morning in late August when the *Germania* sailed into the Port of New York and deposited its 216 bedraggled passengers ashore. Among them were four women, swathed in the heavy black traveling habits of the Dominican order. Huddled together near the midship departure deck, they looked over the bustling crowds moving on the docks below. They had just completed a four-week journey from their home in Ratisbon, Germany (which is now called Regensburg), responding to the need of a burgeoning German-American community. Like most of the newly arrived German immigrants, the four nuns spoke no English.

Months earlier, Dom Wimmer, a Benedictine monk who had years before left Germany and found an abbey in Pennsylvania, had visited the four nuns' convent in Ratisbon. He had appealed to the Mother Superior to send help to the New World. The German Catholic community was in desperate need of teachers for the schools they had just built. Dom Wimmer had painted a picture of a well-established church, a large and supportive community, and a new convent empty and at the ready. He promised to be at the dock to meet the arrival of the *Germania*.

Now the four women stood on the busy dock, surrounded by their modest luggage, and looked around. They grew increasingly nervous. Where was Dom Wimmer? The hours passed as they waited on the dock. Still, there was no sign of their American sponsor.

Hungry, thirsty, sweaty, and exhausted, the sisters finally took matters into their own hands. They had been stood up on one of the most important dates of their lives, but they were undaunted. They stopped a policeman, who took them to a priest, who found someone who spoke German. It turned out that Dom Wimmer had assigned the task of greeting them to a Benedictine priest in Newark, New Jersey, and he had forgotten. So much for the joyous arrival of the new workers in God's American vineyard.

It was an inauspicious beginning, to say the least, and things only grew worse. The Dominicans learned that they would be assigned to a parish on Long Island, New York, and would live under the control of the local parish priests. It was decided that the two choir nuns, who were well educated, would be put to work teaching 140 students in a Catholic school for girls on Long Island. The lay sisters would cook and clean for the priests.

The sisters were treated little better than indentured servants— totally at the mercy of the churchmen who sponsored them. It was immediately clear that no one had prepared for their arrival or given a thought to the facilities that would be needed to house them. Their first "convent" was a dank unfinished basement in the priest's rectory—little more than a glorified crawl space, with a low ceiling and a dirt floor. It was impossible to keep cloister in such a small space; spiritual starvation was added to physical deprivation. During their first winter in America, bitter winds whistled through the cracks in their convent hovel; rain and snow kept the floor muddy and the surfaces damp. Often the sisters would wake in the morning to find their beds covered with a blanket of snow. It didn't stop the work, however.

The German Catholic families in the area were so delighted to have the sisters teaching in the school that an additional one hundred students were enrolled within the first six months after their arrival. In the spirit of obedience and sacrifice, the two choir nuns accepted the daunting task of teaching 240 children. Such a task is an almost unthinkable burden by the standards we enjoy today.

It was miraculous that these four women were able to plant a seed of such tenacity in their new environment that it would grow into a vast tree of thriving communities. Perhaps it was typical of the fervent missionary spirit that the religious orders brought to this country. Imagine if these Dominican nuns, their Benedictine counterparts, the Holy Names Sisters, or any others had remained mired in expectation and rigidity when improvisation and flexibility were the only ways to accomplish the task of building the foundation of the church in the New World.

At least these first missionaries had the familiarity of the known. Customs and practices were still based on familiar European ways. The German-American community continued to grow at a startling pace. By the 1880s, there were more than 5 million German immigrants living in the eastern United States.

But perhaps the truest pioneers were those who agreed to go west, expanding the order's mission to a rugged, barely civilized unknown. On an August morning in 1890, seven young nuns— the eldest being thirty-one, and only one born in the United States—donned their black traveling clothes and boarded a train heading toward Washington State. Not only would they enter unfamiliar land; they would also be asked to take on a new mission—building and staffing a hospital in Aberdeen, an outpost south of Seattle, to treat the loggers and their families. Two of the sisters, trained as teachers, would also staff a school.

As the train crossed the rugged Rocky Mountains and continued on through the breathtakingly lush green lands of Idaho, the sisters must have thought they were seeing visions. There were few places on earth as beautiful as this evergreen land. But as they traveled deeper into Washington State, they passed stretches of devastated forest. Where trees once stood, there were only stumps and mountains of waste. The nauseating stench of smoking lumber mills fouled the air.

Aberdeen was not anything like the lush picture of scented evergreens, sparkling lakes, and majestic mountain peaks they had expected. As the sisters rode the last leg of their journey by steamboat down the murky Chehalis River, they passed miles of stripped land. Aberdeen itself was an ugly town, choked with smoking mills and built on oozing, smelly tidal flats. Their little convent, set atop pilings to prevent flooding from the constantly overflowing flats, was a better accommodation than had been provided for the first sisters who came to New York from Germany. Still, it was a poor dwelling, and the work was hard. Within two weeks of their arrival, the sisters had opened both a rudimentary hospital and a school.

As I read, I realized that the description of the Dominican sisters' early life in the Northwest would easily lay to rest any notions that they were taken care of by the Mother Church. Even as the growing archdiocese placed increasing demands on the sisters to build and staff more hospitals and schools, it was up to the nuns themselves to raise the money. In fact, two nuns were assigned the role of beggars to raise money to support the community. Alms gathering was a mendicant tradition in Europe, and it was adopted in the United States, as well.

Riding on horseback along trails that wove through the deep

forests and rocky land of rural Washington State, the hardy pair of beggar nuns were as tenacious and courageous as Annie Oakley— and their dress was far more limiting. Bears, wolves, and mountain lions often appeared in their path—as did wild, uncouth, and often drunken loggers who hadn't seen a woman in months. The sisters always managed to sidestep any unwelcome approaches, and, in fact, they often shamed the rambunctious louts into giving alms.

Now I was beginning to understand what Sister Joanne had been trying to tell me. They hadn't abandoned their mission *or* their calling. The struggles they faced today, with dwindling members, limited resources, and threatened property, had nothing to do with the strength of the order. The order wasn't dying. They were shedding what they'd never really needed. They were returning to their raison d'être—the core of their purpose.

I thought suddenly of a passage from Nikos Kazantzakis's *The Saviors of God,* one of my favorite books:

> *What is the value of subduing the earth,*
> *The waters, the air, of conquering space and time,*
> *Of understanding what laws govern the mirages*
> *That rise from the burning deserts of the mind?*
> *Never acknowledge the limitations of man*
> *Smash all boundaries! Deny whatever your eyes see.*
> *Die every moment, but say:*
> *"Death does not exist."*

When I arrived back in New York, Paul hugged me to him and teased me, saying, "So, Sister, have I lost you to the nuns yet?"

I shook my head. "You're behind the times, buddy. Women aren't lost to the nuns anymore. They get *found* by them."

Before I left Seattle, I had placed an ad in the *Seattle Northwest Progress,* looking for former Dominicans. I'd been home two weeks when I received an E-mail message:

Would you by chance be the Catherine Schuler who graduated from Holy Angels, in Ballard, in the late 1960s? The Catherine Schuler who was a friend of Bernadette and who wanted to be a writer? If so, you will (I hope) remember me as Sister Carmen, the music teacher. I can also tell you how to get in touch with Sister Elizabeth. Do you remember her? I think she taught senior English. Also how to reach Sister Barbara, and a couple of others.

As simple as that. It was all coming together.

10

Tomorrow Land

Rosary Heights

—APRIL 1997

"YOU'RE WHAT? YOU'RE KIDDING, RIGHT?"

Whenever anyone learned that I was going to a convent, the most common response was envy. You'd think I'd scored the proverbial jackpot. "I wish *I* could get away and spend time in a convent," they'd say, sighing. "I could use the rest." Almost everyone I know is, like me, totally enveloped in personal and professional whirlwinds. My friends are busy, slightly harried, and completely overextended. The most treasured commodity in their lives are the slices of time they are able to hack out for themselves and those they love.

My friends weren't just jealous, though. They were also curious—almost urgently so. Believers and nonbelievers alike, they felt

that there was a rare and undiscovered world that existed in convents, an untouched glimpse into a sort of nirvana. Everyone
wanted to know the secrets of life behind the walls of a religious
order. It was as if by intimately exploring who these women *really*
were—why they would wish to be nuns in this day and age—I
might encounter a new revelation for all who struggle with uncertainty in these careworn times. In our minds, their vocation
seemed to immunize them from the everyday malaise of life. They
seemed inured to depression, the pain of failure, rejection, and the
ugly aftermath of the pursuit of wealth, power, or fame. They were
free from the sharp claws of jealousy and desire, as well as the many
other demons that hound most of us.

There has been a tremendous resurgence of interest concerning matters of faith and belief. Society's quest for spiritual renewal
has emerged from an overwhelming sense that something is missing in our lives—a void exists in which privilege provides no com-
pensation. But generations have been left without a context in
which to place belief—the products of uncertain and quixotic
spiritual searches. The search for higher meaning has too often
been sidetracked by the insistent demands of everyday needs. What
did the sisters know that we didn't? Was the image that appeared
to them when they looked into a mirror the same as the image that
appeared to us? What had they learned? What was it that they
desired? What provided them such a deep source of satisfaction
that they were able to sublimate the common human desires that
drove the rest of us?

How many times had I wondered, How can a woman born in
these times take a vow of chastity? What excitement, what pleasure can be found in living in a community of women, most of
them gray with age? It wasn't just the vow of chastity I pondered
and marveled at; it was also the individual obligation that each of
the sisters assumed. At least the majority of relationships, beyond
family, contain an element of choice. But in a religious order, you
are forced to live with a disparate group brought together to form

a religious community. Whether you wish to or not, you have to see their faces every day. Natural human emotions—anger, frustration, disappointment, and the simple possibility of poor chemistry—don't just disappear because you have chosen the religious life. It will be a never-ending struggle to keep your annoyances in check and remain focused on the higher calling.

Taking a vow of poverty didn't trouble me too much. I hadn't grown up in a wealthy family and I'd spent most of my life living on next to nothing. Obedience was a big problem, though. I bridled at the concept of obedience, not that I wasn't an obedient person—in my own way. But obedience on my own terms seemed a far cry from a *vow* of obedience.

And then there was this undeniable reality: What had happened to this order of women? Why had new applicants become so rare? Their ranks were dwindling; their age averaged out to about fifty-five years old. Sister Joanne's face, so filled with joy and clarity, her incredible energy—what was that about? How did she keep going as she did—her spirits so high, her convictions so unshakable—with the members of her order aging and dying out? The formerly indomitable order of sisters at Rosary Heights gave every appearance of being at the end of something rather than at the beginning.

I tried to pack my questions, biases, and suspicions neatly into my suitcase, along with my trusty tape recorder. Perhaps in the fresh springtime beauty of Rosary Heights, I would have a chance to sort everything out.

However, any thoughts I entertained that my stay would be a gentle retreat from the cares of the world were quickly shattered upon my arrival. Sister Joanne, the soul of efficiency and organization, handed me a sheaf of papers that detailed the complete itinerary of my stay. It had been decided that I would be put to work. These were busy women. As lovely as Rosary Heights was, they didn't just sit around staring out at the mountains and fingering their rosary beads. Every sister's day was packed with service. The

Dominicans, I was gently reminded, had been called to be the foot-washing community. They were responsible for their brothers and sisters—for soothing the suffering of humanity.

As a former master general of the Dominicans was fond of saying, "To be a true Dominican, you need to pray with the newspaper in one hand and the Scriptures in the other." It was a far cry from the days when sisters had to sneak peeks at the newspapers that lined the garbage pails to get a little news.

In an effort to make my time with them fruitful, Sister Joanne had arranged for me to do quite a bit of traveling to the various missions. First, I'd be driving south, to Chehalis, then north to Everett, and even farther north after that to the Arlington area, where I'd spent months working with Elizabeth and Celestine, teaching catechism to the Native American children. I'd also share in the work of the prison ministry, as well as feeding the homeless. I'd get a taste of life at the Intercommunity Center, whose goal was housing and services for the poor, and talk to sisters who had recently returned from missions in Poland, Mexico, and Haiti. And that was just the beginning. In the course of my stay, Sister Joanne hoped to introduce me to most of the sisters in the order, including more than two dozen at a Dominican retirement center in Seattle.

"You'll enjoy talking to our retired sisters," Sister Joanne assured me. "They'll regale you with stories of the wild old days. Oh, by the way, do you remember Sister Claire? She's moved into our retirement home recently. She's looking forward to talking to you. She remembers you from Holy Angels."

"I remember her, as well," I politely replied. Of course she remembers me, I thought wryly. Who doesn't? And how could I forget *her*?

Sister Joanne's brow suddenly furrowed with concern. "Oh dear," she said, "I hope I haven't packed the schedule too tightly. It's just that we've spread out so much, and I wanted you to see everything. There'll be time for you to stay here with us, too, so you can experience our community."

My head was buzzing, but of course I expressed my delight. I'd come here to learn about their life, after all.

Sister Joanne led me across the cobblestone walkway to the carriage house, where I would be staying. My room was small and simple—a nun's room. It contained a bed and a desk, with an old-fashioned sink and towel rack in one corner. A large window faced north onto the familiar forest I'd strolled in my youth. I still remembered feeling dwarfed by the huge evergreens, hearing nothing but light wind, chirping birds, and the rustling of squirrels as they raced from limb to limb. It finally came to me that my senior-year retreat had been in April 1968. It had been almost exactly twenty-nine years since I'd leaned back against one of those trees and wished that I could stay forever. Twenty-nine years and a lifetime since I'd sat on a bench with Bernadette and Tracy and sensed that nothing would ever be the same, that a magical time was coming to an end.

I rose early my first morning in the convent. The sun was just beginning to send waves of light from the east. As quietly as possible, I tiptoed into the large bathroom next to my room and took a shower. I felt shy about making my presence known. It would take me awhile to feel at home.

Sister Joanne had told me to come over to the main house and join the sisters in the kitchen for an informal breakfast whenever I was ready in the morning. I walked across the cobblestones in the dewy dawn and used my key to let myself in the back door. Two of the sisters were already sitting at the table, eating hot oatmeal. One was Sister Hilary. The other introduced herself to me as Sister Martha. Both were wearing bathrobes. Sister Martha was a sweet-faced older woman, with pale, almost translucent skin. I had learned from Sister Joanne that she suffered from non-Hodgkin's lymphoma, but when she greeted me, her face was full of good humor.

I poured myself a cup of coffee and sat down with them.

"Catherine is one of our girls," Sister Hilary explained to Sister Martha.

"Ah!" She nodded, as if all were explained. I started to describe my reason for being there. By then, I'd developed a regular little speech.

"You're just having coffee?" Sister Martha interrupted me. "You should eat. Let me fix you a bowl of cereal."

"No, no, coffee is fine."

Sister Magdalene and Sister Helen drifted into the kitchen and started preparing food. Sister Helen sat down beside me. Sister Magdalene, dressed in a business suit, stopped to remind me that I was going to work with her that morning and said she'd be back for me at eight. Then she hurried out of the kitchen, carrying her coffee cup.

There was a quality about Sister Helen that was fresh and appealing. Also intelligent—but she didn't give much away in her face. She was a native Washingtonian, born in Everett and raised in Hoquiam, where her family was in the logging business. In high school, she'd been one of the last boarders at Holy Angels—another one of "our girls," and she joined the order in 1960. She was fifty-five, but she looked at least ten years younger. She was such a quiet, thoughtful, unassuming woman, it was hard to get my mind around the fact that she was, in effect, the prioress of the order.

Sister Joanne came hurrying into the kitchen, ebullient as ever. She looked horrified when she saw my cup of coffee. "Where's your breakfast? You must have breakfast." I again declined, but she wouldn't hear of it. "At least have some orange juice and a couple of slices of toast." Sister Hilary, finishing her last spoonful of oatmeal, was frowning slightly. "You must eat your breakfast," she said.

Yes, Mother, I thought, feeling the strange but familiar tug of obedience. I'm in the convent now. I can no longer do whatever I wish to.

A large glass of orange juice and a platter of toast was put before me, along with a bowl of jam and a dish of butter. I never eat breakfast, especially at dawn. But as I sipped my juice and nibbled at my toast, I remembered a nun once telling me that the rule of obedience included the dictate that you must eat everything on your plate at every meal. You were not permitted to demur, even if you weren't hungry, or hated what was being served. You also weren't allowed to fast, unless the community decided to fast. That was just a small example of the vow of obedience, setting aside your personal preferences and partaking in the life of the community.

At eight o'clock, I found Sister Magdalene in the parking lot and accompanied her to work.

Sister Magdalene was familiar to me; I'd known a lot of women like her. She was sharp, no-nonsense, and direct. An executive, she was the director of the volunteer program at the Intercommunity Center, which was located in the heart of downtown Seattle. The Intercommunity Ministry had been established in 1994 as a collaborative effort of several communities of religious orders, including the Edmonds Dominicans, the Sisters of the Holy Names, the Sisters of Providence, the Tacoma Dominicans, and the Sisters of Saint Joseph of Peace. The ministry's basic mission was to recruit secular volunteers from the community to work with the sisters in service to the poor. The Intercommunity Ministry included a well-developed housing program for the poor and handicapped, services for AIDS patients and their children, an organization of food and clothing banks, work in Native American communities, and programs to assist migrant workers. Sister Magdalene explained that the ministry was *in* the archdiocese but not *of* the archdiocese. I took this to mean—not necessarily correctly—that the archdiocese didn't contribute to the Intercommunity Ministry but was happy to take credit for its accomplishments.

"I'm sorry if I seemed a bit abrupt this morning," Sister Magdalene said as we swung onto the freeway. "Mornings are usually a time of silence for me. I use it for prayer."

"I wondered when any of you ever has time to pray," I said. "All of you seem to be constantly on the run."

Sister Magdalene let out a long sigh, then smiled at me. "We *are* constantly on the run. It's true. It was much easier in the old days when we were cloistered together. We'd rise early in the morning and have prayer time together. Then we'd go to school together, teach, and go home. We were allowed to talk for an hour, then take time for prayer and study. We'd pray together again, have dinner, and be in our beds by nine o'clock at night. We didn't realize how relatively easy it was then. But now we're all so busy. Sisters running here and going there, with hardly a moment for us all to be together. Sometimes you wonder what keeps us in tune with the fact that we're still a part of a community. We spend so much time on our own that there are days when I have to stop for a second and remind myself to think about the community first. Not that you ever forget, but a lot of times you just feel like you're on your own."

Exactly. That was my question. "So what *does* keep the community together?"

"Prayer," she answered, "keeps us together. Personal prayer as well as communal prayer. We pray together as a community every night before dinner, and the rest of our prayer time is on our own. I couldn't do my work without it. Prayer allows me to have some kind of center. Like my first cup of coffee in the morning. I have a cup of coffee in complete silence before I begin my formal meditation and prayer. It's a little ritual of my own that I use to prepare. Every morning, I focus for a half an hour on centering my thoughts and breathing. I try to remain perfectly still and not allow any destructive thoughts, any negatives, to creep in. I've been doing it for fifteen years and I'm not quite there yet. But I'm working on it."

"That kind of meditation has always been hard for me," I admitted. "Emptying yourself must be so difficult."

"Well, emptying yourself for the sake of being empty leads to only one condition—emptiness. But emptying yourself to become a channel for God's greatness means that you find yourself finally full." She smiled. "I know. It sounds like Buddhism, like a Zen koan, and I admit I've been influenced by those teachings. But basically, it's just good old-fashioned prayer, and it's the only way I've stopped myself from becoming an obsessed workaholic and burning out."

Magdalene's office was an unimposing square building on the

edge of skid row in downtown Seattle. To the west, the deep mewling of ships' foghorns blared along the docks. The monolithic skyscrapers that had been punched into the sky at the center of Seattle's business district were alight with furious activity.

Inside, Sister Magdalene introduced me to the staff and told them about the book I was writing. One of the young men looked up from his desk with interest. "So, are you learning a lot?" he asked.

"I'm learning that the sisters have taken on a tremendous amount of the work that we usually think is being handled by the archdiocese," I said. "It's odd. I'll bet when most people think of the church, they think of the male religious—the Pope, the cardinals, the bishops, the priests. But I haven't seen a single priest around since I've been here. I don't get it."

"I'll tell you a secret," he said, leaning in conspiratorially. "The men of the church have *authority,* and the women of the church have *faith.* That's how it looks to me anyway."

In the course of the morning, Sister Magdalene fielded dozens of phone calls and spent a good deal of her time cajoling potential volunteers or pumping up those who had become discouraged. When not interrupted by emergencies and personnel crises, she clicked away at her computer, writing fund-raising letters. Her office was just like any other—buzzing with activity, the in baskets piled high next to almost empty out baskets. But there was also a sense of overwhelming responsibility, of genuine caring, hanging in the air. And there was something very different about this office: The constant state of anxiety that seemed to line the faces of most working people was absent here.

I mentioned this to Sister Magdalene. "You can see from the attitudes of your staff that something different is going on here. People are hassled, but no one's uptight. Whoever learns that I'm working on this book gets instantly excited by it. Everyone's very interested. They think nuns have some incredible secret. The perception is that you don't suffer from the stress that other people do."

"Maybe our spirituality provides some protection," she

responded thoughtfully, "but the stress is there nevertheless. Our country's changed in the last couple of decades. Government funding is being cut. The welfare system has been dismantled. Even food-stamp allocations are being cut. People are hungry, scared, worried. There are new people on our doorsteps every day. Kids are going hungry. They aren't getting free breakfasts or lunch; they're not getting their shots at school anymore. It's a tragedy and a disgrace. Poor children and desperate parents aren't going to go away. There will be more tomorrow. What are we supposed to do? Ignore them? It's an invitation for stress. But that's where prayer comes in. I think that when Jesus walked the earth, he showed us how to handle it. I don't think we've ever quite been able to achieve what he wanted. I do know that we sometimes fall into this Messiah complex. We so much want to believe that we can change the world overnight. We have to constantly remind ourselves that even Jesus took time to pray and restore himself spiritually."

"Prayer restores your sense of faith, but what about the harsh realities that you deal with day in and day out?" I retorted. "The majority of people are able to find some kind of satisfaction, some meaning in what they do. It sounds like you're fighting a last-ditch battle for people who've been shunted aside. If you're unable to accomplish your goals for this ministry because the programs that once helped to support your work are gone, and if the government agencies do nothing to help you, what are you left with? You really can't win, can you?"

Again, Sister Magdalene sat back and regarded me with her quiet air. An executive with a computer screen flashing behind her, she was unabashedly discussing the meaning of prayer, the meaning of faith. "Well, I think John the Baptist was the model. To prepare the way, you do what you need to do. Being center stage, receiving accolades and encouragement, being slapped on the back, or getting bonuses makes you feel good. It's probably a real morale booster. But that kind of acclaim isn't what we're about."

As Sister spoke, I realized that she was revealing a kernel of *the secret* in what she was saying—the sense of meaning so many longed for beyond the trappings of worldly success.

"So what do you believe your mission is supposed to be?"

"Obedience," she instantly replied. It seemed a strange answer.

"Do you mean obedience to the church? Or to the archdiocese?" Here we were at one of the concepts that gave me a problem—the question of obedience. Did the sisters break their backs at the pleasure of the archdiocese?

Sister Magdalene thought my question was quite funny. "No, no, no," she said, waving a dismissive hand. "I'm talking about the true meaning of obedience. It comes from the Latin word *obediens,* which means 'to listen.' God speaks to us through our bodies, through ideas; God deals with us as we are. Obedience isn't about mindlessly following orders. It's about listening to the right voice."

"Does the archbishop represent the right voice?" I asked, hoping to finally understand the logic of religious obedience.

"There has been a breakdown in communication, some sense of discomfort among the hierarchy of the church," she carefully said. "The hierarchy is not as involved in the community as we wish it would be. The archbishop should be consulting with us more. Not only are we an incredible resource but we know what's really going on out there. He should at least use us as a sounding board. We listen to the people; we understand their worries and fears. But the archbishop feels threatened somehow, I think. He's a truly wonderful man, but he still feels threatened."

"I guess it's up to the women," I said.

Sister Magdalene laughed. "Well, it's the women ultimately who are doing the work of the church. The women—not just religious but laywomen, too—are running the mission. When you think about it, it's always been women who've been in the muck and mire. From the start, we've always been the hands of the church. Maybe it's because women are more accustomed to dealing with community and collaboration. The church spent centuries keeping us from positions of authority. Maybe because of that, we're more able to deal with challenges to any authority we may have. Our relationship to one another—sister to sister—is like a circle. I know what I'm doing here, and if one of my sisters can do it better, she's welcome to my chair. Let her take this mission and run with it. I would want her to do well. I'd help her if I could. I wouldn't be the least bit threatened by someone else's success. Those who've given themselves to God needn't compete with one another. Believe me, Catherine, there's enough need to go around. There's plenty of room for all of us."

You couldn't ask for a more purely meditative environment than Rosary Heights in the spring: the air scrubbed clean by April showers, the flowers blossoming; the fat honeybees lumbering from petal to petal, gathering the sweet nectar of their annual ritual. I could hear the faint crash of the waves against the shore far below, the cawing of seagulls slowly gliding overhead. When the ground became dry enough—maybe in June—civil engineers and excavating crews would come to try to shore up the crumbling hillside. No one was certain whether they'd be successful. After all, what methods could be employed, what materials used, to support the weight of a mountain?

I was trying to take advantage of what little quiet time I had to reflect on what I'd been seeing and hearing. It was, as always, a struggle. Meditation had always been a slippery slope for me. It had always tantalized me, seeming to exist just beyond my grasp. Even in the days when I was attending Mass regularly and was swathed in the sound of choir bells and the smoke of incense, meditative prayer eluded me. I remember kneeling in a pew after receiving Communion, trying so hard to let the Holy Spirit carry me away to some other plane. In the Catholic church, the Eucharist is more than just a symbol. When the priest blesses the Host, a miracle occurs, which is known as transubstantiation. The Host is no longer a piece of bread. It *becomes* Christ's body. When you take the Host, you are, quite literally, taking Jesus Christ—and for a time he is there, dwelling inside you. For all those years when I devoutly believed this was true, I would kneel, close my eyes, and try hard to blot out everything but the presence of Jesus. He was there inside of me. I wasn't searching for understanding. I knew better than that. Transubstantiation is a great mystery. It's beyond understanding. But I was searching for some small rustle in my heart that would tell me he was really there. The mystery of faith was always my crisis of faith.

I couldn't bring myself to ask any of the nuns whether they really believed that Jesus was there—in the Host, in their hearts, in the sky, at the right hand of the Father. Did you have to believe in a personal Jesus to be a Catholic? And did you have to believe it to be a nun? When you prayed, was it to a person, or was it to a universal force? When you lay on your deathbed, did you feel peace, knowing that God was coming to take you after your life of toil?

I recalled an incident when my son, Paul, was eight years old. For some reason, he was desperately fixated on death and the afterlife. There were no ready answers in our household, no fixed certainties. We had chosen to raise our child with a secular ethic, not a rigid dogma.

One night, Paul shook me awake at 2:00 A.M., very agitated.

"I can't sleep," he cried. "I'm too worried about death."

I rubbed the sleep out of my eyes and dragged myself out of bed. I couldn't understand what he was talking about. "Oh, you had a bad dream," I murmured consolingly.

"No," he insisted. "I was *thinking*."

I got out of bed and sat with him in the living room. There was no specific trigger for this anxiety. There had been no deaths in our family. But he was very upset.

"Do you go somewhere after death, or do you just die and that's it?" he asked urgently.

I hedged. "Well, some people believe there is life after death."

"But Mom, do *you* believe it?"

I told him yes, not knowing whether I actually believed it or not. My answer wasn't very convincing, though. He grabbed my arm. "Can you *prove* it? Can anyone *prove* it?"

I shook my head no. "You have to have faith," I said, and he got very upset. "Oh, no, oh, no," he cried. "You can't prove it. You can't prove it."

Paul's crisis lasted several days. He worried and fretted and tossed in his sleep. There wasn't anything I could do. I had failed the ultimate test—been unable to give him the final comfort, the proof that there was eternal life. It made me sad. When I was his age, I was surrounded by the spirit of belief. There was never a single doubt in my mind that God and heaven really existed. I never spent a single sleepless night worrying about whether there was an afterlife. I had the consoling force of certainty all around me. It was written in the catechism, and it was burned into my consciousness:

> Why did God make me?
> God made me to share His goodness and to make
>   me happy with Him in heaven.

It was just as simple as that. I could say it's easy to have faith when you're a young child, before you're really able to think and reason. But as an adult, to have that kind of faith—well, I couldn't comprehend that.

Sister Louise had lost her faith only once, she told me later that day. I was chatting with her in her office at a Seattle Catholic school, and she was telling me about her greatest vocational crisis. It was in the early eighties, when it seemed as though the order was barely surviving a devastating plague. The frequent sight of friends and colleagues, her young peers, with suitcases packed, standing at the door. Leaving. When her best friend, Mary Anne—the bright, beaming, reliable sister, the one she knew the best and trusted the most—had told her she was leaving, it was the saddest day of her life.

Louise steeled herself against her fears and fought her despair for as long as she could. But it wasn't just all the young sisters leaving; the older ones were leaving in their own fashion. The funerals started to eat away at her. During that period, there were a number of funerals. The younger sisters were always assigned to carry the coffins. Because they didn't have male pallbearers, it was necessary for the sisters to carry the coffins. Time and again, Louise hefted her side of the plain wooden coffin and walked it slowly across the cemetery lawn, helping to arrange it finally in the burial plot. The coffins were crude and inexpensive—made of the roughest pine. The handles fitted underneath were unfinished, and they would dig into Louise's hands, depositing sharp splinters and leaving purple bruises. The funerals always made her want to cry. It was a very moving experience to carry your own dead. But carrying coffins became a symbol to Louise. A reminder. Was there any hope? Was there any future for the order? Was she going to spend the rest of her life carrying coffins, picking splinters out of her hands? And who would be left to carry *her* coffin when her time came?

Another sister said one day, as if reading her thoughts, "Do you think we'll burn out first, or are we just going to rust out?"

The problem was, Sister Louise loved the order. She loved her assignment as director of sister formation, arranging for the training and education of the sisters. This was the new face of the Dominican order—women like Louise. She had her master's degree, was well traveled and well schooled. She was the cream of the crop of modern women. The women of the order no longer kept custody of their eyes; they kept custody of an idea. Now their eyes were wide open—they observed everything and acted on what they saw.

But Sister Louise was burning out. She knew if she didn't get help, she would either *rust* out—become one of those closed-off, bitter old nuns who lived in the empty chapel of her mind—or she would catch fire and explode.

Until fairly recently, the order would have scoffed at the idea that a nun who was suffering this way needed something outside the confines of the rule. Keep the rule and the rule will keep you. When the demons threaten your fortress, pray. When you can't shake the despair, have faith and carry on. But times had changed. The congregation understood—if one of the sisters needed some help, she would get it. So Sister Louise was sent on a sabbatical to a center in Spokane, designed for sisters who were having a hard time.

She spent her sabbatical doing individual therapy, group therapy—focusing on personal growth. She studied ballet, art, and time management. She learned—for the first time—healthy communication skills.

For the first three months, she couldn't shake the guilt. What was she doing here? Was she a freak? She was young; why wasn't she working, making a contribution to the order? In time, she realized that she had to do this for the sake of the order. She had to replenish herself or she would have nothing left to give.

Sister Louise had to learn again how to be still. When she had entered the order in 1967, there was a strong belief in the dangers of doing nothing. "Idle hands are the devil's workshop," the novice mistress used to say. She remembered how the young sisters had dreaded "recreation and change" vacations, because even then they had to look busy all the time. If you didn't, something would be found for you to do. There was never any time just to sit and think. Perhaps they were afraid that if you had too much time for introspection, you'd decide you didn't belong there.

Her time away was of great value to Louise. When she returned, she was able to make a real contribution. The cobwebs had been cleared from her mind, the confidence returned to her step.

She was more at peace with the direction of the order. She decided, It's God's problem. If God wants this order to succeed, it will—and in ways we might not even guess at yet.

The Feast of Saint Catherine of Siena
— April 29

Sister Joanne and I were speeding up Interstate 5 in a steady rain. She was at the wheel of a black 1985 Ford sedan on a three-lane highway, cruising at seventy-five miles per hour. Far too fast for the weather conditions and traffic. We had been driving in concentrated silence for about ten minutes when she turned to me and confided, "I just learned to drive last year." I looked at her with surprise and dread. She was handling the wheel with practiced ease, but one never knew whether a driver's style was born of training or feckless audacity. Fearless confidence and ignorant fearlessness can both find homes in the same being.

"All the years I wasted. I was always afraid to drive," she mused. "For the most part, I never needed to. But once I was elected to the Leadership Council, I needed to get around a bit more. A former student gave me driving lessons as a gift." She chuckled gleefully. "You should have seen me. The first few times I went driving with the instructor, he was as white as a ghost. I think my lessons were more like suicide missions! I learned, though. I wasn't a natural, by any means. But I haven't killed anyone yet, either. So I'm proud of myself."

I double-checked to make sure my seat belt was securely fastened, then gave myself over to a higher power. I decided not to worry about Sister Joanne's driving skills. I had already placed my life in her hands. I wanted to talk.

"How did you know that you had a calling?" I asked bluntly.

Joanne smiled happily, trying to recollect. I found myself once again marveling at the satisfaction and peace she radiated. She was about as far as one could imagine from the stereotype of a neurotic or sexually repressed woman. Extremely feminine, she glowed with an unaffected womanliness. She was just Joanne, a woman at ease with her choice in life.

As we drove along the highway, enormous logging trucks speeding past, lifting and depositing torrents of water onto our windshield, Joanne told me the story of the moment she knew that she had a calling. It sounded as though it was straight out of a Hollywood script, but I could tell it was true and heartfelt.

Joanne had always loved the nuns. But her fascination wasn't of the crush variety, the youthful infatuation customarily expected of certain high school girls. Joanne wasn't given to flights of fancy. She'd been rough-hewn by the natural practicality of her Canadian parents. She was grounded in the world, and close to the earth.

Joanne had been taught that God's presence was inlaid in the rough terrain and mountainous peaks of her homeland, the trees and lakes surrounding her. She had never thought of a religious calling as being separate from the world. A calling was part of a promise to care for it, to protect it and love it, take it in your arms as you would a tiny infant and nurture it.

Joanne was the last person anyone would have thought would be attracted to a religious vocation. The girls that God called always seemed to be cut from a special mold. They were more serious and more circumspect than everyone else. But Joanne was a cutup, irreverent and flirtatious. She didn't go to church every day. She had a boyfriend. She was planning to attend college after her high school graduation.

But something happened, something she couldn't explain to anyone. She didn't mention it to her parents, or to the boy she'd been seeing. She sensed that she was waiting for something. She hesitated in applying to different schools. She spent time alone, walking in the woods, trying to catch the faint sound she heard echoing in a deep crevice of her unconscious. Almost without thinking, she began to look into religious orders. She didn't really think she'd consider joining one, but she felt compelled to find out what they were about. She kept telling herself she was merely curious. What harm could it do?

One of the orders she approached was the Sisters of Saint Dominic of the Holy Cross, in Edmonds, Washington. She was invited to visit for a weekend to see the way they lived.

Joanne was instantly taken with Rosary Heights. It was beautiful, tranquil, full of grace. Her two-day stay was an encounter with everything she imagined religious life would be. It was a moving experience, with midnight prayer services, simple food, open, scintillating conversation, and plenty of solitary time to walk and meditate. And the joy of the women, the good humor she discovered among them! Joanne had feared that religious orders bore an overlay of grim sanctity, but the sisters here were so real and warm.

In the background, there were always many white-clad

novices—at least twenty of them—silently going about their routine. She was not allowed to speak to them, nor they to her, but she caught a twitch of smile now and then, a subtle wink. Ah, come on, they seemed to be saying. We see that light in your eyes. It was very dreamlike. Ordinary life as she knew it seemed thousands of miles away. Joanne felt a strange sensation. All the cares and expectations of the real world disappeared, and in the quiet peace that remained was a deep pool of pure joy. And then the thought entered her head like a whisper. This is the place. But she wasn't sure. When she spoke with one of the older sisters about her uncertainty, Sister's response was a gentle smile as she said, "Many are called, but few are chosen."

Joanne asked for a further explanation. The sister said that God called many to his service but that not everyone who was called listened and responded. The few who did were the chosen. She told Joanne that there was nothing to be afraid of. The most important element of a true vocation was free will. "Remember," she said, "God is not a kidnapper who steals young women in the night. He is a kind Father who extends a precious invitation."

Joanne careened off Interstate 5 and we began driving west. The roads were small and winding. We roared past green farmlands and pastures dotted with grazing cows and horses. At one point, we passed a huge field covered with a solid blanket of yellow tulips. It seemed to stretch beyond the horizon, and it was one of the prettiest sights I'd ever seen. Back in 1969, when I had come to stay with Elizabeth and Celestine, it had been winter. I'd never seen the brilliant colors of spring in this part of Washington before.

We pulled into La Conner and drove through the reservation. Sister Ruth lived right in the center of the reservation, and the mission had been steadily developed since the days when the sisters lived across the water on Camano Island. Her house was a small converted trailer, cozy and welcoming. The walls were covered with Sister Ruth's own paintings—richly textured oils and watercolors evoking natural scenes.

Sister Ruth herself was a quiet woman, part Native American.

When she spoke it was in a thoughtful, low voice. She carried an aura of dignity and reserve common to the Native Americans I'd known.

The plan, I had been told, was to attend Mass on the reservation, then have lunch with Sister Ruth. I had assumed we'd be going to the church, but suddenly a young priest appeared on the doorstep, carrying his Mass bag—chalice, Hosts, and prayer books.

The four of us sat around a little table in Sister Ruth's dining room, and Father Harold laid out his materials.

"Today is the feast of our mother, Catherine of Siena," he began, taking me completely by surprise. I had long since forgotten my patron's feast day. "This is a special Mass in her name."

The Mass, said around that table, was a celebration of a community of faith coming together. It made me think of the stories of early Christians gathering around makeshift tables in dank underground caverns to "eat of his body and drink of his blood"— to break bread and drink wine. I suddenly found it easy to pray to my patron saint, easy to ask Catherine to intercede for me.

Chehalis, Washington

I was looking forward to visiting Chehalis, where one of the first outposts of Dominicans had arrived over a century ago. I had never been to this part of the state—a two-hour drive south from Seattle, through a battered terrain of smoking mills and arid land. I was set to meet Sister Perpetua at Saint Helen's Hospital, in Chehalis, the second hospital to be built by the sisters before the beginning of the century. Saint Helen's was scheduled to close soon, and all the chronic-care patients would be moved to a modern hospital that had just recently been built. The work of the sisters would be completed.

Joanne had told me very little about Sister Perpetua—other than that she had served in the hospital ministry for many years and that she would amaze me. I wondered why the other sisters all smiled knowingly when they heard I was going to visit her.

As I pulled into the parking lot of Saint Helen's Hospital in Chehalis in my rental car, I was two minutes late for our first meeting. A tiny figure wearing a short veil and a plain white dress came bustling toward me across the lot. As she got closer, I saw a withered little face that looked as if a hundred years worth of lines had been penciled in, and sharp, piercing blue-gray eyes so deeply buried that they glistened. The lightly marbled beads threw lightning bolts of intention.

"Sister Perpetua," I said, guessing correctly. I grabbed my briefcase and jumped out of the car. She hardly paused, and I followed in her wake at high speed across the parking lot. "We're late," she said over her shoulder, scurrying forward. "We're due at the church for a funeral."

She pulled open the driver's side door of a massive dark blue Ford. It was covered with splatters of mud and had significant body damage. She climbed in. As she fired up the engine, it dawned on me that she planned to *drive* this car. She motioned me to the passenger's side door and the seat next to her. I fumbled for my seat belt as I shot furtive glances in her direction. Her head rose barely an inch and a half above the steering wheel. She looked for all the world like a little girl trying to see out from the bottom corner of a window. She put the Ford into gear and backed rapidly—too rapidly—out of the parking space. She took her right hand off the wheel, made a quick sign of the cross, and said, "Let us pray. O Lord, keep us safe on our journey, so that we may continue to do thy work. Amen." I replied, "Amen." Oh yeah, I concurred. I nodded silently. We were going only about four blocks, but I felt a sudden renewed fervor. This was a prayer I was glad to say.

I quickly discovered that these prayers were a constant of Sister Perpetua's day. As soon as we pulled up in back of the funeral home, she said another prayer, rejoicing in our safe arrival. "Thank you, Lord, for seeing us safely on our journey." She prayed when we got back into the car—"O Lord, keep us safe on our journey"—and again when we sped back into the hospital parking lot, roared into a space with brakes screeching and tires squealing, and narrowly missed tearing off my side of the Ford with a cement barrier. "Let us pray. O Lord, we praise you for your goodness in allowing us to live another day." I was sitting there with my heart racing furiously, panting and thinking, Another *day*? How about another *minute*?

"Let's eat," Sister Perpetua ordered, leading me into the hospital cafeteria. We got into line with our trays. I chose a prepackaged tuna sandwich and a Coke. Sister Perpetua, barely rising above the bottom window of the food display, selected a piece of cake and a brownie. Not a very good diet, I thought to myself. If this is where she eats most of her meals, she can't even see, much less reach, anything *but* the desserts. But I had a feeling she didn't care much for being sensible. Perhaps she'd reached an age where she ate what she liked rather than what she needed. We found an empty table and sat down.

"Let us pray," she intoned as I started to bite into my sandwich. I dropped it on the plate like a hot potato and bowed my head. "O Lord, we thank you for sending Catherine to us this day. Bless her good work, and this food you see before us. Amen."

"Amen," I responded. I picked up my sandwich and took a bite. Sister Perpetua watched me with her piercing little beads of light. Although I was nearly forty-seven years old, I had that sensation that we all experience occasionally—less and less as the years pass—of feeling somewhat daunted in the face of age and wisdom.

"So," she said, taking a forkful of cake, "you're one of our girls."

"Yes." I was getting used to this.

"Maybe you knew my blood sister. She taught at Saint Alphonsus in the sixties."

"Um, maybe. We didn't know the elementary school teachers too well. What was her name?"

"Sister Celestine."

"*You're* Sister Celestine's blood sister?"

"Yes. She passed away, you know." Her forehead briefly

furrowed and her eyes flashed with pain. "Celestine and I were the only girls in our family, and we both entered the convent. I was the first, and she entered four years later."

"I knew Sister Celestine," I said softly, feeling overcome with regret. I hadn't kept my promise to her that last day, standing at the train station. I was supposed to have called her when I got back to Seattle. "I spent some time with her up in Arlington, when she and Sister Elizabeth were working at the Indian reservation."

Sister Perpetua's face lit up. "You knew Celestine. Elizabeth was such a dear friend to her. She's such a lovely woman. She wrote all the music for the memorial service. It was quite something."

She looked at her watch. "Time to give Communion," she said, finishing the last of her brownie and making the sign of the cross, followed by a short prayer. "Jesus our Lord, thank you for this opportunity to fill our minds and souls as well as our bodies. In your name we pray. Amen."

And we were off. Through the cafeteria, then up on the elevator to the floor devoted to stroke victims. She took a little silver box from her pocket that looked like a makeup compact. It contained preblessed Communion Hosts, which Sister Perpetua distributed to the patients. To be honest, I'd never seen this before. I'd always assumed that the hospital chaplain or a local priest was on hand to distribute the Host. It turned out that it had become a common procedure for the sisters to distribute Communion after a priest had properly blessed a bushel of unleavened Hosts and said, "This is my body." After this first time, I saw it again and again. Now I wondered what the priests were doing if not giving the sacrament. It was supposed to be their highest calling. Perhaps there really weren't enough priests to go around anymore.

Sister Perpetua was all business as she marched into the rooms, snapped off the TVs, and announced, "It's time to receive Our Lord." I hovered in the background and watched the quick little ceremonies. Although many of the stroke patients stared at her with blank eyes when she first walked into the room, when the white Host was offered, a tiny change occurred. As each person took it on his or her tongue, there was a glimmer of recognition and a faint sigh of peace.

In addition to making the hospital rounds with Sister Perpetua, I was to spend some time with Sister Katherine, her housemate, whose mission was to serve a destitute Hispanic community living in a run-down trailer park in Chehalis.

Sister Katherine was the polar opposite of tiny Sister Perpetua. A strapping woman in her mid-sixties with a broad, pleasant face and a windblown pile of blond curls, she greeted me with a booming hello and pumped my hand vigorously. Like every other sister I had met, Sister Katherine looked a good ten to fifteen years younger than her actual age. Her shabby brown station wagon was packed full with clothing in all sizes, big containers of dried milk, sewing supplies, and boxes of language tapes. I squeezed into the front seat, and we sped off toward the trailer park, Sister Katherine keeping up a steady stream of conversation. It turned out that she, too, had a blood sister in the order, a sister I had already met over breakfast at Rosary Heights. Katherine and her sister, Adella, had been professed the same year, in 1948. They were very different women. Adella was soft-spoken, with a quiet, almost mystical, beauty. Her sister, Katherine, was bold and outspoken, wearing her generous heart on her sleeve for all to see.

The trailer park was a grim, sprawling ghetto of dilapidated trailers, muddy flats, and barely habitable conditions. Groups of children were everywhere, splashing through the puddles, playing ball, trying to force the wheels of their old bikes through the unrelenting mud that sucked at the tires and sent them spinning out of control.

"My ministry is with the women," Sister Katherine said bluntly. "Not with the men. I don't work with men."

"Why not?" I asked, taken aback by how forcefully she stated it.

"It's simple," she replied. "In this culture, the men are the heads of the household. They dominate the women. The women have no skills; they can't speak the language—although most of the men have a rudimentary grasp of English. They start having children at a young age, and the cycle of poverty continues. The men are not going to change that. They enjoy their status in the family. They know their women will stay with them and do whatever they want because they have no choice. They could never support themselves or their children alone."

She smiled broadly. "When I started working here, I began with the basics. I taught the women to sew. It was a craft, a skill, something they could use to earn money and be more independent. Some of them have become accomplished seamstresses. Then I added language studies. I have every woman in the place learning to speak English. Their husbands are very suspicious of me, especially since I work only with the women. I try to visit the women when their husbands aren't home, but occasionally one of them will be there. You might see it. He'll immediately try to take over the conversation and make himself the center of my visit. I'll be polite, but I'll try to take his wife into the kitchen, where we can have a private conversation." She beamed proudly. "These women are different from the way they were before. I see more strength in them. They are so beautiful—some are just young girls with little babies. My heart goes out to them. I love them. It's a privilege to know them."

As the day progressed, I sensed that I was watching a modern-day saint go about her work. There was certainly nothing dramatic, colorful, or interesting here. This was grim, everyday reality. No heroics, no romantic visions, just mud and squalor. What were the rewards of such a life? Why bother? Why fight against the tide of despair that seems to envelop places like this?

At the last trailer we visited that day, a beautiful young woman with shining black hair greeted us with a flurry of Spanish. She was holding a tiny baby on her hip, and two small children were watching a small TV in the narrow living room. Sister Katherine gave her a bag of baby clothes, a container of dried milk, and a bolt of green material. They chatted in Spanish while I sat quietly. The woman suddenly pointed to me, smiling and nodding.

"She thinks you're a sister," Sister Katherine confided. "Your face has that light."

The day I returned to Rosary Heights from Chehalis, there was a driving rain. As I prepared to leave the little convent, Sister Perpetua hurried out and handed me some envelopes. "Please give these to Sister Joanne. They're important," she said. Then her intense little face softened and she held out a small card—like a holy card. "You loved Sister Celestine, so I thought you'd like to have this. It's her memorial card."

I was deeply touched—and honored. On one side of the simple black-and-white card was an illustration of the Holy Mother holding the infant Jesus, a monk with his rosary beads kneeling before them. The beads extended to the hands of the infant Jesus; a crown sat on the Holy Mother's head. Encircled around them were these words: "TURN THEN MOST GRACIOUS . . . ADVOCATE THINE EYES OF MERCY." At the bottom of the card was printed: "NOW AND AT THE HOUR OF OUR DEATH . . . AMEN." On the other side of the card was this:

In Loving Memory of
SISTER CELESTINE HAUGHIAN, O.P.

Born: December 16, 1917
Professed: January 19, 1935
Died: August 23, 1995

Then there was a simple black cross.

May she live in peace with God.

The traffic on Interstate 5 crawled along, and it felt as if it would take forever to get back to Rosary Heights. When I finally reached the edge of Seattle, I pulled into a diner to get a cup of hot coffee. I felt chilled to the bone. When I emerged, no more than ten minutes later, my rental car was sitting in the lot with the trunk popped open. My briefcase was gone. I stared at the empty trunk in disbelief. My tape recorder, my notes, my address book. Sister Perpetua's important envelopes. Sister Celestine's memorial card. My key to Rosary Heights. I was shaking with cold and anger. What a meaningless crime. I'd had my purse with me. There was no money, nothing whatsoever of value—except to me.

By the time I made a police report and got back on the road, it was late. I arrived at Rosary Heights at ten o'clock that night, shivering and miserable. I rang the front doorbell, and Sister Helen appeared.

"My briefcase was stolen," I blurted out. "I lost my key."

"Oh, you poor thing!" She hustled me inside, and before I knew it, I was surrounded by sympathetic sisters, commiserating, clucking their tongues at the horror of it, pouring me a nice cup of hot tea. Their response was oddly comforting, and I was surprised that I didn't feel much worse about the loss. Ordinarily, I would have been hysterical. But try as I might, I couldn't feel too bad about it. The sisters seemed far more upset for me than I was. Perhaps the spirit of the sisters themselves had entered me. No material loss could be so terrible. It wasn't such a big thing.

"Oh," I said to Sister Joanne, remembering Sister Perpetua's letters. "Could you call Sister Perpetua and tell her they were lost?" I felt worse about that than anything.

The next morning, Sister Joanne told me that the envelopes had contained Mass cards—requests for prayers—and forty dollars. Guessing what my reaction would be, she added, "Don't even think of giving me the money. I won't accept it. If it comes back to us, it comes back; otherwise, it was meant to be." Replacing the stolen money was exactly what I'd planned to do, but she'd cut me off at the pass.

Maybe Sister Joanne had an intuition. After I'd been home for a few weeks, I got a call from my local post office that a package had arrived for me from the post office's Lost and Found Department in Seattle. A big box contained my briefcase. Someone had rifled through it, even opened the envelopes Sister Perpetua had given me, filled with the Mass cards and cash. But the first thing I saw was the edge of a twenty-dollar bill. They hadn't taken the cash; they hadn't taken anything. All I could think was that this was a miracle of the nuns. I imagined some young punk popping my trunk, stealing the briefcase, and looking through it, seeing the Mass cards, the references to nuns, Sister Celestine's memorial card. Maybe he'd cursed miserably. "Oh, great. I just stole some nun's briefcase." Not wanting a theft from a nun on his soul, he tossed the briefcase into a mailbox and walked away, hoping for a better score the next time. Maybe the thief was a former Catholic schoolboy. Maybe he was still held in that viselike grip.

One day, I remained at the motherhouse, planning to spend several hours in the order's archives. They were kept on the ground floor of the carriage house, in which I was billeted during my stay.

The archivist was a cheerful, chatty laywoman named Margaret, whose blood sister, Donna, had once been a member of the order. But, she confided to me, Donna had left a long time ago. And after she left, she had contracted multiple sclerosis.

The archives comprised two rooms—one crammed with files and cabinets and the other filled with artifacts. The artifacts room was like a tiny museum, depicting the history of the order. Most of the items were carefully preserved under glass. There were samples of habits from the early part of the century, a tiny crown of thorns worn in the old bridal profession ceremony, and letters written in the 1800s from the motherhouse in Newburgh, New York. Copies of the Divine Office, a piece of bone from the body of Saint Dominic, and rosary beads worn by Mother Guilelma, the first western prioress, were displayed. There was a large sturdy oak table that had been in the first refectory in Aberdeen, a statue of Mary that had once stood in the garden of Saint Joseph's, the congregation's first hospital, and a cabinet of dolls depicting the various modifications of the habit since the nineteenth century. In another case were copies of the yearbooks from every graduating class at Holy Angels, from 1907 to 1972. There was such a wealth of material that I could hardly take it all in. Reluctantly, I turned away. My real work was with the files.

With Margaret's assistance, I located documents that filled the gaps in my understanding of religious life in this order. I had a special interest in documents from the 1950s and 1960s, times of precarious balance between the old and the new.

Margaret laid a fat binder on the table. "This might be helpful," she said. "It's copies of the order newsletter from the fifties and sixties."

For the next two hours, I lost myself in the vivid portrait of order life that was documented in the *Holy Cross Bulletin:* stories of individual sisters, descriptions of events, pictures of novitiate classes. There were even recipes—angel pie and pineapple delight salad. As I was leafing through the Winter 1961 issue, I suddenly came upon a page that made my heart stop.

"This is *me!*" I gasped.

Margaret looked up from her work, puzzled. "There's a picture of you?"

I pointed with a shaking hand to the page, headlined TOMORROW LAND. There I was, ten years old, standing with Mary Anne Dwyer and the other girls, my wide eyes staring out beneath the tight wimple of my Sisters of the Sacred Heart habit. A large gold locket in the shape of a heart lay against my chest. I had forgotten about my single foray into the secret world of nuns.

I sat for a long time, trying to read the expression on my child's face and thinking about the bizarre coincidence of stumbling upon this picture. I had come to Rosary Heights to discover the secret of the religious women and to shake open a closed chapter of my own life. It had never occurred to me that I would find myself, literally, here in the order archives—a part of their story for all time. Perhaps I was part of the perpetual circle. The sisters and the girls they taught inextricably linked by one's exposure to the other. The sisters were confirmed in their choices by seeing the children's struggles. The children were allowed the rueful opportunity of being placed in the hands of the nuns, a chance to have every aspect of the calling rubbed off on them. I was "one of their girls." I had always been one of their girls. I just hadn't known it.

11

Last Call

THE KING COUNTY JAIL, LOCATED IN DOWNTOWN SEATTLE, IS pretty much like any other jail. It is a cold, imposing box, a fortress with barred windows and watch towers, sitting on a dark, deserted street. Several weeks before my arrival at Rosary Heights, I'd sent my Social Security number and other personal information to the prison authorities. They wanted to run a computer check on my background. Even though I was accompanying Sister Patrice, they weren't taking any chances.

The prison ministry of religious women has sparked criticism among some cynics. They complain that these women are coddling criminals. Like her counterpart, Sister Helen Prejean, Sister

Patrice struggled with hardened hearts both within and without the steel bars of a prison. There were those who were convinced that these men were tricksters. They believed that the nuns were easy prey for these convicts. The most virulent were the new breed of "lock-and-load" Christians—right-wing law-and-order conservatives who considered any humanitarian gestures extended to these "animals" a disgrace.

But Sister Patrice wouldn't listen to them. They didn't get it. A remarkably pragmatic, tough individual, she readily admitted that there were many reasons for jailhouse conversion, and not all of them were inspired by God. But her attitude was clear-cut: The men who chose to attend a religious service instead of fighting, hanging out, or watching TV in the common recreation room were better off than those who didn't. There was always the possibility that, by the repetition of divinely inspired prayers, or by some miraculous osmosis, they would receive the light of God's grace.

Among her other duties at the prison, Sister Patrice officiated at an evening Mass held once each week. Again, there was no priest, so she carried the little silver compact of preblessed Hosts. As we rode up in the prison's elevator, she gave me some fundamentals. "The prisoners' uniforms are color-coded. Yellows are the misdemeanors, and reds are the felonies. You have nothing to worry about, but always keep a little distance between you and the inmates. Believe me, no one's going to bother you. But it's more comfortable for everyone that way."

The room we entered was painted a bleak institutional yellow and contained a table and plastic chairs, but nothing else. A large wire-meshed observation window looked out into the hallway, where we could observe and be observed. Throughout the Mass, I saw guards in the hallway lining up prison ers. They would order them to assume the position, legs and arms spread in an X, and roughly pat them down.

Fifteen men garbed in reds and yellows attended Mass that evening. They were in good spirits, happy to be out of confinement

for an hour. We began the Mass with song. I saw immediately that
singing was hugely favored. The men sang with fervor, called out
requests, and sang song after song, their deep voices rumbling and
rising through the room. "The Battle Hymn of the Republic";
"Come Holy Ghost, Creator Blest"; "To Jesus Christ Our Sover-
eign King"; "Holy, Holy, Holy." It was clear they would sing for the
entire hour if they were permitted. Finally, Sister Patrice cut them
off and read the Gospel of the day.

> On one occasion Jesus spoke thus. "Come to me, all
> you who are weary and find life burdensome, and I will
> refresh you. Take my yoke upon your shoulders and
> learn from me, for I am generous and humble of heart.
> Your soul will find rest, for my yoke is easy and my bur-
> den light."

Sister Patrice asked the men to talk about what the passage meant to them, and what they had discovered in the past
week. I could tell that those who spoke out were mouthing oft-
repeated lines:

"I know now that it's wrong to steal from others. . . . I'll never
steal again. Jesus will provide me with everything I need."

"I used to beat up my wife, but I know now that when I get
out I'll never hurt her again. Jesus has taught me to be loving and
gentle to others."

"It gets so hard in here, but Jesus' words comfort me."

One man announced that he was being released that very
weekend. His release was set for Saturday night at midnight. This
set off alarms for Sister Patrice.

"Is someone picking you up?"

"Yeah, I got a friend coming to get me."

"And you're going straight home?"

He looked at her as if she were nuts. "I been locked up in here
six months. I gotta celebrate a little bit, Sister." The other men
chuckled. Sister Patrice sighed. Would the system never learn?

Releasing men from jail at midnight on a Saturday. Midnight—the witching hour. It was almost like receiving an engraved invitation to commit some stupid crime and return to prison.

When it was time for Communion, Sister Patrice opened her little silver case, removed a host, and held it up. Although a priest had already blessed it, when she said, "As Jesus Christ said to his apostles, 'Take this, all of you, and eat it: This is my body which will be given up for you,'" her spirit lent a renewed authority to the words. It sounded for all the world as if she were a priest saying Mass. A shiver ran down my spine.

She poured some grape juice in a cup and held it up. "Then Jesus said to his apostles, 'Take this, all of you, and drink from it: This is the cup of my blood, the blood of the new and everlasting covenant. It will be shed for you and for all, so that sins may be forgiven. Do this in memory of me.'"

The men rose and arranged themselves before Sister Patrice, their baggy pants brushing across the floor. As each of them received Communion, there was utter peace in the room. There was nothing phony here. It was real.

Bernadette and I were walking together on the grounds of Rosary Heights. She was in town for a few days and had agreed to meet me at the motherhouse. We were both like young girls again. We were exactly the same as we once were. I felt unaccountably grateful to be there with her.

"Do you remember when we last saw each other?" Bernadette asked. She didn't look a day older to me. The same soft brown cap of hair, the slender frame, the serious, sweet face. The only real difference was the new gleam in her eyes—the toughened shell, the independent spirit.

"Of course I do," I replied. "It was in 1973. Christmas. I was pregnant. You were getting ready to join the Sisters of Social Service."

"Do you think we've changed much?" she asked.

"I used to think so. But now . . . no, we're fundamentally the same."

We walked to the edge of the bluff and looked over into the pile of mud and rubble. "Nobody breathe," Bernadette said. I knew what she meant. The hill could go. It was a sobering thought.

She told me a story of an incident that had occurred the previous day at Sunday Mass. Bernadette's family still lived in Saint Alphonsus parish. She laughingly described how the old convent had been turned into a senior center. "That parlor we used to sit in? It's a bingo parlor!"

Then she told me about a confrontation she had had with Father Reilly. "Remember him?"

"Oh, yes," I said with distaste. Father Reilly was one of those priests who was constantly hustling for money—not for the poor, but for building projects. His latest was the construction of a gymnasium to be called the Father Reilly Center.

"After Mass," Bernadette said, "we were in the coffee room, mingling, and Father Reilly came up to me. He was trying to talk me into writing a check for three hundred dollars, right then and there. I was annoyed that he'd chosen this moment to raise money. So I said, 'Sorry, Father. I've already given seventeen years to the church.'"

I laughed. "Good answer! What did he say?"

"He said, 'Oh, you were a nun? Well, the church took care of you for eighteen years. Isn't it time you gave something back?'"

Carmen

After I received Carmen's E-mail, she and I started up regular communications. She was so happy and high-spirited. I didn't remember that about her at all. She explained that the years I knew her when I was in high school were a very hard time for her. She was struggling, unhappy. She was having health problems. I probably never knew the *real* Carmen.

It was a different Carmen, that was for sure. Another reason she seemed so open and happy was that back in the 1960s, the sisters were very circumspect. They kept custody of their tongues as well as their eyes. They put a brave face on in front of the girls who were in their charge.

It seemed amazing to me now, but I never knew that Carmen had a raunchy wit and a quick mind. She was retired from teaching, and she divided her time between giving private music lessons and being a dog trainer. She had a steady boyfriend, a sweet-tempered German shepherd, and a little house in West Seattle.

If I had expected the ex-nuns to be filled with rancor toward their old order, Carmen set me straight. She loved Rosary Heights. She visited whenever she could. She participated in their programs. She kept in touch. She viewed the women in her order as her sisters. Carmen was still one of them, in her own separate way, and she was proud to be so.

She warned me, though, that if I got in touch with Elizabeth, I might find a different attitude. "I love Elizabeth," Carmen said. "But you have to understand, Elizabeth was never one of *us*. Her home was Guilford. She had a hard time at Saint Alphonsus, so I can understand her feelings. Just don't forget—she never really knew the order."

The first time I wrote to Elizabeth, I did so with shaking hands. In a very real sense, Elizabeth was my vital connection with the past. She had been in the back of my mind since the last time I saw her. I had long ago despaired of ever finding her. She and Jim had moved to California, swallowed up, I imagined, by the invisible underground of ex-priests and ex-nuns. In fact, they had moved back to Seattle when their daughter, Faith, was born, and had been there all along. Right in the phone book!

"Dear Elizabeth," I wrote, "I have been looking for you for a long time. Let me reintroduce myself. . . ."

A week later, a letter arrived from Bainbridge Island, across the Sound from Seattle.

Hello there, old friend!

I remember you well. We have often talked about your visit to our little house. Jim and I still laugh about the time you threw out the brown eggs because you thought they were spoiled. After Jim and I left Seattle, we moved to San Leandro, where Jim started a Ph.D. program and I got a job as drama director at San Leandro High School. Those were very happy years. Mother Dominick tried to forbid Celestine from having any contact with us, but Cel ignored her and came to San Francisco for a year for CCD training. She spent every weekend with us. After Faith was born, we moved back to Seattle and settled on Bainbridge Island. Jim got a job as headmaster of a private school in Kent. I decided to pursue my sculpting rather than return to teaching. We have lived here ever since. We are content and happy. We were wrong about one thing, though. The Vatican never came around on the issue of married priests.

Celestine, bless her soul, died in 1995. She suffered so much. In the end, she was barely conscious, but I sat by her bed every day and held her hand. Her death was a great blow, but I'm confident she is watching over us. Why don't you come and see us for a few days? We have plenty of space here.

Love,
Elizabeth

Elizabeth and Jim
Bainbridge Island, Washington—1997
Déjà vu—all over again. Sitting around the table playing spiritual chess with Father Curtis. He'll always be Father Curtis to me, no matter the church's position. Although we hadn't laid eyes on one

another since 1969, we picked up right where we'd left off. To Elizabeth and Jim, I was the same old Catherine—the well-meaning but muddled girl who had once tossed the brown eggs in the Arlington house into the garbage because I thought they'd spoiled.

Jim and Elizabeth still seemed the same to me, too. They'd grown older, of course, and their faces and bodies showed the wear and tear of age. Jim's once-wavy dark hair had transformed itself into a sea of white, and his strong frame had been whittled by the aftereffects of a heart attack he suffered a few years before. Elizabeth remained an animated bundle of energy, although not as slim as she once was. It startled me to learn that she had suffered from a series of health problems in the last few years, including a frightening bout with her vision, which almost led to her going blind. In 1985, she woke one morning, to find that she'd lost almost all of the sight in her left eye. After examining her, the doctors said she had at most three years before she would lose the sight in her right eye, too. This was the worst possible news for Elizabeth, because over the years she had developed a thriving business as a sculptor. She had first learned to sculpt while in the cloister, and she had never stopped. Eventually, she began a series of small fanciful figures, which had caught on. Now they were being marketed all over the world. The prospect of losing her sight terrified her; she wondered if God was telling her he no longer wished her to be an artist. Perhaps he wanted her to do something else. She spent the next two years making molds of all of her designs, so they could still be reproduced even if she went blind. The crisis led her to reevaluate her life, and she began to write, thinking she would still be able to do so even if she became sightless. But then, miraculously, her sight was restored. The doctors couldn't explain what had happened, or why, but her vision returned to normal.

Jim and Elizabeth lived in a secluded wooden-frame house set back in the woods of Bainbridge Island, surrounded by stately evergreens and chirping birds. A small shed had been transformed into a workshop for Elizabeth's art, and two horses contentedly grazed in a lower pasture of their rural property. Their twenty-one-year-old daughter, Faith, a lovely amalgam of her parents, was building a house on the land where she and her fiancé would live after they were married.

Elizabeth spoke in breathless whispers about the terrifying January storm that sent a nearby house, and the young family who lived in it, sliding down a collapsing hill to their deaths. Jim and Elizabeth had their own story to tell about danger and miracles during the worst of the storm. They had huddled in their house, without electricity or heat, and listened to trees falling all around them. Any moment, they expected one of the large evergreens surrounding their house to crash through the roof, but they were spared. The following day, after the storm had died down, they ventured outside to assess the damage. They were shocked by the devastation surrounding them. Enormous trees lay like fallen pins in a bowling alley, jutting every which way and blocking the small road that led from their secluded house to civilization. Knowing that no utility crews would be appearing soon to cut them out of their evergreen blockade, Jim put on his warmest coat and boots, gassed up and oiled his chain saw, and set out to start taking down some of the fallen trees that lay in the path of the main road.

Elizabeth, meanwhile, made herself a cup of tea and went to work in her studio. She soon lost herself in her sculpting work. Hours passed before Elizabeth looked up from the tiny sculpture she'd been creating and realized that it was almost three o'clock. The shadows were beginning to lengthen, and she hadn't seen Jim or heard the chain saw buzzing for almost four hours. Why hadn't she been paying closer attention? Where was he? Suddenly alarmed, she grabbed a coat and went looking for him, stumbling over snowdrifts and fallen branches, calling his name again and again. She heard nothing. Cold, scared, and beginning to panic, she frantically pushed her way through the snow and the dwindling light, determined to find him. She caught a glimpse of red next to a gigantic fallen tree and ran toward it. Jim was sitting on the ground, dazed, his chain saw beside him. He smiled gently when he saw her.

"Oh, hi," he said nonchalantly, trying to rise to his feet but quickly falling back, clutching the side of his head.

"Jim," she screamed, reaching him. "What happened? Are you all right?"

"Huh? I'm fine . . . fine." He again tried to stagger to his feet, but fell back once more.

As she helped get him up, Elizabeth saw the angry gash lying in the center of a rising welt along the right side of his head. Jim knew nothing. One minute, he had been standing there, and the next, he was staring up at the fading light from the ground. They finally figured out what must have happened. Jim had found a tree about to go over, turned away to start the chain saw, and that was all he remembered. Apparently, the tree had chosen that moment to finish coming down. It must have grazed his head, knocking him out cold for almost four hours. If he'd been standing a couple of inches one way or the other, if the tree had fallen differently, his death would have almost certainly been instantaneous.

"Now I know why I believe in the Holy Spirit," Elizabeth said, sighing, and hugged him tightly to her.

As always, Jim loved a good fight. He was never one to walk away from a confrontation, moral or intellectual. He raised an amused eyebrow when I tried to hedge a response to one of his penetrating questions, or tripped over my words in an attempt to get a thought out before he batted my responses out of the park like a grand slam. The chance to chew over some of the great theological questions plainly still gave him great joy. While Elizabeth stirred pots of beef stew, rice, and greens in the kitchen, Jim and I sat at the table in front of the blazing fireplace and talked about the calling.

"The idea of a calling is a very intriguing one," he mused. "There's the mystery, of course. What is it? What must it be like? And then there's the fear. Is God calling me? What for? Maybe a mystery can remain a mystery only as long as it *is* a mystery. There are so many things we don't understand in the universe. Doctors still can't completely explain how the body works. Why should we be able to understand how God works? Everyone wants explanations that are rational and reasoned; everyone wants to define their terms. I think that the calling is like a lot of things we can't explain. Once you try to define it, you put limits on it. And once you do that, the mystery is gone."

"That's the problem I'm facing right now, Jim," I retorted with exasperation. "I'd love just to leave it alone, let it remain an eternal and profound mystery, but I'm writing about it. That's the subject of my book. How do I examine it without trying to define it? Words may lack the power to explain things beyond our kith and kin, but they're what we've been given to work with. When people read my book, they'll be expecting some insight. I don't think my readers will be satisfied if I just dance around the mystery of the calling."

I was being deliberately contentious because I knew exactly what Jim meant. One of the most difficult subjects I'd ever tackled, it was the reason I'd laid down the objective pen of the journalist and jumped into the fray—letting my own soul dangle in the riptide of uncertainty. I knew of no other way to approach the mystery of faith. It wasn't going to happen by osmosis, or by interviewing other people about their experiences. I had to try to remember what it had been like for me, way back when. And I had to come to terms with the calling within me that still existed, that had never been quelled.

"Of course not, but we also use words to evince faith," Jim said quietly. As if reading my thoughts, he added, "If you can communicate the experience of what it was to feel that attraction—that calling—twenty-some years ago, you won't disappoint your readers. I know you, Catherine. You felt an attraction to the religious life, didn't you?"

"Yes, I did," I admitted.

"And now? The attraction isn't there anymore? Or is it?" His lips curled into a tiny smile, the delight of the challenger brightening his eyes. *Check . . . checkmate.*

"Now, you mean?" I repeated stupidly. I hadn't allowed myself to consider that. "I don't really know—well, yes, maybe I do. I've always felt a calling, but to what exactly, I don't know. I mean, I don't want to join a convent, but there's something there." I threw up my hands in frustration. "I don't know what it is. I've always felt it, though, even when I was a little girl."

He nodded with understanding. "I know. You miss something, don't you?"

"I do. But I'm not sure what it is that I miss."

"Well, I miss it, too," he said, gazing into my eyes with real feeling. "I also have a hard time putting my finger on it. But it never leaves you once you've felt it. I'd have a hard time joining a community that said it could fulfill it for me. What if it weren't able to? What then? I'm afraid it would damage what I feel, somehow, and I'd be left dissatisfied and disappointed. I don't want the mystery within me diminished in that way. So the sense that something is missing, unfortunately, is ever present."

This was the Father Curtis I remembered—laying all his cards on the table, telling me his honest thoughts. I felt a curious sense of relief and belonging to be sitting in this house.

Elizabeth appeared just then from the kitchen, carrying a heaping bowl of steaming beef stew. She smiled at me fondly. "I can't believe you're sitting here, Catherine," she said. "It's as though no time has passed at all."

"And yet a whole lifetime seems to have gone by," I murmured.

"You two sound like you're having the same discussion you did almost thirty years ago. Notice how the conversation picks up right from where we left off?"

We sat down at the table and Jim said a short prayer. The food was wonderful and warming.

"Tell me something," Jim said, the twitch of his lip telling me he already knew the answer. "Do you still have it? The calling?"

I took a sip of wine and considered for only a second before I responded. "I have to say yes. I *do* feel called. I've always felt called. I just don't know what it means anymore."

Jim didn't ask me what I thought it meant. Instead, he asked a question that surprised me. "Who is calling you?"

I paused, a forkful of stew halfway to my mouth. "I don't know," I said, wondering what he was talking about.

"Is it *self*?" he prodded.

"Oh, no." I was certain of that. I knew if the calling came from within, I'd surely understand it better. "I don't know who's calling me, and I don't know what's calling me, but it isn't *me* calling me."

"The *Other*, then. It comes from the *Other*." He bit into a thick chunk of homemade corn bread and smiled with satisfaction as he chewed. Elizabeth laughed and raised her wineglass. "Welcome to the land of the *Other*," she saluted me. "The land of the *Other* is Jim's domain. You've made him a very happy man."

I finished chewing my food, swallowed, and smiled at Jim. "Maybe you've got something there. Yes, maybe you're right. It must come from the *Other*."

Jim's face lit up, as if he had successfully guided me to the top of a treacherous mountain without losing me in an icy crevasse. "And that's the mystery," he declared. *"Other?* Who is this *Other*? What is this *Other* who's calling? I sometimes wonder if every human being in the world feels the calling at some point or other. They may not be able to identify it, but there it is. It frightens people, the calling; maybe that's why so many try to drown it out with drugs and alcohol. They want to stop what they're hearing, what they're thinking, what they're *feeling*. But the calling can't be drowned in a sea of alcohol or drugs; it can't be stopped once it's begun—that's the mystery. It is *Other*. Why else do people go through their entire lives with this undefined longing? Why can't they be sated by all their earthly pursuits? Of course,

I think that there are many people who deny it, flee from it. The calling isn't a comfortable experience, it feels dangerous. How could it not?"

I laughed. " 'The Hound of Heaven.' "

"Ah, yes." He smiled. " 'I fled Him, down the nights and down the days . . .' That's it exactly."

We ate in silence for a few minutes. Finally, trying to get to the heart of the matter, I said, "Let's say you're right, Jim. A lot of people are called, but they spend their lives running from it. It terrifies them. If everyone does have a calling, how do you find out what it is? What if you can't figure out your calling? People may long for community of some kind, not necessarily in a religious context, but a community of like souls. They also long for a greater sense of spirituality in their lives. I think a lot of people sense there is something else, something more profound and satisfying than can be provided by their everyday reality. How do they find the answer within themselves—their calling? The longing that most people experience isn't tangible, so it can never be truly satisfied. I think most people walk around with a vague sense of unease. Their lives are a series of unfulfilled longings."

"Fulfillment doesn't always feel good. It isn't something you necessarily experience as well-being." He shrugged.

"That may be so, but most people, including myself, wouldn't appreciate that idea. Our world, our society, has become accustomed to some level of comfort, of satisfaction."

"Even being crucified can be okay if you see beyond the moment, if you're sure of your calling," he replied. "Surety and faith are all; the rest doesn't make any difference," he said.

"That may be fine for you, Jim, but you'd have a hard time selling that to the rest of us. I think that's one of the things that terrifies us so. What if you discover that your calling is a call to martyrdom, self-annihilation, or death? Most people would want to flee from that revelation. Don't you think that there are certain people who are different, who have something about them, something that sets them apart from others? You can't explain it, but they have a kind of light coming off of them, a beacon radiating from their eyes; they have the calling. What do you think?"

"There's a mystery there," Jim agreed. "But ultimately, people define the mystery for themselves by going to the known. They may call the answer to their mystery Yahweh, or Buddha, or Christ the Lord. But it's a mystery that contains elements of the familiar to them."

"You're the one who said you can't define the mystery!" I reminded him. "How can mystery be defined?"

"Catherine, think about it," Jim said patiently. "You were defining it even in high school, when you wanted to enter a convent. Then you started to change your definition when you became involved in the radical antiwar movement. You changed it once more when you decided to marry. Then you had a son to raise. And you're still defining it—or trying to. Why else would you be writing this book? Why else would you be here? Don't you see what I'm saying? It's all part of the same calling."

I stared at him openmouthed. I had never examined the choices I'd made in that light before. "It's all part of the same calling," he'd said.

"And you probably felt uncertain about each step you took— it's only natural to consider the consequences of our actions. Every time we choose one thing, we have to give up something else," Jim added kindly. "Each step along the way, you had a family or community that you moved away from, had to let go of, in order to move on. And you did it every time, didn't you? You broke away, even though you may not have been sure it was the right thing to do. And at the time you did it, it was hurtful, difficult, and painful." He sighed and rubbed his eyes with his hands. "I think if we didn't have that, the conflict that arises from change, the uncertainty of growth, we would never move on in our lives."

"We're a perfect example of that," Elizabeth interjected, reaching for Jim's hand. "If we hadn't been able to see what happened between us as a continuation of our calling, we never would've done it."

Jim squeezed her hand. "And if that had happened, maybe we would never have known what our true calling was meant to be. When Elizabeth and I realized that we belonged together, I didn't feel as if I was making a different choice. It was the same choice. The Spirit was leading us down an unexpected path, but it was part of the same calling. I didn't reject the church, or stop loving God; I continued to follow the voice that I had always followed. My calling has never changed."

It confused me to hear him say that. "Jim, I was there," I said fiercely. "I remember what you thought. Your true calling was to be a priest, but you thought it would be okay to get married, because the church was going to allow priests to marry. You didn't want to stop being a priest. You expected that you'd be able to be a married pastor within five years. That was 1969. Almost thirty years have passed, Jim, and the church is more determined than ever not to let that happen. You'll never be a priest again." My voice had risen to a loud pitch. Maybe it was frustration, or maybe I was just annoyed by Jim's simple acceptance. I wanted to shout, Hey! Reality check!

He wasn't bothered, though. He simply shrugged. "I don't feel that the church has to change tomorrow to meet *my* expectations. I think it will change in time, but I feel comfortable with it. What the church does or doesn't do has nothing to do with my calling. You know, I have real problems with the way the government runs our country, but that doesn't make me any less American. It's the same with the church. The church and the hierarchy that runs it have never been one and the same. The hierarchy are all mortals, and they control the government of the church. It's a very human institution, with all the weaknesses and foibles that implies. But there is something far greater and more profound than that in the church—a spiritual dimension that no hierarchy can control. God fills every nook and cranny with his spirit. He exists, and the Spirit exists, and it doesn't make any difference what Popes, cardinals, or archbishops direct. The hierarchy can do whatever they want. They must know that in their heart of hearts. It will never alter the spirit—the mysterious presence that finds all who seek."

"So," I said, feeling disturbed, "ordination means nothing?" I turned to Elizabeth. "Your solemn vows meant nothing?"

Elizabeth gazed at me, bemused. "My solemn vows meant a great deal to me—they gave me great joy. But, when you examine it, is a vow you take when you are one person valid forever? What if you become another person? What does it mean to take a vow if you change, and grow, and find yourself becoming someone else?"

"Commitment, for one thing," I replied, refusing to give up easily.

"I think there are extremes of commitment. I think not taking one's vows seriously may be an extreme, depending on what you mean," Jim said. "But the other extreme might be feeling that one is defined for life. Are you the same person you were thirty years ago, Catherine? I know I'm not. It would be a shame to think we can be frozen in time, frozen by a choice we made when we were virtually children. 'I've taken my final vows. That's it.' Well, where does that leave you?"

"Last call!" Elizabeth trilled.

"Ah, but there is never a *last call,* is there?" Jim said quietly.

A silence descended over the room. I felt Jim and Elizabeth both staring at me intently.

"Just when you think the party's over," Elizabeth said solemnly, "there's another call." She rose from the table and headed toward the kitchen. "Coffee, anyone?" she asked over her shoulder. "Or how about some brandy?" We all laughed. For some reason, it felt like the funniest joke in the world.

12

The Naked God Quest

"I was trying to find my way to the infinite."

WAS I CALLED? AM I CALLED? HAVE ALL MY YEARS OF SEARCH-ing been an effort to find my way to the infinite? But who is call-ing today? And to what am I called? There is a break in the air, a shiver of waves. Its source is no longer evident.

What can I learn from the women religious who appear before me today? Where are the radiant young brides of Christ, the women who once walked among us as visible signs of God's will in the world? They're still there, aren't they?

They seemed to disappear. They made themselves almost invisible by dressing in the plain clothing of the times—skirts, pantsuits, stockings, and heels. They adopted curls and waves, try-ing to undo years of hair flattening caused by the old headdresses. They smoothed moisturizing lotion into the creases in their foreheads. They began spreading out from the convents, renting apartments in twos or threes, some going it alone. They no longer filled the schools and hospitals. And the children who still received their education from the sisters no longer experienced anything close to what we experienced. When we were children, nuns ruled the schools and the world. The warning jangle of rosary beads has been silenced in the school hallways.

There is a vague nostalgia to see them again as they once were. Perhaps we need the assurance that something in this suffering, material world still carries God's imprimatur. We feel a clutch of longing for a time when faith was symbolized by a flowing white robe and a chant. Recordings of Gregorian and other liturgical chants flood the marketplace. We ache for the ancient rhythms of faith, the eternal signs. Signs have changed. Time has changed them.

Should we be absorbed with visages? Do we require the outer appearance of orthodoxy as a certification of sanctity? We wonder if the old ways were not so righteous as they seemed, and the new ways not as fraught with danger. Something is missing. There is a rent in the seamless story of the call to serve Christ and his people.

Who are these religious women now? we wonder. What is their calling?

Are they called to be a sign to the world? Is fealty and devotion enough?

What is the sign?

Are they called to be a community, living together in service and prayer?

Where are they?

If the lives of nuns are defined by lives of prayer but they no longer join together throughout the day for the hours of the Divine Office, does their attuned and conjoined ability, now sundered, diminish their quest for God? Or ours?

Who are they?

Stripped of the visible accoutrements of their sanctity, no longer automatically deferred to for their pious sacrifices, they live among us, reduced to the anonymity of ordinary women. And yet they possess an essential difference. They are still graced with an extraordinary calling.

"It is the greatest form of humility," one nun observes, "to have no sign to prove to the world that you are holy."

Metamorphosed from the safe cocoon of tradition, the women religious of today have been asked to take flight on uncertain wings. They live their vows of poverty, chastity, and obedience in raw faith.

They must ask themselves if there is a place in the world for nuns. They must ask themselves if they are embraced by the church. The calling to be a woman religious is beyond the work. The work itself, no matter how satisfying, isn't the point. An elderly sister recalls joining an order in 1917, when she was fifteen years old. The prioress asked her, "Would you like to be a nurse, or would you rather be a teacher?" The young girl paused for a moment. Nursing and teaching had never occurred to her before. She finally decided. "I guess I'd rather be a nurse," she said. Eighty years later, her career as a nurse long over, she remains a member of a religious community. Her *calling* was not merely the earthly task she was given. It was much more.

The calling cannot be defined in the choice of a vocation, or a love of God. The desire to confront the mysteries of faith and belief cannot be coaxed by the will or won by the heart. The calling requires a different element from any of the ninety-two that the earth contains. We hope for a defining moment. That moment may never come. There is only the calling. Plain, unadorned, without pretense or planning, the calling appears. It then persists, remains, or diminishes. There are no wishes involved. The marshal of a true calling need not tend the fire. The glow of a calling does not burn beyond an ember. Like an everlasting light, an eternal verity, it remains forever constant. It is only the times that have changed.

Few young girls dream any longer of being nuns and donning the sacred veil. The romance has dimmed even as the missionary need has soared. The women who choose to follow this path today

are not swooning for a vision of Jesus in the night. They are act-
ing in complete faith, and responding to real need. They offer
themselves as sacrificial lambs in the fields of the world. In a sense,
they are the modern virgin martyrs.

So if it is no longer a romantic dalliance, then the call is something far rarer. These literally *are* the chosen few. They possess an
almost fundamental holiness, as though they had been genetically
selected. There is something elemental and mysterious, a quality of
Other. Whatever we posit or imagine, the calling is an event without parallel. The calling acts on us in this world but exists on a
plane outside of our grasp.

I am haunted by the image of the naked God quest, an image
expressed by Sister Sandra M. Schneiders, IHM.

> As many left and few entered, religious who stayed got
> in touch in a new way with the real meaning of reli-
> gious vocation, the naked God quest at the center of
> their hearts. . . . Those who continued to choose reli-
> gious life had now to choose it in purified faith because
> it was largely devoid of compensatory packaging.

The naked God quest is the struggle that exists in a world
largely devoid of community or privilege, comfort or communion.
It is a pursuit of pure faith. Fragile souls tremble before the
unknown. Others plough forward. An ongoing inner battle to
break the mystery never ends. We need human fragments, familiar
trails that will lead us on. Can we ever understand? What does it
mean for us?

How many of us have been drawn to our lives through inci-
dental events, a series of casual confluences? Why do some of us
perform, others direct? Why do some write, others edit? Why do
some doctors choose to be psychiatrists, other neurosurgeons? Ask
yourself. Quietly. Are *you* called?

Think now. Why are you reading this? Are you looking for
something? Does this interest you? *Why?*

I believe we are all called—although we may chafe against the calling. It may not fit our superficial preferences or ideals. None of us is inured from pain, heartbreak, or loss. Some of us may never get to do what we believe we want to do, never get to follow our call. And all along, all we have been doing, and all we *can* do is follow the call. Do you hear it? See it? Sense it? The hound of heaven's footsteps bearing down on you? The *Other* forming your name on *Its* lips?

We are called. The tap on our shoulder may come only once. But in our dreams, in our relationships, in encounters that may not even register, the light falls on us from above, and we experience a flash of perception. That flash is meant to startle us awake deep inside.

In my dream, Bernadette and I are walking along a sloping path littered with rocks. We're breathing hard, picking our way uphill. We're moving toward a group of buildings that are forged into the side of the hills. They are chapels and shops that surround the remains of the house where Catherine of Siena communed with Jesus. We find her cell. It is a tiny space beneath the kitchen. It contains only a crude mat, the brick that was her pillow, and the scourge she used to perform penance on herself. We walk out onto a garden terrace that overlooks the city and sit down without a word. Preparations are being made for lunch. We can hear the sounds, smell vegetables cooking. The palms of my hands ache.

I wake up. My palms ache for days.

In my dream, I am in a great hall with dozens of people. It is some sort of banquet, a celebration. Everyone is eating, drinking, and talking. I walk over to a table covered with pitchers of water. I'm very thirsty. A girl is standing behind the table, serving others, pouring water from a pitcher into outstretched goblets. The girl's hair is long and thick, the color of strawberries. She turns, and I see that it's Tracy. Her blue eyes are sparkling. Her lips are stretched in a dazzling smile, and her teeth gleam. She still looks twenty years old.

"Tracy!" I cry, so happy to see her, so grateful that she's alive. The nightmare of her being murdered wasn't true. "I thought you were dead," I say, sobbing.

She looks at me, puzzled. "Why do you say that? I'm not dead," she says, as if it were a ridiculous idea. "I'm alive. I'm *alive.*"

Then she disappears. I wake up.

I am flipping through the television channels on a Sunday night when I see the face of a nun, dressed in a traditional habit, but with a softened headdress that rests loosely against her forehead. Her eyes are penetrating, yet gentle. She is both ethereal and real—and very familiar.

The nun sits in a chair across from a television interviewer. I realize with amazement that this is the former Dolores Hart—now Mother Dolores. Suddenly, after thirty-five years, she has broken her silence and is speaking to the press.

The interviewer is eager to talk about her opinions and memories of Elvis. Of course. Mother Dolores calls him Mr. Presley. After thirty-five years, the primary question asked concerns Mother Dolores's relationship with a dead entertainer. Elvis was referred to as "the King." Better to ask her of her relationship with the King who brought her to a cloistered life. But Mother Dolores is full of gentle good humor. There is nothing she could be asked that would perturb her. She radiates peace, and her eyes sparkle with a nun's humor. She will not be put on a pedestal, or made a symbol.

Mother Dolores remains a member of the Academy of Motion Picture Arts and Sciences, and she religiously votes every year. The interviewer chews on this piece of information. She leans in closely, with drawn forehead and probing eyes, wearing the mask of the *serious* journalist. "Mother Dolores, you realize, I'm sure, that there is a tremendous controversy concerning morality being waged around Hollywood right now. There are increasing questions about the kind of pictures that are being produced. Tell me. If you could address the members of the Academy, and send them one message, what would it be?"

Mother Dolores lowers her head and ponders the question. Finally, she raises her bright eyes to meet the journalist's and says, very softly and very carefully, "I would like to tell them that Paul Newman should have won for *The Verdict* in 1982," she replies without a hint of irony. After a lifetime of feeling distaste for Sister Martina's pious description of Dolores Hart and her vocation, I finally know who she is. And I like her.

A sister friend in Seattle sends me an article written by Sister Barbara Fiand, of the Sisters of Notre Dame de Namur. Sister Barbara, a professor of philosophical and spiritual theology at the Athenaeum of Ohio, is a revolutionary voice on the subject of religious orders. She is a spiritual archaeologist, who turns the broken relics of the past over in her mind until she can identify their timeless value. In her article, she speaks of the prophetic voice that calls them into the future and challenges them to embrace the "creative dying" of their orders. She tells her fellow sisters not to be intimidated by those who view their current state as negative. She exhorts them not to be timid. "Why are we seemingly so frightened of moving beyond known structures?" she writes. "Because we are unable or unwilling, and afraid to die, the Resurrection escapes us."

Sister Barbara reminds us of the Easter story. As the disciples of Jesus hover at his tomb, heartbroken, betrayed, and forlorn, a man suddenly appears before them, radiant in a white robe. "Why do you seek the living among the dead?" he asks gently. "He is not here. He has been raised up."

Before Christmas, an envelope arrives in the mail. The return address reads "Sister Katherine Diederich, Chehalis." When I open

it, a small card falls out. On the front is a gold-embossed figure of
Mary holding the baby Jesus, and scripted letters that read:

A Spiritual Bouquet

I whistle softly. A spiritual bouquet. It has been at least thirty
years, maybe more, since I received one. I didn't even realize this
was done anymore. The idea of the spiritual bouquet is simple.
Instead of buying flowers for someone, you give them a bouquet
of prayers. These prayers rise to heaven, and the recipient's name is
blessed. A spiritual bouquet may be good for an immediate cir-
cumstance, or the grace it elicits may be held in reserve for you
until you die, when you may *really* need it.

Inside, the card outlines the terms of my bouquet.

> *As a special Christmas Gift to you—*
> *I have arranged to have you and your intentions*
> *remembered in Nine Christmas Novena Masses—*
> *in honor of the divine Infant Jesus.*
> *This Novena will begin on*
> *Christmas Day.*
>
> *The Novena Masses will be offered at the altar*
> *in the Basilica of St. Mary Major in Rome,*
> *where a relic of the Crib of the Infant Savior*
> *is enshrined.*

I am speechless over this wonderful gift. Imagine Sister Katherine thinking of me in this way. They have a relic of the crib! Did
Joseph and Mary take it back to Nazareth from Bethlehem, strapped
on the back of a donkey? The entire incident amazes me. As I focus
in like a laser on this book about women religious, my mind and
soul filled with thoughts of countless women's relationships with

God, my name is being blessed in the Basilica of St. Mary Major in Rome for nine days. Thank you, Sister Katherine.

My son, Paul, calls me on Christmas Day. He has been living and working in Paris for the past year, becoming fluent in the language and studying at the Sorbonne. He and his girlfriend are spending Christmas in Rome, visiting friends. He tells me that on Christmas Eve, they walked to the Vatican, where the lights were blazing and the aura of holiness and joy was in the air. He had one thing on his mind. He wanted to light a votive candle for my father at St. Peter's. Paul has been lighting candles for his beloved grandfather in every cathedral and church he has visited while in Europe. In spite of his secular upbringing, my son has a great instinct for the religious.

He tells me with disappointment that candle lighting is not allowed in the Vatican. But, he adds cheerfully, on Christmas Day he went to another church, the Basilica of St. Mary Major, and lit a candle there.

Coincidence? Miracle? Who can say? I only know that prayers were rising simultaneously to heaven from the center of Rome on Christmas Day, for my father and me—mingling upward on a thin stream of incense and candlelight.

I walk around for days, swathed in an invisible aura of prayers. I am blessed a hundredfold.

Epilogue:
Higher Ground

Rosary Heights

— MARCH 1998

ON JANUARY 15, THE DOMINICAN SISTERS AT ROSARY HEIGHTS observed the first anniversary of the landslide. In the order newsletter, sent to all the outposts, Sister Helen wrote, "I have learned more about geology than I ever taught sixth graders, but more importantly, I am much more aware of the power of nature. Heavy rains, high winds and speeding trains below the bluff demand my attention as never before. And I wait and pray, in awe of nature and trusting in God's care for us."

Not surprisingly, however, the Sisters of Saint Dominic didn't spend the year shivering in their beds waiting for God and nature to decide their fate. In their minds, adhering to God's will did not mean standing still and fingering one's rosary beads. The old adage,

God helps those who help themselves, was applied. The sisters took action. They became amateur geologists.

Today, buried throughout the property, at depths ranging from 76 to 219 feet, are the most sophisticated monitoring devices in the world. They were installed by the United States Geological Survey, making Rosary Heights only the second site in the country to use them. The devices gather data on groundwater pressure, rainfall, and slope movement. The sisters have turned their personal landslide into a geological project. There is even a Web site where anyone can go to keep track of the minute shiftings in the land beneath the motherhouse.*

Sister Andrea has replanted her vegetable garden at a safe distance from the bluff. She considers herself the point nun on the geological project. It appeals to her sense of connection with the earth. She pulls off her boots and hits the Web site at least once a day—like a mother hovering over an asthmatic child.

The orange barriers have been taken down and a permanent fence will be put up in the summer. With El Niño busy to the south, winter this year was forgiving. Life goes on. Change, as ever, is in the air as the order prepares for its elections. Every four years, the sisters return home to Rosary Heights to choose a new prioress. The Edmonds Dominicans have gone back to calling their appointed leader prioress again, after twenty years of using the secular title president. The original change, during the exploratory period of the 1970s, was intended to signify a more democratic system of leadership. The word *prioress* evolved from the Latin word *praecedere,* which means literally "to surpass in rank, dignity, and importance." The traditional prioresses were certainly true to the definition—women of magnificent stature who could reduce young novices to sobbing heaps with a mere glance. Their portraits are all steely eyes and tight, severe lips. To be fair, such a stance was probably just what was needed to tame the wild, unchurched Pacific Northwest. The decision to invoke a new definition of

---

*http://geohazards.cr.usgs.gov/html__files/landslides/woodway/woodl.htm

leadership, in light of the changes brought about by Vatican II, was right for its times, as well.

But there has been yet another shift in the landscape of time—a sense that although the sisters are more engaged in the world than ever before, they have grown into a new spirituality that distances them from the mundane. Perhaps it's because presidents run nations and corporations that the order has abandoned the title. It doesn't really suit the head of a religious sisterhood. *Prioress* has taken on a renewed meaning—one steeped in history, yet modern. A prioress is the first among equals. She wears the mantle in humility—and only for a brief time. The election is held every four years, and no one serves as prioress for more than two terms.

In early March, just before the elections, I visited Rosary Heights. I felt I had to clear up some unfinished business with Sister Hilary—the Mother Dominick of my youth. I had avoided this conversation for as long as I could, but it was obvious that my journey wouldn't be completed without it.

As I turned onto the narrow tree-shaded road and drove the winding path to the front circular driveway, I could clearly remember the terrible jitters I suffered that day, almost exactly thirty years ago, when my father pulled his car up to the front door of the motherhouse and I emerged. I was following my calling then—or so I believed. My interview with Mother Dominick seemed like a mere formality. That it all turned out so differently has been a lingering wound all my life—long after I rejected any idea of joining a religious order. For the most part, Mother Dominick's rejection left a nonfatal scar that flared up only occasionally. With time, the girl I had been and the convictions that beat so strongly in my seventeen-year-old heart were replaced with other convictions. But the uneasy journey I had embarked on nearly two years before had brought everything to the surface. Once I decided to write about what it meant to be called, I couldn't avoid the abrupt and unexpected rebuff of what I thought at the time was my own calling. I wondered, Is the calling to religious life such a fragile thing that it can be dismissed with a word? Surely not—as so many saints, my own patron Catherine among them, demonstrated. What would Catherine have said to a Mother Dominick who told her to go away? I imagine that my patron would have made a bed outside the prioress's door and refused to move until she was allowed in. She was so bold and certain; nothing could have stopped her. Not only was I stopped short by Mother Dominick's edict but I never considered returning—although she had plainly invited me to do so. It was a puzzle that I hoped the former prioress could help me solve.

Sister Hilary came slowly into the library, her footsteps more labored in the year since I last saw her. We sat across from each other, and she leaned toward me, shifting slightly to the right so that her good ear would face in my direction. She had no idea that we had once faced each other across this very room. Sister Hilary didn't remember ever having met me before last year. She only knew that I was "one of our girls," preparing to write a book about the order.

I told her about the first time we met, thirty years ago, and she listened with a bemused expression, her memory unable to capture my face among so many others.

"I was crushed," I said. "I couldn't believe you would reject me and say I might not really have a vocation."

"Is that what you thought?" She raised her eyebrows in surprise. "Oh, my goodness, it was nothing like that." She sighed. "I'm afraid it was simple pragmatism that caused you to be sent away. Nothing more. You see, we always made sure that our sisters received the best educations—often to the master's and Ph.D. levels. But then so many sisters started leaving, and it put a terrible financial strain on us. We had accepted them as young girls out of high school, provided them with higher education, and then they left. It was quite discouraging. We decided that we could no longer afford such an investment. We thought that if a girl truly had a vocation, it could wait."

"I can see that." I frowned. "But it didn't really work, did it?

Once girls like me got out into the world, they didn't come back. Don't you think you lost more than you gained?"

"We prayed about that," she murmured. "It was a true test of faith. Nearly all of our vocations came out of the Catholic high schools. But the world had changed, and it was time we changed, too. I'm sure we made mistakes—turned away girls who would have made fine sisters. God has never allowed us to become complacent."

"Well," I said, "I guess I didn't have a vocation after all."

My words made her smile. "But of course you did—and do. You express it through your writing. Think of this book. . . . You could not have written it if you had followed another path. God's intentions can be hard to fathom. Perhaps you need to listen more closely." She glanced at the clock. "Please stay for lunch," she said. "I think Sister Amanda has put out some tuna fish sandwiches."

The mood was bright at lunch. Everyone was looking forward to the homecoming the following week, when all the sisters would stream in from their outposts near and far. Many of them hadn't been back since the last election, four years ago. There was Sister Michele, who ran a mental-health clinic in Minnesota; Sister Cele, teaching in Santa Barbara; Sister Jean, doing legal services in Anchorage, Alaska; Sister Philomena, caring for hundreds of orphans in Haiti. I remember one of the sisters saying of Philomena, "She loves babies so much. If she weren't a nun, she'd have ten children. When she finally returns to the United States, we'll have to find her some babies, or she won't be happy."

Sister Helen had completed her eight-year term as prioress. She would step down after the election, as would the members of her leadership team, including Sister Joanne. In a world where women in their fifties and sixties struggle to find employment, Helen and Joanne would be out job hunting. It seemed like a terrifying prospect to me. I reminded Sister Joanne how she had once told me that if she had to, she'd go to work as a salesgirl at Nordstrom's.

She laughed. "Oh, dear, did I say that? I don't think Nord-strom's would take me."

Helen and Joanne didn't seem particularly concerned about the sudden uncertainty of their futures. They were accustomed to the cycle of change—even looked forward to it. Joanne's true love was teaching; it had been a sacrifice for her to give it up for eight years. Helen was interested in serving the poor rural communities, similar to the one in which she was raised. "I may try living in an apartment," she said. "I've never done that before."

Youthfulness shined in their faces, defying their years. This, I realized, is one of the qualities that makes nuns such a subject of awe and fascination in the secular world. They possess something that everyone longs for but few are able to achieve. It is the gift of eternal youth. They are forever just beginning, just setting out. They approach life as though they were twenty-year-old girls, exhilarated as they anticipate the unknown adventures that life has to offer. They are armed with a vow of poverty, which frees them from the drive for security and acquisitions. They are obedient to God and the community, and can set aside regrets and resentments. And they are chaste to a singular purpose. Like partners in an old marriage, they don't always feel the romance, but they never doubt their love.

GLOSSARY

Please note that not all terms in the glossary appear in the book. Some definitions have been provided for a better understanding of religious organization.

breviary: A book containing the complete order of the Divine Office for each day.

canon law: Official church law. Canon law was revised in 1917, and again in 1983.

Catholic Youth Organization (CYO): A social and athletic organization for young Catholic school-age children from first grade to senior high school. Funded by the archdiocese and run by lay volunteers, the CYO fields baseball, basketball, football, and other athletic teams. They sponsor field trips, dances, and other social events.

chapter: The governing legislative body of a religious order or congregation.

Confraternity of Christian Doctrine (CCD): Catechism classes for Catholic students not attending Catholic schools. Taught by religious to lay teachers, who then teach the children.

congregation: A religious community whose members are bound by simple rather than solemn vows. Congregations are not chartered directly by Rome. Since 1752, no new religious orders have been permitted by Rome. Unlike religious orders, congregations are subject to varying degrees of government by councils of bishops. Male religious communities founded since 1752 have avoided this interference by organizing as "pious societies," which are not bound by vows. Women weren't permitted to form pious societies. Therefore, all religious communities of women founded since 1752 have been congregations.

constitutions: The rules originally laid down by the founder and later modified by various chapters concerning the basic purpose and daily life of the order or congregation. Constitutions must now be approved by the Sacred Congregation for Religious in Rome.

convent: The community dwelling of members of a religious order or congregation. Current usage limits the term to mean only the home of women religious. During the Middle Ages, convents could also mean a dwelling of male religious.

Council of Major Superiors of Women Religious (CMSWR): A new organization for the conservative American religious communities. Established in 1992.

Divine Office: The official collection of psalms, Scripture, devotional readings, and other prayers, chanted or recited daily by members of religious communities at specified hours of the day or night. Two of the most important hours of the Divine Office are lauds and vespers. Lauds, forming with matins (morning prayers), is the first of the canonical hours, an office of solemn praise to God. Vespers is the evening worship, sung in the sixth canonical hour, considered the late afternoon.

evangelical counsels: The vows and practice of poverty, chastity, and obedience.

Leadership Conference of Women Religious (LCWR): The Conference of Major Superiors of Women, changed after

1971. Still the umbrella organization for the heads of women's communities in the United States.

novice: *Member of a religious community during the first year or years after official entrance and prior to the first profession of vows. Canon law stipulates that all new members of religious orders must have at least one full year of canonical novitiate. The novice doesn't engage in secular studies or an active ministry but instead studies Scripture, theology, and the rules and history of the religious community she is entering. Many congregations require an additional year of novitiate. An active ministry or secular studies may be pursued at that time.*

nun: *A female member of a contemplative religious order. The words* nun *and* sister *are often used interchangeably. They do not always mean the same thing, but the usage is universal. Some nuns are not cloistered, and some sisters are not nuns.*

order: *A religious group officially chartered by the Pope, and exempt from church jurisdiction over its affairs. No new orders have been allowed since 1752.*

Perfectae Caritatis *(Decree on the Adaptation and Renewal of Religious Life): The 1965 Vatican decree mandating that religious orders and congregations adapt and update their lifestyles, according to the spirit of their original founder.*

postulant: *The traditional title given to a person seeking to join a religious community. The postulant usually lives with the community for a probationary period. Some women's religious communities have begun substituting titles such as associate or affiliate for postulant candidates.*

prioress: *The head of a religious order of women in the Benedictine or Augustinian monastic tradition. A prioress* is elected or appointed for a specific term of office. She has less discretionary power than an abbess.

regular clergy: Clergy who belong to a religious order, rather than lay clergy, who live in the world and don't belong to a religious order.

religious: A person who is a member of a religious order or congregation. A woman religious or a male religious.

religious life: Life in a religious community, usually under some form of vows.

rule: The constitution and guidelines that specify the way of life of a religious community.

secular clergy: The parish priests and bishops of a diocese. Secular clergy don't take vows. They can own property. Celibacy and obedience to the local bishop are administrative regulations, not vows.

sister: A female member of a religious congregation. Sister and nun are words that are used interchangeably. But a sister need not be a nun. A nun is under solemn vows, whereas a sister may not be.

vow: A formal promise in which a person binds him- or herself to a strict set of codes and obligations. Usually made by a member of a religious community, there are usually three vows required: the vow of poverty, the vow of chastity, and the vow of obedience.

ABOUT THE AUTHOR

CATHERINE WHITNEY is the author of a number of books, most recently *Guilty* (as coauthor with Harold Rothwax) and *Eat Right 4 Your Type* (with Peter D'Adamo), both *New York Times* best-sellers.